D0947281

The Mexican Spy Company

To my wife, Pat

The Mexican Spy Company

United States Covert Operations in Mexico, 1845–1848

by

A. Brooke Caruso

McFarland & Company, Inc., Publishers
Jefferson, North Carolina, and London

British Library Cataloguing-in-Publication data are available

Library of Congress Cataloguing-in-Publication Data

Caruso, A. Brooke.
    The Mexican Spy Company : United States covert operations in
Mexico, 1845–1848 / by A. Brooke Caruso.
      p. cm.
    Includes bibliographical references and index.
    ISBN 0-89950-630-5 (lib. bdg. : 50# alk. paper) ∞
    1. United States — History — War with Mexico, 1845–1848 — Secret
service. 2. Spies — United States — History — 19th century. 3. Spies —
Mexico — History — 19th century. 4. Espionage, American — Mexico —
History — 19th century. 5. Mexican Spy Company. I. Title.
E415.2.S43C37   1991
973.6'2 — dc20   91-52745
                                                              CIP

Manufactured in the United States of America

McFarland & Company, Inc., Publishers
  Box 611, Jefferson, North Carolina 28640

Contents

173695

Preface

This is a study of United States government covert operations on two separate levels — strategic and tactical. The study encompasses a specific time, the inauguration of President James K. Polk to the end of the Mexican War, and a specific area, the republics of Texas and Mexico.

Covert operations are studied on the strategic or presidential level to show the power of the secret presidency, and on the tactical, battlefield level to demonstrate the effect these operations can have on the outcome of a war. To accomplish this, the covert operations must be identified and quantified.

James K. Polk is an excellent example of a president who used covert operations to increase his power and influence as he intrigued in foreign affairs and pursued secret policies. Polk also was adept at denying any relationship to an unsuccessful secret operation or raising the banner of national defense to hide his secrets from any congressional investigation.

General Winfield Scott in his campaign from Veracruz to Mexico City demonstrated the effectiveness of tactical covert operations. With the use of advanced information, Scott fought a campaign of maneuver rather than attrition.

The covert operations, whether on the presidential or battlefield level, were some of the most imaginative and successful in United States espionage history.

Treaty with Spain (1819)

Article III

The boundary line between the two countries, west of the Mississippi, shall begin on the Gulph of Mexico, at the mouth of the river Sabine, in the sea, continuing north, along the western bank of that river, to the 32d degree of latitude; thence, by a line due north, to the degree of latitude where it strikes the Rio Roxo of Nachitoches, or Red River; then following the course of the Rio Roxo westward to the degree of longitude 100 west from London and 23 from Washington; then, crossing the said Red River, and running thence by a line due north, to the river Arkansas; thence, following the course of the southern bank of the Arkansas, to its source, in latitude 42 north; and thence, by that parallel of latitude, to the South Sea. . . .

The two high contracting parties agree to cede and renounce all their rights, claims, and pretensions, to the territories described by the said line, that is to say: The United States hereby cede to His Catholic Majesty, and renounce forever, all their rights, claims and pretensions, to the territories lying west and south of the above-described line; and, in like manner, His Catholic Majesty cedes to the said United States all his rights, claims, and pretensions to any territories east and north of the said line, and for himself, his heirs, and successors, renounces all claim to the said territories forever.

United States Plenipotentiary
John Quincy Adams

Part I

Texas

Chapter 1

Prologue: 1825–1845

When Mexico won her independence from Spain in 1821, she was a huge country, stretching from the Sabine River to the Pacific Ocean, from 15 degrees North latitude to 42 degrees North latitude, an area of over 1,600,000 square miles. By 1848 the United States of America had acquired more than half (900,000 square miles) of this newly independent nation. Mexico knew she had problems when President John Quincy Adams (1825–1829) attempted to acquire all or as much of the northern Mexican province of Texas as he could. Just his interest in this territory was enough to cause alarm in Mexico.[1] During his presidency, Adams made no less than three attempts to induce Mexico to sell this land to the United States but with no success. The Mexican people were so against selling vast portions of their homeland that Joel Poinsett, the United States minister to Mexico, did not even carry out his instructions for submitting the last proposition.[2]

President Andrew Jackson (1829–1837) had disagreed with Adams on many issues, but was in complete agreement with him on buying the Mexican province of Texas. Jackson continued the effort to purchase Texas from Mexico over a period of several years and under great secrecy. But Jackson was not only interested in the province of Texas, he was the first American president to make the Mexican ports of Monterrey and San Francisco objects of American continental acquisition.[3] It was Jackson's dream of an empire that the United States would someday expand over "all Spanish North America."[4] Andrew Jackson, whether in or out of office, for the next two decades would be a continuous threat to the security of Mexico.

Two American presidents making numerous offers to purchase their land disturbed and offended the people of Mexico. This emerging giant that was their northern neighbor was a frightening reality to the newly independent country. In 1830 the Mexican government enacted a decree forbidding entrance to Mexico from the north without a Mexican passport, forbidding the introduction of slaves into Mexico, and from a practical point of view, forbidding all American colonization in Texas.[5]

The Mexican decree did not stop Americans from crossing the border into Mexico, nor did the United States government do anything to hamper this movement. As these people were illegal aliens and had no rights, it was in their best interest to push for a change in government. The only way they could establish their position was to provoke a revolution.[6] Even the legal American settlers had little empathy with the Mexican people. The United States minister to Mexico reported to President Jackson in 1833 that Stephen F. Austin told him all the American settlers anticipated a separation from Mexico at some future time.[7]

Sam Houston was sent to the Mexican province of Texas in 1833 by President Jackson to negotiate the protection of American traders on the border with the Indian tribes.[8] Houston was a close friend of Andrew Jackson and had served under him in the War of 1812. Houston was elected governor of Tennessee in 1827, but did not serve out his term. His marriage in 1829 ended in disaster when his wife left him only three months after their wedding. Houston resigned his position as governor and went to live with the Cherokees, with whom he had lived for three years when he was a teenager.[9]

Houston went to Texas because he thought it was the land of opportunity for Americans, and he stayed. The stage was set, and the players were taking their places for the Mexican-American confrontation. The Mexicans were proud people who had no intention of giving up their land. On the other side of the border, the Americans considered the continent theirs by special self-ordained rights and could not understand the Mexican arrogance.

As the number of American illegal aliens in Mexico grew, the inevitable Mexican-American confrontation drew closer. It came in 1936, when the Mexican army was ordered to restore Mexican control of the province. General Antonio López de Santa Anna sought and obtained from the Mexican Congress a decree directing that all foreigners taken in arms against the government should be treated as pirates and shot. General Santa Anna laid siege to the Alamo on February 23, 1836, and General Don José Urrea captured the settlement of San Patricio on 27 February 1836. The Mexican army was on the move as a killing machine: no foreigners were to survive in Texas.[10]

Washington-on-the-Brazos, a small town of five to six thousand people, 150 miles northeast of San Antonio, was the birthplace of the Texas Republic. The Americans met here in an unfinished loft over a barroom on 1 March 1836 and drafted a declaration of independence. They used Thomas Jefferson's declaration, changing words and details to fit the time and place. The next day the Mexican province of Texas was declared an independent republic. The Americans knew this was a war of survival or extermination. The immediate danger prompted quick action.[11]

On 3 March 1836 Sam Houston was appointed head of an army that did not exist. Houston was an excellent choice to raise and lead the rebel army. Not only was he a close friend of President Jackson and a very successful politician in Tennessee, but he was in prime physical condition. Houston stood 6 feet 3 inches tall and weighed 240 pounds. He was physically impressive.[12] After his appointment he immediately departed from Washington-on-the-Brazos for Gonzales, a town 60 miles east of San Antonio. Here Houston found a total of 374 men. The best of this group was a company of 50 Kentucky riflemen, which Sidney Sherman had brought at his own expense from the United States. Houston commissioned Sherman a lieutenant colonel in the Texas militia.[13]

Sidney Sherman had been a successful businessman in Newport, Kentucky, but sold his business and used the money to equip a company of volunteers for the revolution. Sherman was 30 years old when he led his troops into Mexico in December 1835. The Republic of Texas awarded him for his services from 18 December 1835 to 16 December 1836 with a land certificate for 1,280 acres.[14]

At the battle of San Jacinto, Colonel Sherman commanded the left wing of the Texas army, opened the attack, and has been credited with the battle cry, "Remember the Alamo." The combined American and Mexican forces only totaled approximately two thousand men. Nevertheless, the victory was a turning point in the balance of power in the west. The road was open for America's march to the Pacific Ocean.[15]

John Quincy Adams believed President Andrew Jackson was party to a conspiracy to promote the revolution in the Mexican province of Texas. Adams contended that Jackson influenced events in the following manner:

1. Recruiting for the revolutionary army was openly carried on in the United States.

2. Armed reinforcements for the revolutionary forces marched boldly through the United States and crossed the border without restraint.

3. Munitions were sent from the United States without interference from the United States government.

4. Jackson stationed a large body of troops on the Mexican-American border, ostensibly to check possible Indian raids into the United States. Troopers from this force deserted to join the Americans fighting in Mexico. Adams suspected no very vigilant effort was made to prevent these desertions.[16]

American revolutionaries declared Texas independent on 1 March 1836, and by June 1836 they had won de facto independence. Mexico would not recognize the Republic of Texas or even admit it existed, but Mexico was powerless to change the fact of its existence.[17]

The 6,640 qualified voters in the Republic of Texas held their first election in October 1836. Sam Houston was elected president in a land-slide, gathering 5,119 votes. The proposition to seek annexation by the United States was overwhelmingly supported by a vote of 3,277 to 19. Houston strongly supported annexation in his inaugural speech.[18]

Sam Houston was not elected president of a strong, well-organized nation. Texas was a struggling frontier community of less than 40,000 peo-ple. The people were subsistence farmers. The towns were frontier set-tlements with mud streets and at most a few thousand people. The Republic had no banks and no currency.[19] Texas was very weak and vulnerable, but she was far away from Mexico City and very close to the United States. The separation of the province of Texas from Mexico was only possible due to the efforts of the American people. Without the men, money, munitions, and moral support given to the American revolu-tionaries in Mexico by their fellow citizens in the United States, there is little doubt that the Americans would not have been able to gain or main-tain their independence. [20]

Depending on your point of view, the separation of Texas from Mexico was either an excellent example of the Jeffersonian pattern of ex-pansion or a very successful covert operation. The Jeffersonian pattern of expansion envisioned a colony of Americans, planted on vacant though alien soil, which emerges into a free and independent republic.[21] As a covert operation the migration of Americans into Mexico would be described as one of the most successful examples in all history of what might today be called "infiltration and subversion."[22]

General Santa Anna was captured at the battle of San Jacinto. Many people wanted him executed for the murder of 342 American prisoners of war at Goliad on 27 March 1836 and for other war crimes, but President Jackson convinced President Houston that Santa Anna was worth more alive than dead. On 25 November 1836 Santa Anna, accompanied by Colonel Juan Nepomuceno Almonte, and a small escort crossed the Brazos River en route to Washington, D.C. The party traveled to Plaque-mine, Louisiana, and boarded the river steamer *Tennessee* for a 20-day voyage up the Mississippi and Ohio rivers. They landed at Louisville, Ken-tucky, on Christmas Day, 1836. From here Santa Anna traveled through Kentucky, West Virginia, and Maryland. At Frederick, Maryland, he met General Winfield Scott, who was then being tried by a court-martial for alleged transgressions during an earlier campaign in Florida. Santa Anna and Scott conversed amicably for nearly an hour. Santa Anna arrived in Washington on 18 January 1837 after a journey of approximately 1,700 miles.[23]

During the trip and his stay in Washington, Santa Anna delighted in presenting himself as a gracious and cultivated man of impeccable manners, which was just the opposite of American expectations. Santa Anna had been depicted in the press as a fire-breathing monster who ate children.

President Jackson received General Santa Anna in grand style. Jackson gave a dinner for Santa Anna which was attended by the diplomatic corp and high-ranking government officials. There were official greetings and receptions. Most important there was a long, private conversation between Jackson and Santa Anna with a few close advisers present. Texas was discussed. Santa Anna said Jackson offered him 6 million pesos if Mexico would recognize the independence of Texas. Jackson said Santa Anna proposed the cession of Texas to the United States for a fair consideration. Both agreed Santa Anna did not have the power to decide these matters. These decisions would be in the hands of the Mexican Congress. During this conversation Jackson outlined a more far-reaching proposal to Santa Anna. This proposal was the implementation of his continental policy. He suggested to the Mexican leader that the United States might extend her borders to run "the line of the U. States to the Rio grand — up that stream to latitude 38 north & then to the pacific including north California." Jackson offered compensation of $3.5 million for the Mexican land that would become the property of the United States.[24]

President Jackson placed the corvette *Pioneer* at Santa Anna's disposal for his return to Mexico. Santa Anna took a steamer from Baltimore to Norfolk, where he boarded the *Pioneer* and departed for Veracruz, arriving 12 February 1837. Santa Anna became quite an admirer of Andrew Jackson and never forgot the friendly way in which he was received by him.[25]

What effect this trip through the United States had on Santa Anna is left to conjecture. Jackson impressed him, but did he meet James K. Polk? Congressman Polk was the speaker of the House, and a key force in the Jackson administration at the time of Santa Anna's visit. Like General Scott, Polk and Santa Anna's paths would cross, and any knowledge of the other would have been advantageous.

On 1 March 1837 the United States Senate recommended to President Jackson that Texas be formally recognized. Jackson on 3 March nominated Alcée La Branche of Louisiana to be chargé d'affaires to the Republic of Texas. The Senate confirmed the appointment the same day, which was also the last day of the Jackson administration.[26] Why did it take the United States a year to recognize Texas, or the more puzzling question, why was Texas still independent and not part of the United States?

The answer can be found in President Jackson's determination to have all foreign nations treat the United States with due respect. He demanded scrupulous adherence to all treaties and agreements and was prepared to go to war with any nation to right any wrong against the United States. In taking this high-road position President Jackson was very sensitive to any issue that would put the United States in the wrong. In the Spanish-American Treaty of 1819 the United States abandoned its claim to Texas. Jackson desperately wanted Texas, but unless he could buy it from Mexico or Mexico would recognize the Republic of Texas, Texas was out of reach. Jackson had put himself in a box.

Texas formally requested annexation on 4 August 1837. Their request was denied by President Martin Van Buren (Jackson's handpicked successor). Van Buren's position was that the United States was bound by treaty to recognize Mexico's claim to that territory. Andrew Jackson believed Texas to be the key to the United States reaching the Pacific Ocean, but he agreed with President Van Buren that the treaty ruled out annexation. Jackson was still in his box. This rejection infuriated the Texans, and they just as formally withdrew the request for annexation on 12 October 1838. However, at such times that Texas found itself weak, disorganized, and threatened by Mexico, it forgot the rebuttal and turned once more to the fatherland, to see what the sentiment was for annexation; but the United States was not interested.[27] If annexation was not a success, recognition was. Texas's independence was recognized by several countries, including the United States, Great Britain, France, and Belgium.[28]

From 1836 to 1841 Mexico suffered from internal problems, and was not in a position to threaten Texas. However, in 1842 the Mexican army started probing the defenses of Texas. In March the Mexicans took San Antonio and two other positions, but retreated before the Texans could counterattack. The Mexicans and Texans had a brief fight near the Nueces River during July, and in September San Antonio was captured again.[29]

By December 1842 Texas was in trouble. The population was only 70,000 to 75,000. Public resources were exhausted, and there was not a regular soldier in the field. It was doubtful that Texas could maintain her independence if Mexico could mount a sustained, well-led offensive, and there was no outside interference.[30] But it was not to be. Britain and France became interested in Texas, and Mexico had too many other problems. For the time being Texas was able to muddle through.

With the British and the French interest came United States interest. Treaties that were so important in 1837 were ignored. On 16 October 1843 Secretary of State Abel P. Upshur sent a note to Isaac Van Zandt, Texas representative to the United States, informing him that President John Tyler was prepared to present the annexation of Texas to the Congress in the strongest possible terms.[31]

In June 1843 President Tyler by recess appointment made William

Sumter Murphy minister extraordinary to Central America and chargé d'affaires to Texas. The Central America title meant little, but for a year Murphy was the United States representative to Texas. William Murphy had practiced law in Ohio, and was a brigadier general in the militia. He was always known as General Murphy.

During January 1844 negotiations for annexation looked promising when Secretary of State Upshur assured President Houston through William Murphy, that a clear two-thirds of the United States Senate was in favor of the treaty. President Houston at once obtained from the eager Murphy a promise of military protection by the United States pending the conclusion of the negotiations, and Murphy went so far as to order an American vessel to Veracruz to warn other United States naval units that they would soon be needed to repel a Mexican invasion of Texas.

Murphy's initiatives were too much for the Tyler administration. Murphy was informed that he had pledged the president to action unwarranted by the Constitution. However, by the time this dispatch reached Texas on 11 April 1844, the treaty of annexation had been signed. When the treaty came before the Senate for ratification, it was rejected, as was the confirmation of Murphy's appointment. In announcing the rejection of the treaty and his recall to the Texas government, Murphy quipped, "The tail went with the hide." Within a few weeks he died of yellow fever at Galveston. He was 48 years old.[32]

The Senate on 10 June 1844 rejected the annexation treaty for domestic political reasons. This forced Tyler to change direction, and he set course for the House of Representatives.[33] Within two days of his defeat in the Senate, Tyler sent all the papers dealing with the treaty to the House with a message that included the following: "The power of Congress is, however, fully competent in some form of proceeding to accomplish everything that a formal ratification of the treaty could have accomplished."[34]

To support his annexation policy President Tyler appointed Tilghman A. Howard as United States representative to Texas in June 1844. Howard was a friend of Andrew Jackson, and had worked for Houston when Houston was governor of Tennessee. Shortly after his arrival in Texas, Howard died of yellow fever, the fourth out of five United States representatives to die at their post during the short period since Texas had been recognized. President Tyler received word of this in September 1844, and immediately appointed Andrew Jackson Donelson to the post.[35]

Former President Jackson reversed his opinion concerning annexation. The Treaty of 1819 was still alive and well in every legal sense, but the British and French interest in Texas was a threat to the security of the United States. Jackson became a prime mover for annexation and expansion to the Pacific Ocean. His influence in the upcoming events would be significant. Knowing Jackson's position on annexation, President Tyler asked Jackson to use his influence to have Donelson agree to go to Texas. Tyler told Jackson that Donelson was chosen officially because he knew Houston personally, but, basically, he was chosen because he was a member of Andrew Jackson's family and in Jackson's close confidence.[36]

Donelson was raised in Andrew Jackson's home. He served as General Jackson's aide-de-camp and citizen Jackson's confidential secretary. When Jackson was elected president, Donelson accompanied him to the White House as his private secretary. Donelson had all the right contacts in the United States and Texas. He was an excellent choice to promote annexation in Texas.[37]

In his continuing effort to expand the United States, President Tyler sent Duff Green to Mexico in 1844. Green was "to aid in conducting the negotiation for the acquisition of Texas, New Mexico and California." Upon his return from Mexico, Green reported that Mexico would never willingly sell her land to the United States, and, therefore, must be "chastised." To accomplish this, Green proposed to employ "the Indians of the United States and Texas in the invasion of Mexico and revolutionize the country from the Rio Grande to the Pacific under the flag of Texas."[38]

Duff Green was born in Kentucky, but in 1816 at the age of 25 moved to Missouri, where he was successful in business and became a general in the militia. Green moved to Washington, D.C., in 1825, and purchased a newspaper, the *United States Telegraph,* which he used to support Andrew Jackson for president in 1829. In 1840 Green supported William Henry Harrison for president, and was largely responsible for John Tyler being placed on the Whig ticket.[39]

After Green's diplomatic venture in Mexico, President Tyler in September 1844 appointed him United States consul at Galveston, Texas. Green and Galveston did not match. Duff Green as owner and editor of the *United States Telegraph* was a prominent figure in American affairs, and he was an active, outgoing person. The United States consul received no salary, and the amount of American business at Galveston was insignificant. Green was not only a personal friend, political supporter, and confidant of Secretary of State John C. Calhoun, but his son was married to Calhoun's daughter. Yet, for some reason this man agreed to accept a nothing post in the wilds of Texas.[40]

Duff Green did not get settled in Galveston before he was off to Washington-on-the-Brazos, arriving in early December 1844. Green had business with the members of the Texas Congress and President Anson Jones. Jones, who succeeded Houston, had just been sworn in on 9 December 1844. Green's business with these gentlemen had nothing to do with the duties of the United States consul. Green was trying to secure a charter for the "Del Norte Company." The business of this company was to conquer and occupy California and other portions of northern Mexico for the benefit of Texas. In other words, to start a war between Mexico and Texas. When President Jones refused to agree to this scheme, Green threatened to start a revolution in Texas. Jones recalled the United States consul's exequatur by proclamation. Green apologized and disclaimed any intention to interfere with the government of Texas. His apology was accepted by Jones, and Donelson who was now on station reported that the unpleasant affair was quickly forgotten.[41] Green was United States consul at Galveston only from October to December 1844, but in that short time Green claimed, "an arrangement was made for a movement in Texas which would enable the United States to interpose and thus obtain the concessions wanted."[42] On 28 February 1845 Green was paid $1,000 from the fund for the contingent expenses of foreign intercourse for his services as a bearer of dispatches to Mexico and Texas.[43] The official record does not mention covert operations.

Green's activities were closely followed by the British. Charles Elliot, the British chargé d'affaires, reported to his government from Galveston on 8 February 1845 that Green had become a Texas citizen, and had traveled to Corpus Christi on a business trip with Colonel Henry Lawrence Kinney, who was engaged in trade with the Mexicans across the frontier.[44]

Kinney was having a busy month. On 11 February 1845 he sent President Jones a translation of a letter General Arista had written to Kinney. Based on this letter Kinney believed he could conclude an armistice with Mexico for an indefinite time, and he was prepared to travel to Mexico for that purpose. Jones immediately answered Kinney's letter. He agreed with the information provided by General Mariano Arista, but owing to a recent change of government in Mexico, Jones did not believe this was the time for negotiations. Jones did not want to discourage Kinney if there was a chance, and wrote, "But if, through your facilities of communications, you can ascertain the views of the Mexican Government in relation to this subject, any favorable proposition they may make to us shall be as favorably considered." Jones then detailed his plan for a truce. Jones's final instructions to Kinney were if he should see or communicate with General Arista, he was to find out Mexico's conditions for a truce and impress upon Arista the need for some immediate action.[45] The president of Texas was looking for options. The Green affair exposed a U.S. plan to have Texas invade Mexico, providing the United States the opportunity to intervene, and to obtain through military means the land Mexico would not sell. For Texas, peace with Mexico made continued independence instead of annexation a more viable policy.

The convolutions contrived at Washington-on-the-Brazos were

matched or exceeded at Washington-on-the-Potomac. Horace Greeley wrote from Washington, D.C., on 22 February 1845 of President-elect Polk's effort to save Texas annexation from defeat, and to gain its passage in the Senate through pledges on his part to use Senator Thomas Hart Benton's bill for the annexation process. Greeley summarized, "The President elect is the master spirit of the Texas intrigue, and is concentrating his influence, power and patronage wholly on this point."[46]

President-elect Polk promised certain senators in late February 1845 that he would proceed to annexation under Senator Benton's plan, which provided for new negotiations with Mexico over the boundary question. This action was prompted by the Texas claim that its boundary, which, as a province of Mexico had never extended beyond the Nueces River, now extended all the way to the Rio Grande. This claim caused greater concern in Mexico than the annexation legislation. If the United States were to insist on this boundary, then in addition to the loss of Texas, which in reality had had an independent existence from Mexico for nine years, Mexico stood to lose still more land.[47] The senators would not accept the House plan which annexed Texas with her unsettled boundary, and the possibility of war with Mexico. The senators voted for the annexation bill, and it would not have passed without their vote.[48]

The House plan to annex Texas included the following conditions:

1. The boundaries of the new state were to be decided by the United States;

2. The ownership of all public lands in Texas was to be held by the state, not the federal government;

3. Texas ceded to the United States all property and means pertaining to defense;

4. Texas would retain all the public funds, debts, taxes, and dues of every kind;

5. Four other new states, plus Texas, could be formed from this original state.[49]

On 27 February 1845 the Senate passed the annexation bill. This bill basically gave the president the option of using Benton's plan or the House plan. President Tyler, in a surprise move, did not leave the execution of the annexation bill to the new administration. On 3 March 1845, his last day in office, Tyler sent Donelson instructions to present the House of Representatives's plan, not Senator Benton's plan, to the Republic of Texas. Tyler also instructed Donelson that the terms of the United States were to be accepted precisely as they stood, so that all danger incident to delay could be avoided. Prior to sending the instructions, President Tyler informed President-elect Polk of his decision. Polk offered no opinion or resistance.[50] The new administration had no intention of showing its cards until it was in power.

The American revolution in Mexico created the Republic of Texas, and only the support of the American people kept the republic alive. During the revolutionary period, President Andrew Jackson denied to the world any involvement in the violent overthrow of a friendly neighbor, but the men, munitions, and money flowed across the border, unfettered from any government interference.

The background to the American revolution in Mexico was that Mexico refused to sell a vast portion of its northern territory to the United States. This land was considered crucial by President Jackson to the continental expansion of the United States. Adventurers, like Sam Houston who was a very close friend of President Jackson, moved into Mexico as illegal aliens. American dissatisfaction with Mexico due to a variety of grievances both real and imagined, such as racial and religious prejudice, was fanned into revolutionary fever. The Mexican government sent troops to restore order. Americans defeated Mexicans, and proclaimed a republic. Various forms of covert operations, e.g., disinformation, subversion, support of insurgents, and paramilitary operations, were all quite visible, but responsibility for these operations was denied by President Jackson. The essence of covert operations is the ability to deny responsibility.

When Mexico refused to sell President Tyler New Mexico and California, Tyler sent Duff Green to Texas on a covert operation to start a war. When the operation failed, Green apologized and Tyler denied.

Prior to the administration of James K. Polk, the United States government was deeply involved in covert operations in Mexico. Polk would follow in the footsteps of Jackson and Tyler with even more determination and imagination.

Notes to Chapter 1

1. Justin H. Smith, *The Annexation of Texas* (New York: Barnes and Noble, 1941), p. 8.

2. Bennett Champ Clark, *John Quincy Adams* (Boston: Little, Brown, 1932), p. 389.

3. George Ballentine, *Autobiography of an English Soldier in the United States Army* (New York: Stringer and Townsend, 1854; reprint ed., Chicago: R. R. Donnelly and Sons, 1986), p. xxxvii.

4. Robert V. Remini, *Andrew Jackson and the Course of American Democracy, 1833–1845* (New York: Harper and Row, 1984), 3:2.

5. Smith, *Texas*, pp. 9–10.

6. Ibid., p. 17.

7. Ibid., p. 12.

8. Ibid., p. 26.

9. *Encyclopaedia Britannica*, 1956 ed., s.v. "Houston, Sam."

10. Walter Prescott Webb, ed., *The Handbook of Texas* (Chicago: R. R. Donnelly and Sons, 1952), 1:704–705.

11. T. R. Fehrenbach, *Lone Star* (New York: American Legacy, 1983), p. 222.

12. Ibid., p. 224.

13. Ibid., p. 214.

14. Webb, *Handbook,* 2:603.

15. Fehrenbach, *Lone Star,* pp. 232–233.

16. Clark, *Adams,* p. 390.

17. Fehrenbach, *Lone Star,* p. 243.

18. Ibid., p. 246.

19. Ibid., p. 247.

20. Smith, *Texas,* pp. 30–31.

21. R. W. Van Alstyne, *The Rising American Empire* (New York: Oxford University Press, 1960), p. 103.

22. Ballentine, *English Soldier,* p. xxxix.

23. Oakah L. Jones, Jr., *Santa Anna* (New York: Twayne, 1968), pp. 73–74.

24. Remini, *Andrew Jackson,* pp. 364–366.

25. Jones, *Santa Anna,* pp. 74–75.

26. Remini, *Andrew Jackson,* pp. 367–368.

27. Smith, *Texas,* p. 63.

28. Ibid., p. 76.

29. Ibid., p. 38.

30. Ibid., p. 40.

31. Ibid., p. 128.

32. *Dictionary of American Biography,* 1981 index, s.v. "Murphy, William Sumter," by H. Donaldson Jordan.

33. Smith, *Texas,* p. 282.

34. Charles A. McCoy, *Polk and the Presidency* (Austin: University of Texas Press, 1960), p. 86.

35. Smith, *Texas,* p. 361.

36. Remini, *Andrew Jackson,* p. 506.

37. *Dictionary of American Biography,* 1981 index, s.v. "Donelson, Andrew Jackson," by Thomas R. Abernethy.

38. Richard R. Stenberg, "The Failure of Polk's War Intrigue of 1845," *Pacific Historical Review* 4 (March 1935): 44.

39. *Dictionary of American Biography,* 1981 index, s.v. "Green, Duff," by Fletcher M. Green.

40. Smith, *Texas,* p. 212.

41. Ibid., p. 377.

42. Stenberg, "Polk's Intrigue," p. 44.

43. U.S. Congress, House, *Contingent Expenses of State Department,* H. Doc. 11, 29th Cong., 1st sess., 1845.

44. Ephraim Douglass Adams, ed., "British Correspondence Concerning Texas," *The Southwestern Historical Quarterly* 20 (1917): 63–64.

45. Anson Jones, *Memoranda and Official Correspondence Relating to the Republic of Texas* (New York: D. Appleton, 1859; reprint ed., New York: Arno, 1973), p. 432.

46. Richard R. Stenberg, "President Polk and the Annexation of Texas," *Southwestern Social Science Quarterly* 14 (March 1934): 340.

47. McCoy, *Polk*, p. 94.
48. Stenberg, "Polk's Intrigue," p. 41.
49. Smith, *Texas*, p. 332.
50. Ibid., p. 353.

Chapter 2

The Secret War

James K. Polk's political life had its foundation in Jeffersonian principles and the Democratic Party. Jeffersonian principles must be viewed as only applying to white American males. The Whig Party was his enemy, and the battle was continuous, personal, and foul. Polk was a die-hard party man. As speaker of the United States House of Representatives and as governor of Tennessee, he was a party leader. This was the party of Jackson, and Polk was a Jacksonian through and through. Jackson was a close friend and supporter. In May 1844 Andrew Jackson asked James Polk to visit him at the *Hermitage*. When Polk arrived, Jackson told him former President Martin Van Buren had cut his throat "politically" by declaring against annexation, and should not be the Democratic Party candidate for president. Jackson believed the candidate for president "should be an annexation man and from the Southwest." It was Jackson's opinion that Polk was that man, and pledged his support.[1]

On 4 March 1845 James Knox Polk was inaugurated as president of the United States. He was the eleventh president, and at the age of 50, the youngest. Polk had worked extremely hard to win this office. Throughout his career he prepared diligently for every political battle, and if he lost, he did not quit — he just worked harder. When he was young, his poor health (gallstones) and his mother's strong religious influence forged a hardness and determination that was reflected in every aspect of his political life.[2] The new president was ambitious, introverted, and iron-willed, and his large, restless, steely grey eyes, set in deep sockets, gave him a formidable appearance.[3]

Polk's political career provided him with the opportunities to master the art of manipulating men through apparent cordiality and candor. He created the impression of complete agreement, and then made commitments that he subsequently failed to honor. Ultimately this modus operandi left him distrusted and disliked, though it was a major factor in many of his short-term successes.[4]

Polk is considered one of the most assiduous of presidents. He was up at dawn, worked throughout the greater part of the day, and often continued at his desk long into the night. Previous presidents usually went home when Congress was not in session. Polk changed that. He stayed in Washington, and demanded the same of his cabinet.

Polk put his own stamp on the presidency. His propensity for hard work, and his determination to achieve his goals made him the controlling force of his administration. He established the right of the president to know the operational details of the smallest segment of his administration. For the first time it was the president's right and duty to control personally the departmental activity of the executive branch.[5] Polk considered himself responsible for the conduct of every action, anywhere in the executive branch, and was determined to control the decisionmaking process within the executive branch. He was kept informed routinely of these activities through normal channels.[6] When this did not happen, Polk would be furious, and demand the matter be set right immediately.

Polk described in his diary on 28 December 1848 his concept of running the ship of state—"No President who performs his duty faithfully and conscientiously can have any leisure. If he entrusts the details and smaller matters to subordinates constant errors will occur. I prefer to supervise the whole operations of the Government myself rather than entrust the public business to subordinates, and this makes my duties very great."[7]

The cabinet was a very important management tool for Polk. All issues were discussed at regularly scheduled meetings, and when necessary, crisis management meetings were convened on short notice. Polk made the decisions after the issues were discussed, and insisted on the support of his cabinet in the implementation of these decisions. Polk's diary records over four hundred such meetings.[8]

On 7 March 1845 President Polk wrote secretly to Donelson, directing him not to act on Tyler's instructions of 3 March 1845. There would be no action taken on the annexation bill until the cabinet meeting on 10 March. At this meeting the cabinet voted for the House of Representatives's plan. Polk concurred with the cabinet, in spite of his previous promises not to use the House plan. Instead, the chief executive told the cabinet that instructions should be sent immediately to Donelson, confirming Tyler's choice. Secretary of State James Buchanan prepared the instructions, and they were entrusted to Archibald Yell for delivery.[9]

Archibald Yell was a very highly qualified messenger. He had fought with Andrew Jackson against the British at New Orleans and the Seminole Indians in Florida. Jackson admired Yell for his courage, and rewarded him with a succession of federal appointments. The people of Arkansas also admired him. He had served as governor of that state, and in 1845 took his seat as a newly elected United States congressman.[10]

Yell departed from Washington, D.C., on 10 March 1845. He carried more than Secretary Buchanan's written instructions. As President Polk put it, Yell had facts which would aid Donelson in his mission, but which were so highly classified they could not be trusted to paper. Yell was the bearer of secret oral orders, instructions and or facts to Donelson.[11]

Yell met Donelson in New Orleans, and delivered the written instructions and the secret oral orders. Yell did not return to Washington, D.C., as would be expected of a newly elected congressman; instead, he and Donelson sailed to Galveston, Texas, arriving on 27 March 1845. Donelson set off for Washington-on-the-Brazos to deliver the United States plan for annexation to the Texas government. Near the Texas capital, Donelson met the British and French chargés on their way to Galveston. He was curious about the purpose of their journey, but his questions elicited no answers.[12]

The British and French chargés had good reason to be secretive. They had just concluded what they considered a diplomatic coup. At a secret conference the previous day at Washington-on-the-Brazos a deal had been consummated. Texas agreed not to be annexed for 90 days in order to provide an opportunity for the British chargé, Charles Elliot, to travel to Mexico to negotiate a peace treaty. Texas had specified various conditions necessary for it to accept a peace treaty, the major one being Mexico's recognition of Texas independence. This secret arrangement was approved by President Anson Jones and Secretary of State Ashbel Smith.[13]

A. J. Donelson arrived at Washington-on-the-Brazos on 30 March 1845, accompanied by Archibald Yell. President Polk had sent Congressman-elect Yell to deliver a message as a private citizen visiting Texas, but this was his cover. A strong supporter of annexation, Yell had many friends in Texas. He was Polk's own secret agent, and the object of his covert operation was the annexation of Texas.[14] As a private citizen without official ties to the administration, he used his influence to persuade Texans that it was in their own best interest to join the Union.

Upon his arrival in the Texas capital, Donelson delivered the United States annexation proposition to President Jones. Donelson expected action but found delay. The Texas president informed Donelson that he would take no action until he consulted his cabinet on how to handle the question of annexation. This was the same day the British chargé left Galveston for Mexico on his quest for a peace treaty recognizing an independent Texas. President Anson Jones needed to play for time, if he wanted to provide the people of Texas with an option to annexation.[15]

On 27 March 1845 Secretary Buchanan wrote Charles Anderson Wickliffe that the president deemed it necessary to employ a confidential agent to counteract the efforts of the British and French governments in Texas, and Wickliffe was the president's choice. He was to proceed to

Texas as soon as possible, and once there, contact Donelson. Only Donelson was to be made privy to Wickliffe's official status. In Texas, Wickliffe was to use his best judgment on when, where, and how to convince the authorities and people that their "reunion" with the United States was in their best interest. Secret Agent Wickliffe would be compensated $8 per day from time of departure to return, plus travel and other expenses. Wickliffe was instructed to obtain receipts for expenses whenever he could. Buchanan wanted regular reports from him, but only if they could be transmitted with perfect secrecy and security. Wickliffe was advanced $1,000 on account.[16]

Who was this secret agent that President Polk was sending to conduct covert operations in Texas? Charles Anderson Wickliffe was born in Kentucky in 1788. He was a lawyer who very early in his life established a reputation as a drunken carouser and a high-stakes gambler. Owing to his haughty and disdainful disposition, he was commonly referred to as "the Duke." Wickliffe's political life was long and varied: United States House of Representatives, ten years; lieutenant governor of Kentucky, three years; governor of Kentucky, one year; and postmaster general under President Tyler, four years. In his last term in Congress (1831–1833), Wickliffe was thrown from his carriage, and was a cripple for the remainder of his life.[17]

In his letter of 28 March 1845 to Donelson, President Polk discussed secret agents Yell and Wickliffe. Polk wrote that Archibald Yell, who had departed for Texas on 10 March 1845, would have facts which would aid Donelson in his mission, but which were so sensitive they had to be carried in the mind and not trusted to the written word. Donelson was also informed of Polk's sending Charles A. Wickliffe in two or three days to deliver information that had just been received. Wickliffe had Polk's confidence and "will be able to give you [Donelson] valuable information." Wickliffe's cover was the same as Yell's. They were in Texas at their own initiative and for private reasons.[18] President Polk kept his official representative, Donelson, informed of the covert operations being conducted in Donelson's area of responsibility, operations being controlled from Washington, D.C. Thus informed, Donelson was able to deny any involvement in covert operations against Texas, and at the same time provide the secret agents assistance as necessary.

In April 1845 with these secret agents on station in Texas, Secretary Buchanan attempted to derail the intrigues of the British and French diplomats in Texas. He instructed Donelson to assure the people and government of Texas that they could rely on the United States to deal fair and square with them.[19] With the official representative declaring the United States would keep its promises to Texas, the secret agents started making promises. Yell and Wickliffe promised large federal appropriations for Texas after annexation. There would be money to buy up Indian lands, to improve harbors, to build roads, and to do whatever was desired. Yell and Wickliffe teamed up to canvas the settlements. They traveled throughout Texas, speaking at the annexationist meetings that were being held everywhere.[20] By 23 April 1845 proannexation meetings had been held in many places, while no antiannexation meetings had been held anywhere. The Galveston *News* of 22 April reported hearing from nearly twenty county meetings, and all wanted annexation immediately.[21]

Secretary of the Treasury Robert J. Walker was also working for annexation. As a United States senator, Walker was one of President Tyler's foremost allies in the fight for Texas annexation. He was an expansionist, and in the cabinet constantly urged the acquisition of all the territory the United States could acquire, including all of Mexico.[22] Memucan Hunt, a former minister of Texas to the United States, was a friend of Secretary Walker, Hunt's correspondence with Walker reveals that Secretary Walker had arranged to finance a public relations campaign in Texas to promote annexation. Hunt had asked Walker for $10,000 to employ "some half dozen speakers," and $5,000 for printing and transmitting publications throughout Texas. Hunt met Archibald Yell when he arrived in Texas, and he wrote Walker that he and Yell were fighting "what is termed the British party in Texas."[23]

Texas Secretary of State Ashbel Smith in a letter to President Jones dated 9 April 1845 described Archibald Yell as a pleasant gentleman who some citizens considered to be an "unofficial minister" accredited to the citizens of Texas in general. William B. Ochiltree of Houston wrote President Jones on 11 April informing him that "Governor Yell of Arkansas" had departed Houston by stage on his way to Washington-on-the-Brazos. Yell was definitely on the road and spreading the word.[24] The word was disinformation.

Charles Elliot, the British chargé, wrote President Jones on 5 April to keep him informed of his progress. Elliot departed Galveston in a ship bound for Charleston, but when the ship was out of sight of land, the HMS *Eurydice*, commanded by his cousin, Captain Charles George Elliot, R.N., came alongside, and he transferred to his cousin's ship for the trip to Veracruz. Elliot hoped to be reported by those "watching eyes" in Galveston as headed for Charleston, and arrive in Veracruz unobserved. President Jones noted on the margin of Elliot's letter that a man wearing a white hat arrived in Mexico a few days after the date of the letter.[25] The HMS *Eurydice* arrived off Veracruz on the evening of 11 April. Her captain immediately departed for Mexico City. Accompanying him was an inconspicuous man in a white hat. His elaborate precautions did not provide Elliot the cover that he desired. The "watching eyes" were reporting from Galveston, Charleston, and Veracruz. Three days later, after having been duly robbed en route by highwaymen, the cousins arrived at the capital.[26]

In the middle of February 1845, Navy Secretary John Y. Mason had Commodore Robert F. Stockton, U.S. Navy, come to Washington, D.C., from his duty station at Norfolk, Virginia, for a briefing on his forthcoming cruise. Secretary Mason issued orders dated 28 February 1845 to Commodore Stockton to sail his squadron to the Mediterranean Sea. The purpose of the cruise was to show the new warship *Princeton* in the principal ports of the Mediterranean.[27]

When the administration changed, so did Stockton's orders. The new Secretary of the Navy George Bancroft issued new orders on 2 April 1845. Stockton was ordered to report to Commodore David Conner in the Gulf of Mexico with his squadron of *Princeton, Saratoga, St. Mary's,* and *Porpoise.* Commodore Conner was commander of the Home Squadron which was stationed off the coast of Mexico in order to implement American foreign policy if required. During the second week of April 1845, Stockton sailed the *Princeton* to Philadelphia to take on board more weaponry. The peaceful cruise in the Mediterranean was forgotten, and preparations were made to make the *Princeton* combat ready. When Stockton returned to Norfolk his orders were changed again.[28]

Secretary Bancroft's order to Commodore Stockton, commanding a squadron of United States vessels in Hampton Roads, was dated 22 April 1845:

> You will proceed with the vessels that have been placed under your command to the vicinity of Galveston, Texas, and lay as close to the shore as security will permit. You will take one of the vessels into the port of Galveston, and there display the American flag; or more if the bar will permit.
>
> You will yourself go on shore, and make yourself acquainted with the dispositions of the people of Texas, and their relations with Mexico, of which you will report to this Department.
>
> After remaining at or off Galveston as long as in your judgment may seem necessary, you will proceed to join the squadron of Commodore Conner, off Vera Cruz.[29]

On 28 April 1845 the *Norfolk Beacon* reported, "The U.S. Squadron under command of Com. Stockton consisting of the steam frigate *Princeton,* sloops of war *St. Mary's* and *Saratoga,* and brig *Porpoise* sailed from Hampton Roads yesterday morning with sealed orders. Their destination doubtless is the Gulf of Mexico."[30] True as it stands, but the difference between the destination being Veracruz and the destination being Galveston was enormous — geographically, politically, and militarily.

Robert Field Stockton (1795–1866) was born in Princeton, New Jersey. He was the grandson of Richard Stockton, a signer of the Declaration of Independence. Stockton joined the navy as a midshipman in 1811, and served during the War of 1812 under Commodore John Rodgers. From 1816 to 1820 he served on ships stationed in the Mediterranean Sea, where he participated in the war against the Barbary pirates, and also fought two duels with British naval officers. To the crew of his ships he was known as "Fighting Bob" Stockton. In 1821 Stockton sailed to the west coast of Africa for the American Colonization Society and obtained land, which later became Liberia.[31]

Stockton inherited the family homestead at Princeton in 1821, and lived there on leave of absence from the navy for a decade. He devoted his time to the organization of the New Jersey Colonization Society, of which he was the first president, and invested his private fortune in the construction of the Delaware and Raritan Canal, serving as its first president. Becoming involved in New Jersey politics, Stockton allied himself with Andrew Jackson, and became one of the general's most intimate friends.[32]

In 1838 Stockton was promoted to captain, and returned to active duty. He was ordered to the ship-of-the-line *Ohio* as commanding officer, and departed for a tour in the Mediterranean Sea. In 1840, while on leave, Stockton took part in the presidential election campaign, speaking in most of the counties of New Jersey on behalf of William H. Harrison. After Harrison's death, Vice President Tyler became president and offered Stockton the secretary of the navy post in his cabinet, but Stockton declined the offer.

With John Ericsson, later designer of the *Monitor*, Stockton drew up plans for the *Princeton*, the first warship to be driven with a screw propeller. Stockton designed two twelve-inch guns, larger than any in use, for the *Princeton*, and named them "Peacemaker" and "Oregon."[33] Secretary of State Upshur was killed on 28 February 1844 when one of these guns exploded during a Potomac River cruise for President Tyler and his cabinet.

Robert Field Stockton was not your ordinary naval officer. He was one of the wealthiest men in New Jersey and an important public figure. Stockton had a reputation for getting things done in a flamboyant and unconventional manner. He was described as an "egregious braggart" who was "bombastically aggressive."[34] He was the type of man who sought risk, responsibility, and action. When it came to the United States of America, he was an avid expansionist and an extreme American nationalist. When it came to the presidential campaign of 1844, Stockton was probably James Polk's most important and influential supporter in New Jersey.[35]

While Stockton and his squadron were en route to Galveston, A. J. Donelson was busy spinning a web of disinformation in Texas. Donelson convinced the new Texas Secretary of State Ebenezer Allen of a Mexican military threat on the western frontier of Texas, the magnitude of which put the independence of Texas at risk. Donelson persuaded Allen to write a letter asking the United States for protection. With United States troops handling the defense of the Republic of Texas, annexation could not be far away. The letter was sent to President Jones for approval, but Jones did not believe there was a threat, and the letter was not sent. The president knew the British were in Mexico City negotiating a peace treaty in his behalf. In his view, the United States wanted to send troops to Texas when there was not a hostile foot, either Indian or Mexican, in Texas. The object was not to protect Texas, but to ensure a collision with Mexico.[36]

Other threats from the United States sailed across the Gulf of Mexico to Texas. The New Orleans *Commercial Bulletin* declared the United States must occupy Texas, as President James Madison occupied West Florida, if Texas rejected the United States annexation offer. The New Orleans *Picayune* took the position that if the people of Texas were prevented from the opportunity to express their will by President Jones and his British and French conspirators, President Polk would be justified in using military force to end "the tyranny of foreign dictation."

Sam Houston was opposed to the United States terms for annexation. He wanted boundary negotiations with Mexico or independence. Houston was the one man in Texas who had any chance of stopping the American steamroller. But, considering the subtle military threats coming out of United States newspapers, articles in newspapers suggesting the possibility of Houston for president of the United States, a private letter from Andrew Jackson which was delivered by Donelson, and the knowledge that the majority was for annexation, Houston decided it was in his own best interest not to fight, and opted out of the game. He arrived at Galveston on 4 May 1845, bound for the *Hermitage* to discuss his political future with Andrew Jackson.[37]

Archibald Yell informed President Polk of Houston's arrival in Galveston in his letter of 5 May 1845. Charles Wickliffe wrote Polk on the same day. Wickliffe had undertaken a trip to the Rio Grande, but the ship encountered very heavy winds, and Wickliffe and his "confidant" (possibly H. L. Kinney) became too sick to continue. Prior to the bad weather, Wickliffe had collected some excellent information. He described for Polk the geographical features and the military significance of Corpus Christi and Brazos Santiago, and explained the need to occupy both or at least one of these places. To occupy Corpus Christi or Brazos Santiago it would be necessary to transport the troops by ship because they could not be marched over land at certain seasons due to the harshness of the land and the weather.[38]

Donelson reported to Secretary Buchanan from New Orleans on 11 May 1845: "Governor Tell [Yell] who has spent some time in Texas, and is familiar with the influences at work there, and with the probable course of action which will settle the question of annexation, is the bearer of this communication, and may be safely relied on for details which may not have been given in my previous dispatches."[39] Information of a delicate nature was only passed by trusted individuals and not entrusted to paper.

Commodore Stockton's squadron anchored off Galveston on 12 May 1845.[40] Stockton's activities during his stay in Galveston in no way reflected his written orders. Yell had secret oral orders. Wickliffe had secret oral orders. Did Stockton have secret oral orders? Richard Stenberg in his article, "The Failure of Polk's War Intrigue of 1845," described what he considered Stockton's and Wickliffe's secret orders. They were sent to instigate Texas to seize the "disputed" territory west of the Nueces River, and start a war with Mexico in which the United States would immediately join in "defense" of Texas.[41]

Duff Green was still in Texas, pushing for annexation, and eager to expand the United States at the expense of Mexico when Stockton and Wickliffe were there, and with them pushed for the invasion of Mexico.[42] President Jones was kept informed of the attempt to manipulate the foreign policy of the Republic of Texas, and was very interested in the meetings held by Stockton, Wickliffe, Major General Sidney Sherman, commander of the Texas militia, and others, which resulted in the active preparations at Galveston for organizing volunteer forces to invade Mexico.[43]

Wickliffe reported to Secretary Buchanan on 20 May 1845 from Galveston. He described his visit to Brazos County where he did not see or hear one man who was opposed to annexation. From a source in the San Antonio area and another source who had a secret correspondence by way of San Antonio with Mexico City and other cities on the border, Wickliffe was informed of Mexican preparations for military action of some kind in the area between the Nueces River and the Rio Grande. Wickliffe wanted to visit this area. He had a contact who was well acquainted with General Arista, and it was hoped that General Arista would tell this man the truth concerning the intentions of Mexico. Wickliffe's contact, with whom he had confidence in his fidelity and character, had come from Kentucky and made a fortune in trading with Mexico. Major General Sherman had agreed to accompany Wickliffe on his trip. Commodore Stockton was fully informed of Wickliffe's plan and would provide the transportation. Wickliffe reported to Buchanan that Commodore Stockton had agreed to sail his squadron to Corpus Christi and Brazos Santiago. While the ships were in port, Major General Sherman was to visit the frontier posts on an intelligence collection mission. If this mission verified Wickliffe's information, Sherman would call out the militia to repel the Mexicans. The cruise was delayed due to adverse winds and never did reach Corpus Christi.[44]

Commodore Stockton wrote Navy Secretary Bancroft from his flagship *Princeton* on 22 May 1845. He had sent for Major General Sherman, and "He [Sherman] has consented to call out the troops, to clear and protect the boundary — he is to leave this place [Galveston] to morrow to advise with the President on the Subject." Stockton then requested more provisions and powder be sent to Pensacola or New Orleans. Stockton had used no significant amount of powder at the time of his request, and there is no reason to doubt that the ship chandlers of Galveston could satisfy the normal provision requirements of his squadron. Stockton would need extra provisions and powder only if he was going to supply a large number of personnel, not including his squadron, on short notice. Bancroft did not bat an eye, but immediately replied, "Orders will be given to furnish powder and supplies at Pensacola on your requisitions."[45] Bancroft did not ask why powder and provisions were needed, or how much powder and provisions were needed.

On the same day Commodore Stockton also wrote to Commodore David Conner, the senior United States naval officer in the Gulf of Mexico. Stockton revealed to Conner that he had come to Galveston "under private instructions, copies of which I presume are enclosed by the Department to you, which I fear will keep me here longer than I wished. If however war should be declared in the mean time, I will as soon as possible be by your side."[46]

A. J. Donelson, in a report from New Orleans dated 24 May 1845, described to Secretary Buchanan the events taking place in Texas. He made clear that no means were omitted "to hasten the official action of the Texian Executive." To counteract the British and the French, Donelson wrote, "I had secret and timely information of every movement calculated to produce delay, and was able to look without apprehension on the mission of Smith, as well as the extraordinary efforts of the French and British Ministers to make the execution of our proposals impossible." Using newspapers as a source, Donelson informed Buchanan of Stockton's arrival in Galveston, and his plan to sail to Brazos Santiago in a joint venture with Major General Sherman to stop the Mexican troops if there should be a belligerent movement on that frontier. Donelson saw no probability that such a movement was yet to be expected from Mexico. "Such an idea is contradicted by all the reports received here from that Government." Donelson hoped that the military force under Stockton would not disturb "this posture of affairs."[47]

Commodore Stockton wrote Secretary Bancroft from Galveston on 27 May 1845. This letter clarifies the requisition for provisions and powder, and the "private instructions." The letter purports to disconnect the United States from the actions of an individual, but in reality, connects the individual with the Polk administration.

> Since my last letter I have seen Mr. Mayfield late [Texan] Secretary of State—who says that if the people here did not feel assured that the Boundary line would be the Rio Grande three fourths and himself amongst the number would oppose the annexation—But I need hardly say another word on that subject; Its importance is apparent—But it may perhaps be as well for me in this way to let you know how I propose to settle the matter without committing the U. States—The Major General will call out three thousand men & "R. F. Stockton Esq." will supply them in a private way with provisions and ammunition—
> Yours
> [signed] R. F. Stockton[48]

Commodore Stockton's letter basically informed the secretary of the navy that in a friendly foreign nation he was raising an army and supplying it with United States provisions and ammunition to invade another friendly foreign nation. It was time for the immediate recall of Commodore Stockton, an investigation into his activities, and the convening of a general court-martial, unless Commodore Stockton had secret orders to do what he was doing. Stockton was not recalled, there was no investigation, and no general court-martial.

Stockton, Wickliffe, and Sherman had several meetings on board the *Princeton*. At these meetings they planned their covert operation, i.e., the invasion of Mexico, and the disinformation operations needed to justify the invasion. Dr. J. H. Wright, passed assistant surgeon of the *Princeton*, was selected to represent Stockton, and present the proposal to President Anson Jones.[49] Major General Sherman accompanied Dr. Wright to Washington-on-the-Brazos.

The Texas president was born in Great Barrington, Massachusetts, on 20 January 1798. His family was very poor and very large. Anson Jones was the thirteenth of fourteen children. At nineteen he started studying medicine, but his studies were constantly interrupted by the effort to make a living. After ten years of hard work, disappointment, failure, and frustration, Anson Jones received his degree of doctor of medicine from Jefferson College, Canonsburg, Pennsylvania, in 1827. After five unsuccessful years practicing in Philadelphia, Jones moved to New Orleans where he started drinking and gambling. In 1833 he landed at Brazoria, Mexico, with $17 in his pocket. Brazoria needed a trained physician, and Jones was welcomed. He established a busy practice, and became a respected member of the pioneer community. Jones served as a physician and soldier in Houston's army, and fought at the battle of San Jacinto.

When Houston was elected president of the new republic he sent Jones to Washington, D.C., as the new nation's representative. After that

Jones was elected to the Texas Senate, and became its presiding officer. When Houston was reelected president, he appointed Jones secretary of state. The two men were too unlike to become close friends, but Houston evidently trusted him. Anson Jones was elected president in September 1844 only with the powerful support of Houston. Jones, a plain, friendly, well-meaning man, was 46 years old when he was sworn in on 9 December 1844.[50]

Sherman and Wright met with President Jones on 28 May 1845, and spent the next three days discussing the covert operation. Major General Sherman represented himself and his associates in the militia. Dr. Wright informed Jones that he was the surgeon of the *Princeton* and the secretary of Commodore Stockton. Under the list of officers on board the *Princeton*, the Commodore's secretary was J. P. Norris.[51]

Wright told Jones he was sent by Commodore Stockton to propose that Jones authorize Major General Sherman to raise a force of two or three thousand men, or as many as might be necessary to attack, capture, and hold the Mexican town of Matamoros. Commodore Stockton would provide assistance with his squadron, under the pretext of giving the protection promised by the United States to Texas by William S. Murphy in 1844. Stockton would supply the necessary provisions, arms, and ammunition for the troops, land them at strategic points on the coast, and would agree to pay the officers and men to be engaged.

Wright informed Jones of Stockton's consultations with Major General Sherman, who approved the plan and was present to say so. The people from Galveston to Washington-on-the-Brazos had been spoken to about the plan and approved it unanimously, and all that was waiting was the sanction of the government. Major General Sherman confirmed Dr. Wright's statement, and hoped President Jones would approve of the plan.

President Jones asked Dr. Wright for written instructions from the commodore. Wright answered that no written instructions would be forthcoming, but Stockton would visit Jones, and describe the operation personally if Jones desired. Jones asked if Andrew Jackson Donelson knew of the plan. Wright would only say that the operation was secret, and had the sanction of the United States government. President Polk did not wish to be known in the matter, but Polk approved Stockton's plan, and as evidence of that to Jones, Charles Wickliffe, Polk's personal agent in Texas, was associated with Stockton. Jones was told that President Polk wanted Texas to place herself in an attitude of active hostility toward Mexico, so that, when Texas came into the Union, she might bring a war with her, and this was the object of the proposed expedition to Matamoros.

Wright then explained to Jones that Commodore Stockton was very wealthy, and had the resources to support the expedition personally, and it was desirable that it should appear to the world as his individual enterprise. But Jones was to understand the United States government was at the bottom of it.[52]

On the second day of the discussions, word was received from Captain Hayes of the Texas Rangers that some 7,800 Mexican troops had arrived in northern Mexico, including those in Monterrey and along the Rio Grande, and that a body of Mexican soldiers, numbering about 100, had marched to a point on the Nueces River. Captain Hayes intended to start the next day with 50 men to give battle to the invaders on the Nueces. This purported "intelligence" was designed to force Jones to approve Stockton's plan. Captain Hayes was one of those who had joined with Stockton in Galveston in the preparation of the operation. There was no attack by the Mexican army, and no counterattack by Captain Hayes; instead, there was a disinformation attack as part of the overall covert operation.[53]

After being told the whole plan Jones said, "So, gentlemen, the Commodore, on the part of the United States, wishes me to manufacture a war for them"; to which Wright and Sherman replied affirmatively. Jones then had a private conversation with Sherman. The militia commander again urged Jones to approve the covert operation, saying it was extremely popular among the people, and he would have no trouble raising the men if Stockton provided provisions and pay.

Jones needed time for the British chargé Elliot to return from Mexico with the hoped-for peace treaty. The peace treaty would give Texas the luxury of options. President Jones told Wright he would need a few days longer to think about the proposal, plus Congress would convene on 16 June 1845 and he wanted their advice on the matter.[54]

A. J. Donelson returned to Galveston where he would have had the opportunity to meet with Stockton and Wickliffe. His report to Buchanan from Galveston dated 2 June 1845 does not mention the mission of Wright and Sherman; instead:

> I adverted in my last dispatch from New Orleans to the presence of Capt. Stoktons [sic] squadron here, and to a rumour that he had sailed to Santiago, to cooperate with Genl Sherman of the Texan Militia in defending the occupation of the Rio Grande. This was not correct. Capt. Stockton weighed anchor, at this port, a few days ago, for the purpose of examining the coast, but he has since returned.[55]

Wickliffe explained to Polk in his letter of 3 June 1845 the rationale of Stockton's plan. During April, May, and June, Wickliffe, Donelson, Yell, Green, Stockton, and Sherman were emphasizing the danger of invasion (possibly at British instigation), and the need for American intervention; so the excuse of an expected Mexican attack across the Rio Grande was ready at hand to rationalize a preemptive invasion.[56]

Ebenezer Allen wrote President Jones on 5 June 1845 of some "unaccredited and informed" agents acting in the pretended behalf of the United States, endeavoring to take advantage of the crisis to push Texas into war with Mexico. Allen stated that Major General Sherman told him of Donelson's approval of an immediate Texas military occupation of the territory west of the Nueces River, "but not as Minister of the United States." Allen only had indirect news from Stockton who, in urging military operations on the part of Texas, seemed only to act through others, holding himself in the meantime, "wisely aloof."[57]

Ashbel Smith told of the promises of lavish projects by Donelson, Yell, Wickliffe, and Stockton. He cited the following as examples: clear out rivers, deepen harbor entrances, build lighthouses, erect military works, fortifications for the defense of the coast, and important works of internal improvement. Employment, wealth, and prosperity would reign in the annexed land. Washington, D.C., was going to make them all rich. The secret agents used bribes, disinformation (lies), and promises of public offices to obtain support for annexation and the invasion of Mexico.[58]

The agents of the United States in Texas sent numerous reports to their controllers in Washington, D.C. Archibald Yell reported to President Polk, Commodore Stockton reported to Secretary Bancroft, A. J. Donelson reported to Secretary Buchanan, and Charles Wickliffe apparently had the discretion to report to Polk or Buchanan.[59]

In late May 1845 Wickliffe wrote Buchanan of the need for light draft vessels to be used as coastal vessels between the Sabine and the Rio Grande rivers, and as transports up the rivers. Wickliffe also recommended the immediate stationing at Galveston of a quartermaster, to make all necessary preparations for the subsistance of the troops in advance of the order for their march.[60] Wickliffe was providing excellent information for the invasion of Mexico.

While the American agents continued their various operations to persuade the people of Texas that annexation and invasion of Mexico was in their own best interest, Jones waited. He waited for the return of the British chargé from Mexico with propositions of peace and an acknowledgment of Texas independence. Even if these propositions were not acceptable to the Texans, he felt it would halt any movement for an invasion of Mexico.

Elliot returned from Mexico and delivered his dispatches to Jones at the Texas capital. President Jones formally announced the agreement with Mexico on 4 June 1845 and proclaimed the end of the war. Wickliffe reported that this proclamation came "like a peal of thunder in a clear sky."[61] President Jones was able to "declare my independence of Com. Stockton and Mr. Wright, Gov. Yell, Major Donelson, Mr. Polk and Mr. Buchanan."[62]

The British chargé, upon landing in Galveston, learned from a very reliable source that Commodore Stockton was using every means available to induce President Jones to immediately issue a proclamation calling out volunteers for the purpose of occupying the disputed territory to the Rio Grande. President Jones confirmed this when Elliot delivered the Mexican agreement, and told Elliot that he would issue no proclamation nor authorize any movement of troops unless Mexico made a movement upon Texas.[63]

Wickliffe reported to Polk on 4 June 1845 that President Jones was against annexation and would not allow military operations on the border. In Wickliffe's opinion, Mexico's peace offer would be rejected by the people. Elliot would inform General Arista in Mexico of this rejection, and Mexico would cross the Rio Grande. The people of Texas in this situation were ready to defend themselves but did not have the resources.[64] Wickliffe was reporting what he hoped would happen and produced a poor report.

On the same day Stockton wrote Bancroft a very optimistic letter, which was also a very poor intelligence report. In it he asserted that Jones approved of his "army of occupation," and that he (Stockton) was hard at work to induce the authorities to call the Texas volunteer army into the field. When Polk received these confusing reports, he took action. Buchanan and Bancroft were directed to send dispatches by personal messenger to Wickliffe and Stockton to urge the Texans to attack the Mexicans in the disputed area.[65] It was all to no avail. In this instance the problem of communications would defeat Polk, if this was not already accomplished by Jones, the British, the French, and the Mexicans. It took three to six weeks for a report to travel from Galveston to Washington, D.C., and for an answer to make the return trip. Events overtook Polk's dogged determination to have Texas enter the Union at war with Mexico.

Colonel James Morgan wrote President Jones on 12 July 1845: "Your proclamation came like a clap of thunder upon some folks. Sherman was very disappointed. No one appeared to me more upset by your proclamation than Com. S. I met him at Galveston. We had an hour or more conversation. He was evidently disappointed!"[66] General Edwin Morehouse, who had just arrived from the western frontier, informed Jones that the people of the west were glad Jones stopped Sherman from sending Texas troops for their protection. In his letter of 17 July 1845, Morehouse reported an American sent to Monterrey saw General Arista and said there was "no news or stir amongst the Mexican troops." Morehouse agreed, and he wrote, "It is all a humbug as to the Mexicans concentrating on the frontier."[67]

Wickliffe departed Galveston for Washington-on-the-Brazos on 13 June 1845 to join Donelson. He would remain there while the Texas

Congress had the subject of annexation under consideration. Wickliffe's report to Buchanan was prepared on the same day. He believed the efforts of Jones and the British to defeat annexation would be overcome by the devotion of the people of Texas to their "Fatherland." Buchanan was informed of the activities of Colonel Kinney of Corpus Christi, who, with 60 men, had set out to investigate a rumor of Mexican troops crossing the Rio Grande and marching north to take possession of Kinney's ranch.[68]

Donelson had communicated his plan for Texas to request military support from the United States to Secretary Buchanan. On 15 June 1845, Buchanan wrote Donelson that the president believed it was preferable that Texas herself should drive the Mexicans from her territory. If Texas would take the initiative, the United States would have to bear the expense of such an expedition.[69] The same scenario was repeated over and over—Texas come into the Union at war with Mexico.

President Jones could provide an option, but as far as annexation was concerned, the Texas Congress was controlled by Donelson. On 18 June 1845, a joint resolution, which accepted the United States plan for annexation and sanctioned the calling of the annexation convention, was adopted unanimously. By similar vote the projected peace treaty with Mexico was promptly rejected by the Texas Senate. The convention was scheduled to assemble at Austin on 4 July 1845.[70]

Wickliffe arrived at Austin on 1 July 1845, and from here on 5 July he sent his last report to Buchanan. Knowing that it would please the administration to have the question of annexation settled on 4 July, Wickliffe suggested this to the members of the convention. The suggestion was favorably received, and the annexation bill was passed with one dissenting vote on 4 July. Wickliffe informed Buchanan that it was his intention to set out for the United States as soon as he was able to travel.[71]

The Texas convention that accepted the United States annexation offer had only one member who was born in the Mexican province of Texas—José Antonio Navarro of San Antonio. Eighteen members came from Tennessee, eight from Virginia, seven from Georgia, six from Kentucky, and five from North Carolina. Scions from several distinguished American families, several former members of the United States Congress, a chief justice of Alabama, and a former Mississippi governor were all involved in the decisionmaking process.[72] In 1844 an outburst of land speculation lured thousands of American settlers to Texas, and its population reached 100,000 at the time of annexation.[73]

Some Texans saw the final months of the Republic as a sordid affair. The last president of Texas, Anson Jones, believed the secret of Donelson's control of the Texas Congress was the lavish promises of office to its members. Jones was told by a reliable source that there was not a single member who was not approached in this manner. Ashbel Smith described the road to annexation as, "the bribery and corruption of some noisy politicians, by promises of office made to them contingent on annexation by the secret agents of the Federal Government, Governor Yell and Mr. Wickliffe, and the system of detraction of the offices of our own Government for the purpose of destroying the confidence of the people of Texas in them."[74]

Commodore Stockton left Galveston on 23 June 1845, after his covert operation to have Texas invade Mexico collapsed in the wake of President Jones's peace proclamation. Stockton, still flying his flag on the *Princeton*, did not report to Commodore Conner, but sailed up the east coast of the United States and arrived at Annapolis on 3 July 1845. Immediately after the *Princeton* dropped anchor, Dr. Wright was sent to Washington with the Texas joint resolution to accept annexation and Stockton's report to Bancroft.[75] Stockton introduced the assistant surgeon to Bancroft by writing, "Doctor Wright was sent by me to Washington during the recent session of the Congress of Texas — as well as on a previous occasion. You will find him an intelligent gentleman, well acquainted with recent occurrences in Texas."[76]

Secretary of the Navy Bancroft wrote to Stockton the same day, "You have leave to come to this city, if your convenience and other circumstances make it agreeable to you. The President would be pleased to converse with you on the events of your cruise."[77]

Bancroft wrote Stockton on 7 July 1845, and the letter bore the notation, "now at Washington." Stockton was not relieved, reprimanded, or court-martialed for his actions in Texas. Instead, he was invited to Washington for a chat with the president. We know he went to Washington because Bancroft's letter of 7 July places him in Washington.

It was decided that the *Princeton* should return to the Gulf of Mexico as soon as possible. As Stockton had no desire to be under Commodore Conner, and believed the real fighting would be in California, he was detached from the *Princeton*, and in August 1845 given command of the *Congress*.

After his cruise to Texas, Stockton believed that there would be war with Mexico, even though Mexico had conditionally recognized Texas independence. During his talk with President Polk, he expressed his reasons for expecting war in the near future. Polk concurred with Stockton on war with Mexico, and displayed his confidence in the ability of Commodore Stockton not only by giving him command of the *Congress*, but by sending him to California to command the United States Pacific Squadron. It was thought that California would be the proper theater for a man of action.[78]

An excerpt from a letter Stockton wrote Bancroft on 24 October 1845, provides evidence of Stockton's secret orders and of the several conversations Bancroft and Stockton had during Stockton's stay in Washington. "Having performed in the best way I could the duty assigned to me in Texas, I returned to the United States, to bring glad tidings of annexation, and to explain to you my views (the importance of which I no doubt overstated) in regard to our relations with Mexico. During those conversations I stated to you that I thought Mexico would probably, when ready, commence hostilities."[79]

The Texas chargé in Washington, D.C., gave Anson Jones direct and positive assurance that Stockton's covert operation had the sanction of the United States government. William D. Lee, the Texas chargé, wrote Jones on 13 September 1845, describing the anger of President Polk, Treasury Secretary Robert J. Walker, War Secretary William L. Marcy, and newspaper editor Thomas Ritchie when President Jones did not agree to Stockton's plan, and did not authorize Major General Sherman to invade Mexico. The letter was lost, but Jones and William Lee had frequent conversations on the subject in November 1850. Lee concurred with Jones on the contents of the letter.[80]

President Jones considered the missions of Yell, Wickliffe, Stockton, Wright, and Donelson to be all the same — convince Jones to manufacture a war with Mexico. When Jones would not cooperate, Wickliffe traveled from Galveston to Austin urging violence and rebellion against the government of Texas.[81] The determination of the Polk administration — personified by Polk himself — and its secret agents led Jones to this conclusion: "The war with the United States and Mexico was inevitable, only because the United States had predetermined it should be so; and solely for that reason."[82] The annexation of Texas and the Mexican War were two different matters. If Polk had not wanted California from the start of his administration there would have been no difficulty with Mexico over Texas.[83]

In his report to Congress on 1 December 1845, the secretary of the navy stated that the Home Squadron under Commodore Conner was increased by the *Princeton, Porpoise, St. Mary's,* and *Saratoga,* under the command of Commodore Stockton.[84] Bancroft said nothing of these ships being in Galveston instead of Veracruz, or of Stockton in the *Princeton* returning to Annapolis. Disinformation at its best, but who was the enemy?

When he was able to travel Charles Wickliffe returned to the United States. Wickliffe was paid $1,571.50 on 24 December 1845, for compensation and expenses out of the State Department "contingent expenses of foreign intercourse" fund.[85] Archibald Yell received $833.19 from the same fund on 23 May 1845.[86]

James Polk was very adept in choosing and handling secret agents.

When possible Polk chose people he knew and trusted, and it was his procedure to personally brief and debrief his secret agents.

When A. J. Donelson returned from Texas, he stayed at the White House as Polk's guest. Donelson was debriefed by Polk and members of the cabinet on Texas and Mexican affairs at the 20 September 1845 cabinet meeting.[87] Charles Wickliffe and Polk had a long conversation concerning Texas affairs on 2 February 1846.[88] Governor Archibald Yell discussed John Slidell's mission to Mexico with Polk in early February 1846. Yell had access to Polk and a debriefing seems logical, even though it is not mentioned in Polk's diary.[89]

As the last president of Texas, Anson Jones surrendered his authority to the newly elected governor of one of the United States on 19 February 1846. Jones took his own life in the old Capitol Hotel in Houston on 9 January 1858.[90]

On 29 March 1846, Senator Samuel Houston, former president of Texas, called on Polk who was very pleased to see him. Polk had served in Congress with Houston, and always considered him his friend. After the visit Polk described Houston as thoroughly Democratic, and fully determined to support Polk's administration.[91] But all things change, and by February 1847 Polk was informed by a representative from Texas of Houston's dissatisfaction with the administration. Polk had heard this from other sources, but he believed Houston had no cause to be dissatisfied. The problem, in Polk's appraisal of the situation, was Houston's aspiration to be a presidential candidate and Houston's dissatisfaction with Polk's efforts to promote Houston.[92]

At the outbreak of the Mexican War, Archibald Yell left Congress, and was commissioned colonel of the 1st Arkansas Volunteer Cavalry. Yell would not return to his seat in the House of Representatives. On 23 February 1847, he was killed at the battle of Buena Vista.[93]

When Polk received word in April 1847 of the death of Archibald Yell, he wrote in his diary "my old esteemed friend, Col. Archibald Yell, of the Arkansas mounted Regiment. I deeply deplore his loss. He was a brave and good man, and among the best friends I had on earth, and had been so for 25 years."[94]

Notes to Chapter 2

1. Remini, *Andrew Jackson*, 3:500–501.
2. Charles G. Sellers, Jr., *James K. Polk, Jacksonian, (1795–1843)* (Princeton: Princeton University Press, 1957), p. 40.
3. Remini, *Andrew Jackson*, p. 118.
4. Charles G. Sellers, Jr., *James K. Polk, Continentalist, 1843–1846* (Princeton, N.J.: Princeton University Press, 1966), p. 127.

5. McCoy, *Polk*, p. 82.

6. Ibid., p. 81.

7. Milo Milton Quaife, ed., *The Diary of James K. Polk* (Chicago: A. C. McClurg, 1910), 4:261.

8. McCoy, *Polk*, pp. 62–63.

9. Smith, *Texas*, p. 353.

10. *Dictionary of American Biography*, 1981 index, s.v. "Yell, Archibald," by David Y. Thomas.

11. Stenberg, "Polk and Texas," p. 353.

12. Smith, *Texas*, pp. 434–436.

13. Jones, *Texas*, p. 473.

14. David M. Pletcher, *The Diplomacy of Annexation* (Columbia: University of Missouri Press, 1973), p. 192.

15. Ibid., p. 192.

16. John Bassett Moore, ed., *The Works of James Buchanan* (Philadelphia: J. B. Lippincott, 1909), 6:130–131.

17. *Dictionary of American Biography*, 1981 index, s.v. "Wickliffe, Charles Anderson," by Robert Spencer Cotterill.

18. Stenberg, "Polk and Texas," p. 353.

19. George Ticknor Curtis, *Life of James Buchanan* (New York: Harper and Brothers, 1883; reprint ed., Freeport, New York: Books for Libraries, 1969), p. 588.

20. Fletcher, *Diplomacy*, p. 194.

21. Smith, *Texas*, pp. 442–443.

22. *Dictionary of American Biography*, 1981 index, s.v. "Walker, Robert John," by H. Donelson Jordan.

23. Glenn W. Price, *Origins of the War with Mexico* (Austin: University of Texas Press, 1967), p. 106.

24. Jones, *Texas*, p. 449.

25. Ibid., p. 443.

26. Smith, *Texas*, p. 423.

27. Price, *Origins*, pp. 75–76.

28. Ibid., p. 76.

29. Ibid., p. 48.

30. *Pensacola Gazette* (Florida), 10 May 1845.

31. *Encyclopaedia Britannica*, 1956 ed., s.v. "Stockton, Robert Field."

32. *Dictionary of American Biography*, 1981 index, s.v. "Stockton, Robert Field," by Charles O. Paullin.

33. *Encyclopaedia Britannica*, 1956 ed., s.v. "Stockton, Robert Field."

34. Cardinal Goodwin, *John Charles Frémont* (Stanford, Calif.: Stanford University Press, 1930), pp. 121–122.

35. Price, *Origins*, p. 48.

36. Jones, *Texas*, p. 67.

37. Smith, *Texas*, p. 443.

38. James K. Polk Papers, *Presidents' Papers Index Series*. Washington, D.C.: Library of Congress, 1969. Reel 38.

39. William R. Manning, ed., *Diplomatic Correspondence of the United States — Inter-American Affairs 1831–1860* (Washington, D.C.: Carnegie Endowment for International Peace, 1937), 12:409–410.

40. Price, *Origins*, p. 108.

41. Stenberg, "Polk's Intrigue," p. 46.

42. Smith, *Texas*, p. 447.

43. Jones, *Texas*, p. 48.

44. Manning, *Correspondence*, 12:412–415.

45. Price, *Origins*, p. 119.

46. Ibid., p. 120.

47. Manning, *Correspondence*, 12:419–420.

48. Alstyne, *Empire*, p. 138.

49. *Pensacola Gazette* (Florida), 10 May 1845.

50. Smith, *Texas*, p. 374.

51. *Pensacola Gazette* (Florida), 10 May 1845.

52. Jones, *Texas*, pp. 48–49.

53. Price, *Origins*, p. 127.

54. Jones, *Texas*, p. 49.

55. Manning, *Correspondence*, 12:422–424.

56. Pletcher, *Diplomacy*, p. 198.

57. Jones, *Texas*, pp. 466–468.

58. Stenberg, "Polk and Texas," pp. 351–352.

59. Smith, *Texas*, p. 440.

60. Manning, *Correspondence*, 12:421.

61. Pletcher, *Diplomacy*, p. 196.

62. Price, *Origins*, p. 113.

63. Ibid., p. 131.

64. Ibid., p. 128.

65. Ibid., p. 139.

66. Jones, *Texas*, pp. 478–479.

67. Ibid., p. 479.

68. Manning, *Correspondence*, 12:433.

69. Stenberg, "Polk's Intrigue," p. 58.

70. Smith, *Texas*, p. 456.

71. Manning, *Correspondence*, 12:445.

72. Fehrenbach, *Lone Star*, p. 266.

73. Alstyne, *Empire*, p. 105.

74. Jones, *Texas*, p. 516.

75. Price, *Origins*, p. 149.

76. Robert Field Stockton Letterbook, 12 August 1843 to 16 February 1847 (Princeton, N.J.: Princeton University Library).

77. C. T. Neu, *Annexation of Texas in New Spain and the Anglo-American West* (Lancaster, Penn.: Lancaster, 1932), 2:93.

78. Samuel John Bayard, A *Sketch of the Life of Com. Robert F. Stockton* (New York: Derby and Jackson, 1856), p. 93.

79. Ibid., p. 95.

80. Jones, *Texas*, p. 491.

81. Ibid., p. 95.

82. Ibid., p. 69.

83. Jesse S. Reeves, *American Diplomacy under Tyler and Polk* (Baltimore: John Hopkins University Press, 1907), p. 189.

84. U.S. Congress, Senate, *Report of the Secretary of the Navy*, 29th Cong., 1st sess., 1845, p. 646.

85. U.S. Congress, House, *Contingent Expenses of the State Department*, H. Doc. 8, 29th Cong., 2nd sess., 1846, p. 24.

86. U.S. Congress, House, *Contingent Expenses of the State Department*, H. Doc. 11, 29th Cong., 1st sess., 1845, p. 26.

87. Quaife, *Polk Diary*, 1:37.

88. Ibid., 1:207.

89. Ibid., 1:231.

90. *Dictionary of American Biography*, 1981 index, s.v. "Jones, Anson," by Robert G. Caldwell.

91. Quaife, *Polk Diary*, 1:309.

92. Ibid., 2:363–364.

93. *Dictionary of American Biography*, 1981 index, s.v. "Yell, Archibald," by David Y. Thomas.

94. Quaife, *Polk Diary*, 2:451–452.

Part II
Mexico

Chapter 3

Dentist, Merchant, Secret Agent

James K. Polk had made political commitments to annex Texas and all of Oregon prior to the election of 1844. However, his real objective was California, which had not been mentioned by either of the parties in the presidential election campaign.[1] After his inauguration Polk told Secretary of the Navy George Bancroft that the acquisition of California was one of his chief goals. Polk understood what he wanted, but could not understand why Mexico did not agree. Polk was willing to buy, but Mexico was not willing to sell. Polk's plan for the expansion of the United States at the expense of Mexico could only reach fruition by war. It was impossible to suppose Mexico would willingly dismember itself.[2] What Mexico did not understand was that Polk was different from his predecessors. For this misjudgment Mexico would pay in blood and land.

United States relations with Mexico during the Polk administration were divided into two distinct phases. During the first phase, which lasted less than a year, Polk attempted by a mixture of diplomacy and force to secure for the United States the territories of New Mexico and California. The second phase was war. If Mexico would not sell, the desired territory would be taken by force.[3] The term "To conquer a peace" was coined to express Polk's policy. He wanted war with Mexico in order to force the Mexicans to hand over their land as a part of the peace treaty.

At the same time President Polk was sending secret agents into the Republic of Texas, he was also sending them into the Republic of Mexico. Secretary of State Buchanan's letter of 28 March 1845, to William S. Parrott described the suspension of diplomatic relations between Mexico and the United States, and the desire of President Polk to restore such relations. The president deemed it expedient to send a secret agent to Mexico for this purpose, and William S. Parrott was selected.[4]

The president's choice for this covert operation had practiced dentistry for many years in Mexico City, and then went into the import business there. As a businessman he lived above his means and ended up bankrupt. His only asset was a huge claim against the Mexican government. The claim, which was based largely upon the seizure of a lot of

bottled English porter, was initiated in 1836, and there was correspondence at various times from the United States minister to the
secretary of state concerning this matter. Parrott had presented his claim
before the commission of 1839,[5] and to the House Committee on Foreign
Affairs of the Twenty-Seventh Congress.[6] There were people in the administration who advised against sending Parrott because of his claim, but
Polk thought differently.

Polk considered Parrott a well-qualified person to be his secret agent
in Mexico. Parrott knew the language, the people, and the leaders. He was
energetic, intelligent, and had a stake in the outcome. Parrott was a very
voluminous reporter, but he had one serious defect in this area — his hand-
writing was atrocious.[7]

Waddy Thompson, United States minister to Mexico, wrote to Secretary of State Webster concerning Parrott's claim on 8 November 1842: "As
to the . . . claim of Mr. Parrott, it may be, and no doubt is just to some
extent but I cannot for bear to say that it is exaggerated to a disgusting
degree. To assert such a claim would subject both me and my Government to ridicule if nothing worse." Thompson painted a colorful picture
of Parrott's life in Mexico for Secretary Webster. He described Parrott's
dental career, and his entrance into business where his troubles began;
and Parrott's luxurious life-style as a businessman, which ended in
bankruptcy. He was at one time to all appearances possessed of a large fortune, but it was a deception; he was living on borrowed money. When the
time to pay arrived, there were various lawsuits between him and his
creditors, and this is where Parrott's claim against the Mexican government originated. Thompson explained, "for erroneous decisions of the
courts (as I understand it) he now claims redress from the government."
Parrott's claim of $690,000, including principal and interest, grew to
$986,880 when presented to Waddy Thompson, and the only support for
the claim was information provided by Parrott. To show how outrageous
Parrott's claim was, Thompson selected one item as an example: ". . . is
for 56, dozen bottles of English porter (worth when seized in 1836 — with
interest at 8 per cent from that time) — less than $1000 — for which a
charge is made of value of Porter . . . $1690 — Interest from 1836.
$6570 — Total $8260. Now am I with a drawn sword to demand the payment of this claim, I doubt not that the same process of exaggeration has
been applied to all other items."[8]

In November 1843 Waddy Thompson reported to Abel P. Upshur,
the new secretary of state, that negotiations concerning American claims
against Mexico were still proceeding. Thompson had examined the Parrott claim thoroughly, and did not hesitate to say that 2 percent on the
amount claimed would be a large allowance.[9] Thompson was wrong. Parrott finally did much better than 2 percent; he was awarded $114,750.[10]

Owing to Parrott's claim, Jesse S. Reeves in *American Diplomacy Under Tyler and Polk* wrote, "The selection of William S. Parrott as an agent for the reestablishment of diplomatic relations was a strange one." Reeves believed that Polk and Buchanan were probably ignorant of the matter, and selected Parrott because he had lived in Mexico.[11] A different viewpoint would be Parrott coming to the attention of Polk just because he had a claim. When Polk sent John Slidell to Mexico in November 1845 to negotiate, Slidell was to propose paying off the claims of American citizens against Mexico with the money the United States would pay Mexico for the northern provinces. If Mexico would not cooperate, Polk was ready with drawn sword to demand payment. Polk did not concern himself with the problems of the Mexican people or their government. It would have been reasonable conduct for him not to ponder the hostility engendered in Mexico City by Parrott's claim.

Parrott was to proceed without delay to Mexico. His mission was "to reach the President and other high officers of the Mexican government and especially the Minister of Foreign Affairs" and convince them it was in their best interest to restore friendly relations with the United States. He was to reveal his official character only if the Mexican authorities agreed to "renew our diplomatic intercourse" and only then "to state that the United States will send a Minister." He was to report as often as he could obtain safe and secret opportunities. His compensation was $8 per day, plus travel and other expenses, and vouchers would be appreciated. Parrott was advanced $1,000.[12]

Polk's concept of friendly relations was Mexico selling her northern provinces to the United States and accepting the Rio Grande as the border. However, this was not Mexico's concept of friendly relations with the United States. Buchanan's letter to Parrott represented the final step in the process of recruiting, briefing, and setting up communication and logistic procedures prior to the insertion of the secret agent into the target country.

As soon as Congress passed the joint annexation resolution, General Juan Nepomuceno Almonte, the Mexican minister, demanded his passport from the secretary of state, and left New York for Mexico by ship on 3 April 1845. Dr. William S. Parrott, United States secret agent, was a fellow passenger.[13]

Parrott was involved in a personally dangerous covert operation. Mexico at the time was a dangerous place, especially for a foreigner, and more especially for an American, but most especially for an American secret agent. Parrott was completely on his own. He had no safe house, no emergency exit route, no emergency communications, and no gold with which to bribe his way out. No backup of any kind was provided. Dangerous or not, from 26 April to 18 October 1845 Parrott sent at least

32 reports to Secretary Buchanan. These reports took from three to seven weeks to reach Washington, D.C. (see Figure 1, p. 47).

I have taken excerpts from Parrott's reports, and arranged them by the month and day. After each month there is a summary that includes comments on Parrott's reporting, and how his reports related to concurrent events and the reports of other intelligence collectors.

April 1845

26 April

> I reached this city on the 23rd....
> ...intense excitement among all parties and classes on the question of the annexation of Texas to the United States....
> War with the United States seems to be the desire of all parties rather than see Texas annexed to the U.S....
> In a separate package I forward four Govt papers, selected from the files, which contain the only matter of interest worthy of transmission.

29 April

> Contrary to an opinion expressed by some in Washington, that my being a claimant on Mexico, would operate to the prejudice of the Government, I have found a most hearty welcome from all quarters....

Summary

In Washington Parrott was given a specific intelligence collection requirement by Buchanan. The secretary of state wanted to know the lasting power of the present Mexican government and the causes of the last change in government. Parrott's experience in Mexico enabled him to satisfy Buchanan's requirement immediately upon his arrival in Mexico. He reported there would be no stability for years to come. The reasons for this included the character of the people, their manners, morals, institutions, and the climate.

Despite his "most hearty welcome," Parrott understood his delicate position. He informed Buchanan of his security procedures—"My instructions are deposited in safety, I keep no copies of my communications to the Department, so as not, under the most unfavorable turn things might take to be taken by surprise—."

Charles Elliot, the British chargé in Texas arrived in Mexico on 11 April 1845. His mission was to stop annexation by negotiating a peace

Figure 1. Parrott's Reports from Mexico City

Date Sent	Date Received in the Department of State
26 April 1845	28 May 1845
29 April 1845	19 May 1845
13 May 1845	2 June 1845
22 May 1845	23 June 1845
29 May 1845	23 June 1845
30 May 1845	23 June 1845
10 June 1845	17 July 1845
10 June 1845	17 July 1845
17 June 1845	Unknown
24 June 1845	17 July 1845
29 June 1845	17 July 1845
5 July 1845	1 September 1845
12 July 1845	1 September 1845
15 July 1845	1 September 1845
22 July 1845	1 September 1845
26 July 1845	25 August 1845
30 July 1845	25 August 1845
16 August 1845	Unknown
23 August 1845	15 September 1845
26 August 1845	Unknown
2 September 1845	11 October 1845
4 September 1845	11 October 1845
6 September 1845	11 October 1845
13 September 1845	17 October 1845
18 September 1845	17 October 1845
25 September 1845	7 November 1845
29 September 1845	21 October 1845
4 October 1845	7 November 1845
11 October 1845	7 November 1845
11 October 1845	Unknown
18 October 1845	9 November 1845

treaty between Texas and Mexico. On 29 April Parrott confirmed the activities of the British and the French in Mexico by forwarding to Buchanan a request of the secretary for foreign affairs to the Mexican Congress to treat with Texas.[14]

In April Parrott collected intelligence on the Texas annexation question, future stability of the Mexican government, activities of the British and French, and the status of the Mexican-Texas peace treaty. From the 29 April report we know that Buchanan and others in Washington were aware of Parrott's claim against the Mexican government. What is not known is who opposed Parrott's selection.

May 1845

13 May

The excitement against the Government and people of the United States . . . still prevails, although I am inclined to believe, not with the same intensity —

. . . the foreign Department. . . as it is now sold to the British interest, and cannot be approached by us. . . .

Mr. Shannon will leave this city to morrow morning, and it has been intimated to me through the Govt circle that I will not be permitted to remain after his departure. . . .

The English have even gone so far as to make believe that I have millions at my disposal, with which to prevent their schemes, and to promote that of the annexation of Texas to the United States. . . .

Great Britain has greatly increased her Naval Forces in the Pacific, the object of which, as stated, is, to take possession of, and hold upper California, in case of a war between the U.S. and Mexico —

22 May

It is not yet known, whether or not, I will be permitted to remain here. . . .

The "iniciativa" of the Government for power to treat with Texas, passed the senate . . . upon which an express was immediately sent to Vera Cruz, with dispatches to be conveyed to Texas. . . .

It is not now certain that any important change in the Cabinet can take place without a revolution, as general Paredes has informed the President ad-interim, that he will oppose any change, should its complexion be more liberal than it now is —

29 May

The Government has not yet granted my letter of security, nor has it informed me that my presence here is disagreeable to it; although it is the general impression that I am a secret agent — some say spy, of the Govt of the U.S.

. . . no hope of approaching directly or indirectly, the present Secretary of State, on the subject of my mission, as he is in the hands of the British Minister.

30 May

The opposition regards the robbery of a high public functionary, such as Mr. Shannon with shame, and call upon the Government to organize a police sufficiently strong to protect the public highways. . . .

Summary

Parrott's reporting in May stressed two important areas: Mexican attitude toward Texas annexation instead of independence, and the strength of British influence in Mexico.

He reported a confusing affair which gave rise to much excitement. The French minister, Baron de Ciprey, was fired upon, then arrested, and his secretary of legation badly beaten. Parrott hoped to clarify the situation when he procured "the french version of the affair."

Parrott also reported on the activities of Congress, political parties, and the departure and robbery of Mr. Shannon, the United States minister to Mexico. During May he sent Buchanan a wide variety of newspaper articles.

Parrott informed Buchanan that he was too vulnerable and exposed to keep copies of his letters or even notes, so there would be defects and repetitions in his correspondence. As a security precaution, Parrott wrote, "I can keep nothing written before me; I have therefore to write in haste, without preparation, and often without revision, as opportunities offer." Safe and reliable communications were difficult from Mexico City to Washington, D.C. Parrott considered the most expeditious and safe channel of communications to be the United States consul in Havana, Cuba.[15]

June 1845

10 June

> ... I have found means to communicate indirectly, with that portion of the Cabinet who now possess the greatest share of public confidence; from intelligence obtained through this channel, it does not seem that the present administration, has any intention or desire whatever, to come to an open rupture with the U.S. To the contrary, it is preparing the public mind for the worse, namely, the annexation of Texas to the American Union —

17 June

> Yesterday there was another alarm of revolution, which proved to be false; the public mind however, is fully prepared, and really expect a *True revolution*, which it is, unreservedly, said, is well nigh at hand. . . .
>
> I have satisfactorily ascertained, through the indirect channel of communication, . . . that the present Government will not declare war against the United States, even if Texas be annexed, provided the force of public opinion does not compel it to do so —

... as to the physical means necessary to carry on a war, with the slightest probability, of even, partial — they do not exist; *Money*, they have none —

24 June

I have, for a long time, been personally acquainted with very many, of the present members of Congress of both houses. I see them often, and have them frequently to breakfast or dine with me. In this way I have been able to ascertain that an act declaratory of war with the United States, cannot pass Congress, should it be even urged by the Executive....

There is not a reasonable man in power or in representation among them, who does not give up Texas as lost to them, by its annexation to the United States....

I have never known this country to be in a more unsettled state than now, and my knowledge of it dates, from the date of its independence.

29 June

... it may reasonably be inferred, that the main object of my mission will be accomplished, namely that of preventing a declaration of war, by Mexico, against the United States — ...

I will not regret, my having been placed for a while, in the most unpleasant of situations, regarded as I have been, the secret agent of our Government; my every movement watched, my every expression of language caught and reported.[16]

Summary

Parrott's June reports informed Buchanan of his well-placed sources, of Mexico's inability to wage war, the instability of the country, and the Mexican hope for a war between the United States and Britain.

John Black, United States consul at Mexico City, wrote Buchanan on 3 July 1845 concerning Parrott's activities. Black, at the request of Parrott, on 12 May applied to the Mexican government for a "Carta de Seguridad." It was not granted, and no reason was given. The fee for the letter was returned to Black. He was told the decision had been referred to the president for his decision, but as of 3 July nothing had been heard. Black reported Parrott was considered by the government to be a secret agent of the United States who had $1 million to be used for bribes. Black wrote, "on what grounds this belief is formed, I am not aware. Neither do I know what they consider to be the nature of Mr. Parrott's secret mission."[17]

July 1845

5 July

... the command of General Paredes has moved from Lagos to San Luis Potosi, and the postmaster general informs me, that this force had been ordered to the Northern Frontier, which is not improbable; but the difference between receiving orders to march, and of the march itself, is very great in this country, and especially at this time, when there is not even money in the public Treasury to pay the troops in the City. The case of Col. Yuricastra is an example. About two months ago, this officer was ordered to upper California, with a command composed of 900. men, to embark at Acapulco; but up to the present date he has not been able to get away for want of funds —

12 July

This Government, it would seem, entertains, at times, some thought of resorting to the extremity of declaring war, against the United States....

The Government is beset on all sides; With the war fever raging at its greatest height, the public Treasury exhausted, the national credit gone, the current and prospective revenue, mortgaged to foreign and domestic creditors, with symptoms of disaffection, visible in all quarters; What can it do?

... I cannot believe the extremity of war will be restored to.

15 July

The Editorial of the official organ, as of the 12th inst, is rather more warlike than usual, and the general opinion is, that the Government will be forced to adopt the alternative of war, provided Texas be annexed to the U.S.

22 July

... an order was prepared (16 July), that I should leave the city within three days & that I should embark at Vera Cruz. This information was communicated to me before the order could be prepared, and resulted in *this*, that I have not yet received the order —

... which in my opinion amounts to this, that it does not intend to declare war, unless it can have the assistance of England its inability to meet such a contingency, alone, openly and boldly, it feels; the opposition has forced it to what it has done, and its purpose now is to gain time....

26 July

> Nor would it be surprising if a favorable report should also be made on that of war. . . . It would there fore be well to prepare for such a contingency, especially as orders have been given to concentrate a respectable force on the Frontier of Texas.
>
> . . . yet from the long acquaintance I have had with this people, I cannot do less than to express my conviction that nothing but a severe chastisement would secure our people, in future, from such vexatious annoyances and insults as those to which they have hitherto been exposed. . . .
>
> . . . it would be far better, that Mexico should declare war now, than that she should propose to open negotiations for the settlement of pending differences; among these, that of *tracing* certain geographical lines drawn upon the maps of the north west coast of America, is not the least important; these lines could be satisfactorily run in a case of war; but not in a negotiation, now, nor at any future period.

30 July

> As yet I have not received my passport, and if I do not have it sent me very soon, it may not be sent at all—I have been told, that the Government is fearful of the consequences of sending me out of the country, in such a summary manner—
>
> They will not make the formal declaration of war if it can be avoided; but as I have before stated they will make a run upon Texas, if they can find the means necessary to get so far; of this you may be assured— Troops are now moving in that direction, under the command of Genl Filisola, an Italian—and the command has been given to a *Foreigner,* who is to be the victim of any disaster which the Mexicans may meet with, in the encounters they may have—[18]

Summary

Parrott's July reports covered troop movements, intentions, and capabilities of the Mexican government, reaction to the Texas Congress vote for annexation, the status of the war and money bills, British influence, regulations for raising local military forces, continued hope that "a war between the United States and England, growing out of the Oregon question—is inevitable—," and the possibility of Parrott's deportation. Parrott's intelligence reports of 12 and 26 July were confirmed by friends of Secretary Bancroft. William Kemble wrote Bancroft on 29 August and 3 September 1845 of the dilemma faced by the Mexican Congress. Kemble's contact was Peter Hargous, a member of an American firm that had been doing business in Mexico for a long time.[19]

In his 30 July report Parrott received information of the deliberations of the government council "from a reliable source," and "from another source." Concerning letters of marque Parrott had information from both an unreliable and a reliable source. Parrott's grading of his sources provided Buchanan and Polk with another tool to evaluate the information he collected.

Parrott's report of 5 July informed Buchanan of troops being ordered to upper California. From Thomas O. Larkin in Monterey, California, Buchanan received more information. Larkin wrote on 10 July 1845 that he had received information of an expedition of troops fitting out at Acapulco "for the purpose of putting out of office, the California Officers and reinstating the Authorities of Mexico." Parrott's report was received on 1 September 1845 and Larkin's on 11 October 1845.[20]

August 1845

5 August

> Another portion of the force destined to California has left for Acapulco to embark; Col. Yuricastra, it is said will soon follow—The military education of this Gentleman was finished in France, and it is said by well informed persons, that his command and political influence, in California, will be turned to french account, under the direction of the french Legation here—He certainly takes with him a large number of frenchmen, for some purpose or other—

16 August

> . . . if a minister from the United States should arrive, he would be received.[21]

26 August

> The present Cabinet, I am well informed, desires to settle the differences, pending between the two Governments, by negotiation—and that it would make overtures to that effect, if it could act *freely*; but to day it cannot, because of the existence of an obstinate opposition to all its measures—. . .
>
> The command of General Filisola, instead of marching *forward* to the Frontier, has been marched *back* and quartered on two estates south of San Luis Potosi, without the means of subsistence—. . .
>
> The authorities of upper California have sent commissioners to the General Government, to say, they will not receive supplies of *men* from the central power; that they can defend themselves, and that all they want are, arms and ammunition—This looks as if they were disposed to set up *business* on their *own* account—. . .

I have good reasons to believe that, an Envoy from the United States would not only, be well received; but that his arrival would be hailed with joy — . . .

The insubordination of the command of Genl. Filisola, seems to have found its way to the command of Genl. Paredes. The officers refuse to march to Texas, and it is feared they will march upon the City and upset the present Government — [22]

Summary

In August Parrott reported an "American squadron" before Veracruz, and an "American General on the Frontier of Mexico proper" would further diminish the war fever. General Taylor had just landed at Corpus Christi, and Parrott's report reflected the Mexican claim of the Nueces River as the border.

When Parrott sent his opinion concerning the reestablishment of diplomatic relations, John Black, United States consul in Mexico City, and F. M. Dimond, United States consul in Veracruz, expressed the same view to Buchanan.[23] However, Parrott's view on the Mexican military was being contradicted in Washington by an unusual source, Baron Gerolt, Prussian minister to the United States. In early August Secretary Bancroft at the president's request went to see Baron Gerolt. The Prussian minister told Bancroft he would give him all of his intelligence, concealing only his informant's name. Gerolt had letters from Mexico City, dated 28 June 1845, that he had received via Havana and Charleston. Baron Gerolt told Bancroft that General Arista with 3.000 men, chiefly cavalry, had been directed to move toward the Rio Grande, and at San Luis Potosi, General Paredes with 7,000 men had been directed to move forward in small divisions toward the Rio Grande. Polk wrote Buchanan on 7 August 1845, "the information from Mexico comes in so authentic a shape as to entitle it to entire credit. The strong possibility is that a Mexican army of 8,000 or 10,000 men are now on the western borders of Texas."[24] The Prussian minister's Mexican correspondent was regarded as entirely trustworthy by Polk and Bancroft, or he reported what they wanted to hear. In Chapter two it was seen that the Mexican troop concentration was "humbug."

September

2 September

The assembly of upper California has sent in an initiative for Federation — . . .

The initiative of war with the United States, sleeps in the Chamber of Deputies, where it will not soon be disturbed — . . .

. . . appearances of *fight* must be kept up for a while. . . . A war with the U.S. is no longer talked of. . . .

4 September

Of one thing you may be assured — and it is, that Mexico will not commit an act, that will give to the United States, the *right* of *conquest* —

6 September

Yesterday an express arrived from General Arista, informing the Government that he had the "Yankees" in view — He gives a detailed statement of their Force, position &c &c, at a place called Kings "Rancho."

I am still confident, the Government is waiting to hear how England takes the annexation of Texas, question — before she will make overtures to the United States, to come to an amicable arrangement of pending differences —

. . . I have been very precise in stating . . . that in a treaty of *limits*, for the sake of peace and good neighborhood, the United States would, no doubt, be disposed, as had been officially stated to meet Mexico, in a negotiation, upon the most friendly and *liberal* terms — They do not seem to relish this; — They fear it will not *save their National Honor* —

13 September

The official organ, which has been silent for several weeks on the subject of war with the United States, came out yesterday, more hostile than is its wont to be —

18 September

The monthly demands on the general Treasury for the army and pensioners of the city only, amount to about $600,000 — while the receipts from all sources, do not exceed $200,000 per month! — . . .

The conductors of some of the public journals, with whom I am acquainted, have informed me that *war* was out of the question. . . .

I feel confident, that if I were to make myself known to the Government, I would receive assurances that would terminate my mission; but from the tenor of my instructions I find that such a step should be taken only, when *sure* of success —

25 September

The information I obtained from a confidential person whom I requested to be present on these occasions. . . .

29 September

> The whole number of General Arista's command, on the frontier, does not exceed 3000. men, and these cover a line of about 140. leagues....
>
> General Paredes remains stationary at St. Luis Potosi, and the Government finds it necessary to keep him there no doubt, to overawe the two factions now striving for supremacy, the one for Santa Anna, the other for the federative form of Government—
>
> ... the disposition publickly manifested, to treat with the United States, is becoming more and more popular; so much so, that I am no longer suspected, watched and shunned; to the contrary, I am now regarded and treated in a friendly manner, even by those whom at first looked upon me as an enemy—[25]

Summary

Parrott's September intelligence reports described Mexico's financial and military problems, lack of support for war with the United States, the hope for British support or aid, and Parrott's roller coaster ride of friendly welcome, threat of deportation, and return to friendly conditions.

On 16 September President Polk told the cabinet that he had dispatches from Dr. Parrott, the United States secret agent in Mexico. It was Parrott's opinion that Mexico would not invade Texas or declare war against the United States, but would reestablish diplomatic relations with the United States. Polk informed the cabinet that the United States consuls at Mexico City and Veracruz concurred with this view. The cabinet agreed it was expedient to reopen diplomatic relations with Mexico, and, to that end, a representative should be sent to Mexico as soon as possible. Polk wanted this decision kept a "profound" secret, fearing that the British or French might take measures to thwart the mission objectives.[26]

John Slidell was chosen for this secret mission. When directed, he would depart Pensacola in a navy ship, and proceed to Veracruz without disclosing his official character. His mission was to establish a permanent boundary with Mexico. As a minimum he was to purchase upper California and New Mexico, but the desired boundary was the Rio Grande to El Paso and from there west to the Pacific Ocean. The United States would pay Mexico $40 million for this land.[27]

To set all this planning in motion, Secretary Buchanan wrote John Black, United States consul in Mexico City, on 17 September 1845. Black was directed to consult with Dr. Parrott on the best way of communicating with the Mexican government to ascertain if they would accept an envoy from the United States to settle all the questions in dispute between the two governments. Parrott was described by Buchanan as a discreet man, well acquainted with public affairs who possessed the secretary's confidence. Buchanan wrote, "preserve the most inviolable secrecy in regard to your proceeding, making no communication to any person with the exception of Dr. Parrott not indispensable to the accomplishment of the object." Black was to get the Mexican response to F. M. Dimon, United States consul in Veracruz. A United States naval vessel would be waiting to carry his dispatch to the United States.[28]

Parrott's reports of 5 July and 5 August on the subject of troops at Acapulco were expanded on by Thomas Larkin in September. On 29 September Larkin wrote to Buchanan the following: "We are expecting from one to two thousand Mexican soldiers from Acapulco, the first of last month they were preparing to sail for California, it is supposed that the funds are furnished by some English House in the City of Mexico, with what truth this report is founded, cannot be known."[29]

October

4 October

I have ascertained, without doubt, that every member of the present Cabinet, are in favor of an amicable arrangement of pending difficulties with the United States — . . .

As yet not a dollar, has been raised under the 15,000,000 — loan, nor is there a dollar in the public Treasury, To day 6000-dollars could not be raised to send to San Martin, to prevent the troops at that place from starving —

11 October

Quite an animated discussion took place in the Chambers on the 8th inst, in *secret session*, in consequence of the arrival of so many Yankee Ships at "Sacrificios" — . . .

General Paredes has made a requisition for $400,000 — which cannot be sent him in the present exhausted state of the Finances — . . .

The police of the city is a complete nullity, robberies and assassinations are of nightly occurrence, we are compelled to go armed for our own personal safety, which is far less now, than at any former period within my recollection — . . .

I have been able to *persuade* one of the Editors of the "Voz del Pueblo" (opposition) of the folly of waging war with us — . . .

The Baron de Ciprey [French ambassador] and suite, left on the 9th inst; I have played an active, but silent, part in bringing about the actual state of the relations existing between his Govt. and this . . . .

It is gratifying to me in the extreme, to receive the assurance, contained in your note of the 17th ulto. received yesterday, that the President as well as yourself, were not dissatisfied with me — in the discharge of an important and responsible trust —

18 October

> I leave this city in the morning, with despatches for your department,
> having finished, satisfactorily, all the business entrusted to my manage-
> ment by the Government in March last.[30]

Summary

On 15 October 1845 the minister for foreign affairs, Manuel de la
Peña y Peña, sent a letter to Consul Black—"my government is disposed
to receive the commissioner of the United States, who may come to this
capital, with full powers from his Government, to settle the present
dispute, in a peaceful reasonable and honorable manner."[31] The Mexican
government demanded that the United States naval force depart the
Veracruz area before a commissioner would be received. The United
States agreed, and the force was dispersed.[32] During October both Parrott
and Black reported to Buchanan their lack of confidence in each other.
Each apparently feared Buchanan might appoint the other as special envoy. At the 11 October meeting with Peña, Black was told the Mexican
government would receive Waddy Thompson, but not Joel Poinsett, Anthony Butler, Parrott, or Commodore Conner.[33] Black wrote Buchanan
on 18 October of his visit to the minister for foreign affairs to obtain a
passport for Parrott to carry dispatches to the United States. The minister
did not desire Parrott to return as commissioner, because he was well
known and the prejudices existing against him could not easily be re-
moved. Buchanan received this letter on 7 November 1845. Black wrote
on 28 October to report Parrott's departure and rumors that Parrott would
return in two months as minister or as secretary of legation. Black believed
these rumors originated from Parrott. Buchanan received this report on
23 November.[34]

With his covert intelligence collector closing up shop in Mexico City,
Buchanan sent a "well done" to his overt intelligence collectors, whose
reports had given Polk and Buchanan a reference line with which to
evaluate the information they received from Parrott. Buchanan sent letters of appreciation to the following: F. M. Dimond, United States consul
at Veracruz; John Black, United States consul at Mexico City; J. P.
Schatzell, United States consul at Matamoras; and Franklin Chase,
United States consul at Tampico.[35]

On 6 November 1845 Bancroft called on Polk with dispatches from
Commodore Conner, commander of the Home Squadron. The commodore reported the Mexican government was willing to renew diplomatic
relations and to receive a minister from the United States. At the

8 November cabinet meeting it was agreed to keep the appointment of a minister to Mexico secret for the time being.[36]

W. S. Parrott, United States secret agent, arrived in Washington, D.C., on 9 November 1845, and went directly to the State Department to deliver the Mexican note agreeing to receive a minister from the United States.[37]

Polk debriefed Parrott the day after his arrival. Parrott confirmed Polk's opinion that the Mexican government was anxious to settle the present dispute, and even expressed the opinion that Mexico would sell California and New Mexico. The same week Bancroft learned from Commodore Conner of the present Mexican regime gaining stability and of the effect the presence of the United States Army on the frontier and the United States Navy at Veracruz was having. Conner wrote: "All parties are becoming sensible of the danger of rushing into war, without preparation and without resources."[38] Commodore Conner apparently had his own intelligence resources in Mexico.

After debriefing Parrott, Polk asked him to return to Mexico as secretary of legation, and Parrott agreed.[39] He was paid $3,076.65 for his services as a secret agent from the fund for the contingent expenses of foreign intercourse on 13 November 1845.[40]

Polk signed the commission for William S. Parrott to be secretary of legation to Mexico on 20 November 1845. This commission was prepared by Nicholas P. Trist, chief clerk of the State Department, and its existence was unknown to any other officer of the government except for the cabinet. Parrott's commission was kept secret so the British, French, and other foreign governments could not create to any "extent an influence to embarrass or thwart the attainment of the objects of his mission." Parrott departed for Mexico the night his commission was signed. He took the "Southern Boat" to Pensacola where he was to deliver instructions to Minister Slidell.[41]

Slidell was chosen for this mission for a variety of reasons. He had been a strong supporter of Polk in the presidential elections, Secretary Buchanan considered him well qualified for the mission, and he had an excellent knowledge of the Spanish language.[42] John Slidell was born in New York City in 1793. He graduated from Columbia College in 1810. Partly because of business failure and partly because of the scandal resulting from a duel, he left New York City in 1825. Slidell went to New Orleans where he established a successful law practice and was a member of the United States Congress from 1843 to 1845. In the election of 1844 Slidell and other Democrats transported "floaters" (a floater is a person who illegally casts a vote at each of several polling places) from New Orleans to Plaquemines parish, and thereby assured a majority for Polk in Louisiana.[43]

Slidell arrived at Veracruz on his secret mission in November 1845. Secretary of Legation Parrott followed Slidell in the company of Lieutenant Archibald Gillespie, USMC, who was traveling covertly to California with secret messages for Thomas Larkin, United States consul at Monterey, and Brevet Captain John C. Fremont.[44] Lieutenant Gillespie was traveling in the guise of a British representative of MacDongal Distilleries.

When Consul John Black reported Minister Slidell's arrival at Veracruz, the Mexican government backed off by saying it had not expected Slidell until January, and it was unprepared to negotiate. Parrott was declared persona non grata.[45] Slidell's mission was doomed to failure because no Mexican government could sell half the country and still be a government. Polk wanted California. He sent Slidell to buy California and New Mexico, not to talk about Texas or the "present dispute" as the Mexicans called it. To Polk, Texas was not negotiable; it was part of the United States, and it extended to the Rio Grande, not the Nueces.

At the time the Slidell mission was conceived, Polk recorded in his diary his determination to take New Mexico and California by war if Mexico should refuse to yield a minimum of territory to satisfy private American claims (like those of Parrott) against Mexico. These private claims were very much in evidence in the proposed negotiations. If Mexico did not sell her land to settle American claims against her, then Polk would have public support to declare war to take the land.[46]

Notes to Chapter 3

1. Alstyne, *Empire*, p. 137.
2. Stenberg, "Polk's Intrigue," p. 42.
3. McCoy, *Polk*, p. 94.
4. Moore, *Buchanan*, 6:132–133.
5. U.S. Congress, Senate, *Claims Presented under Conviction of 4 July 1868*, S. Ex. Doc. 31, 44th Cong., 2d sess., pp. 42–43.
6. U.S. Congress, Senate, *Claims on Mexico*, S. Doc. 411, 27th Cong., 2nd sess., 10 August 1842.
7. George Lockhart Rives, *The United States and Mexico* (New York: Charles Scribner's Sons, 1913), 2:63.
8. Manning, *Correspondence*, 8:524–525.
9. Ibid., 8:572–573.
10. Reeves, *Tyler and Polk*, pp. 269–270.
11. Ibid., pp. 271–273.
12. Moore, *Buchanan*, 6:132–133.
13. Reeves, *Tyler and Polk*, p. 268.
14. Manning, *Correspondence*, 8:712.
15. Ibid., 8:714–719.
16. Ibid., 8:722–730.

17. Ibid., 8:732.

18. Ibid., 8:733–743.

19. Pletcher, *Diplomacy,* p. 260.

20. Manning, *Correspondence,* 8:735.

21. Rives, *United States and Mexico,* 2:63.

22. Manning, *Correspondence,* 8:746.

23. Justin H. Smith, *The War with Mexico* (New York: Macmillan, 1919), 1:89.

24. Curtis, *Buchanan,* p. 590.

25. Manning, *Correspondence,* 8:748–754.

26. Quaife, *Polk Diary,* 1:33–34.

27. Ibid., 1:34–35.

28. Moore, *Buchanan,* 6:260–261.

29. Manning, *Correspondence,* 8:755.

30. Ibid., 8:756–766.

31. Ibid., 8:760.

32. John Bach McMasters, *A History of the People of the United States* (New York: D. Appleton, 1910), 7:434.

33. Pletcher, *Diplomacy,* p. 277.

34. Manning, *Correspondence,* 8:766–767.

35. Moore, *Buchanan,* 6:282.

36. Quaife, *Polk Diary,* 1:91.

37. Ibid., 1:93.

38. Pletcher, *Diplomacy,* p. 287.

39. Quaife, *Polk Diary,* 1:93.

40. U.S. Congress, House, *Contingent Expenses of the State Department,* H. Doc. 11, 29th Cong., 1st sess., 1845, p. 29.

41. Quaife, *Polk Diary,* 1:100.

42. Ibid., 1:232.

43. *Dictionary of American Biography,* 1981 index, s.v. "Slidell, John," by Wendell H. Stephenson.

44. Reeves, *Tyler and Polk,* p. 282.

45. Pletcher, *Diplomacy,* p. 355.

46. Stenberg, "Polk's Intrigue," p. 43.

Chapter 4

Polk/Santa Anna
Joint Covert Operation

After Texas agreed to annexation, elements of the United States Army moved into the state. Brevet Brigadier General Zachary Taylor's command set up camp at Corpus Christi in August 1845. This force was ordered on 13 January 1846 to move to the north bank of the Rio Grande. However, for a variety of reasons, movement from Corpus Christi to the Rio Grande did not commence until 8 March 1846.

During this time between orders and movement, President Polk had a very interesting visitor. Polk wanted to buy northern Mexico, and his visitor presented himself as the representative of the man who could sell northern Mexico. The visitor was Colonel Alejandro J. Atocha, and the man he represented was General Antonio López de Santa Anna.

Colonel Atocha was born in Spain and had lived in Mexico and the United States. During his residence in New Orleans he became a naturalized citizen of the United States. The New Orleans city directory of 1834 lists him as a broker with his office at 53 St. Louis Street, and his residence at 272 Bourbon Street. The city directory for 1838 lists his residence as 241 Bourbon Street.[1] Atocha had been a supporter of General Santa Anna when he was dictator from 1841 to 1844. When Santa Anna was overthrown, the new government deported Atocha in February 1845.[2]

President Polk first met Atocha in June 1845, when Atocha called at the White House to press his claim as an American citizen for damages against Mexico. When he called again in February 1846, it was for a different reason. Atocha told Polk that he had recently come from Havana where he had seen Santa Anna.[3] President José Joaquín Herrera deported Santa Anna in December 1844. Santa Anna went to Havana and lived in forced retirement on a large hacienda outside the city. A year later the Herrera government fell, due to the belief that it was going to agree to sell part of the national domain to the special envoy from the United States, John Slidell. General Mariano Paredes y Arrillaga rebelled against the Herrera government on 14 December 1845, and entered Mexico City on

2 January 1846 as dictator.[4] During these coming and goings Santa Anna continued to plot his return to power.

Colonel Atocha arrived in New Orleans from Havana, Cuba, on 22 December 1845 aboard the steamship *Alabama.* That night he stayed at the St. Louis Hotel, where he was registered as A. Y. Atocha of New York. (The "Y" is most probably a typographical error in the *Daily Delta* of 23 December 1845 in their list of arrivals at principal hotels.)[5] Seven weeks later he would be in Washington, D.C.

On Friday 13 February 1846 Colonel Atocha called on President Polk at the White House. His reason for the visit was to inform Polk in a secret and confidential manner of his discussions with the former dictator of Mexico, General Santa Anna. Atocha told Polk that Santa Anna was in favor of a boundary treaty with the United States. To adjust the boundary between Mexico and the United States, Santa Anna believed the Rio Grande should be the Texas line, and the "Colorado of the West" down through the San Francisco Bay to the sea should be the Mexican line on the north, and that Mexico should cede all land east and north of these natural boundaries to the United States for $30 million.

In Santa Anna's opinion, the United States would never be able to bring Mexico to the bargaining table without the presence of an imposing military force. Santa Anna was surprised that the United States naval forces had been withdrawn from Veracruz in the fall in 1845, and that General Taylor's army was kept at Corpus Christi instead of being stationed on the Rio Grande.[6]

Atocha could not continue describing Santa Anna's proposed joint covert operation because people were waiting to see the president. He departed saying he would call again in a few days.

At his regular Saturday cabinet meeting, Polk told of his conversation with Atocha. The cabinet discussed sending a secret agent to confer with Santa Anna. Polk recommended Governor C. P. Van Ness, former minister to Spain, but no further action was taken at this meeting.[7]

Colonel Atocha returned to the White House at an early hour on 16 February 1846 and spent almost an hour with Polk. Again their meeting was interrupted by the press of other business, but Polk told Atocha to return at 1430, and they met for more than an hour.

Atocha described the problem. Generals Paredes, Almonte, and Santa Anna were willing to sell half their country, but the people of Mexico were unwilling. To resolve this, the people had to see that the treaty was necessary to save Mexico from war with the United States. In order to convince the people of the magnitude of the threat, the United States Army should move from Corpus Christi to the Rio Grande, and a strong naval force should be displayed at Veracruz.

If conditions were right, Santa Anna felt that he could probably return to Mexico in April or May. Santa Anna's last words to Atocha as he was leaving Havana were, "when you see the President tell him to take strong measures and such a treaty can be made and I will sustain it."

Only one final item was required of Polk to ensure the success of this joint covert operation—money. Santa Anna and Paredes would need money to pay the military while the treaty was being ratified by the United States Senate. The generals would need at least $500,000 in hand to sign the treaty. This would be enough to keep them in power for a few months until the balance was paid.[8]

Atocha recommended President Polk transfer John Slidell, United States minister extraordinary to Mexico, from Jalapa Enríquez to a United States warship at Veracruz. Slidell had been waiting in Jalapa for the Mexican government's decision to accept or not accept his credentials. From this position of strength, Slidell would then demand the payment due United States citizens in their claims against Mexico. It was a well-known fact that the Mexican government did not have the funds to satisfy these claims. Surrounded by strong military forces, the threat would then be so great that the Mexican people would agree to the boundary treaty.

Polk listened to everything Atocha had to say, but did not disclose his own views or send any word to General Santa Anna through Atocha. Polk did not have confidence in Colonel Atocha: "He is evidently a man of talents and education, but his whole manner & conversation impressed me with a belief that he was not reliable, and that he would betray any confidence reposed in him, when it was his interest to do so."[9] To prove his bona fides, Atocha asked Polk to see Brantz Mayer of Baltimore. Mayer had been the secretary of legation to Mexico from 1841 to 1843, and was the author of several books on Mexico. Atocha claimed to be very intimate with this gentleman, and believed that he would vouch for his reliability.[10]

During the Polk administration, cabinet meetings were held every week on Tuesday and Saturday. On 17 February at the regular cabinet meeting President Polk related his conversation held on Monday with Atocha, and it was discussed by the cabinet. At this meeting Polk expressed his opinion that it would be necessary to take strong measures toward Mexico before the differences could be settled. Polk then proposed that John Slidell be further instructed to demand an early decision of the Mexican government on whether they would receive him or not, and if the Mexican government would receive him, then whether they would without reasonable delay pay the amount due to American claimants. If the Mexican government refused to do one or both, Slidell should leave the country. Rather than returning to the United States, as previously instructed, he should board a United States warship at Veracruz, and remain there until further advised.

If Slidell ended up on the warship, Polk intended to send a strong message to Congress requesting authorization to have Slidell demand the Mexican government pay the American claims. If this was refused, he wanted authority to take redress into his own hands by aggressive measures. Secretary of War Marcy, Secretary of Treasury Walker, and Secretary of Navy Bancroft all agreed with Polk's evaluation of the situation and his proposed actions. Secretary of State Buchanan was the only dissenter.[11]

Polk took no action on the proposed dispatch to John Slidell. He wrote Buchanan on 19 February that he had decided to wait for a few days, in the expectation that he must very soon receive information from Slidell.[12]

At the 28 March 1846 cabinet meeting, dispatches from Slidell indicated that he would soon be received by the Mexican government. Polk told the cabinet the greatest obstacle to a treaty at this time was authority to make a prompt payment at the signing. General Paredes led a military dictatorship whose soldiers had to be paid, fed, and clothed to keep their support. Polk felt he could deal with whomever was in power, and was not saving his bribe money for Santa Anna. The president wanted $500,000 to $1,000,000 available to Minister Slidell to put on the table at the signing of the treaty. The problem was the appropriation had to be obtained from Congress in secret.[13]

That same day Polk discussed the problem with Senator Thomas Hart Benton. Benton agreed money was needed to bribe Mexican officials to sign the treaty, and the use of the money as a bribe needed to be kept secret. To make his point, Polk used the example of the practice of Congress in placing a secret service fund (fund for contingent expenses of foreign intercourse) at the discretion of the president. He proposed the appropriation be considered in executive session (closed session), and then in open session be passed without debate. Benton concurred, as did Senators Allen, Cass, and Calhoun, to whom Polk posed the same question.[14]

A dispatch received from the United States consul at Veracruz was read at the regular cabinet meeting on Tuesday 7 April 1846. It stated that Slidell would probably not be received by the Mexican government and would return to the United States (the warship option was apparently dropped). Polk told the cabinet if Slidell was not received and returned to the United States, he would ask Congress to pass legislation to take the remedy for the injuries, injustices, and wrongs into their own hands. The cabinet concurred. That night word was received from Slidell confirming the report. The government of Mexico would not receive him, and he had demanded his passport.[15]

While Slidell was traveling home from Mexico, Polk was fighting

Congress to keep expenditures for covert operations a presidential secret. This battle started when Polk directed Secretary Buchanan on 11 April 1846 to provide information as requested by the House of Representatives in relation to the expenditure of the secret service fund during the period Daniel Webster was secretary of state.[16]

On 15 April 1846 Buchanan brought Polk the report on expenditures of the fund "for contingent expenses of foreign intercourse" settled by presidential certification between 4 March 1841 and the retirement of Daniel Webster from the Department of State. After studying the report, Polk called a cabinet meeting, at which it was decided not to give the information to Congress. Polk did not want to expose the secret expenditures of this fund.[17]

President Polk sent a message to Congress on 20 April 1846 stating his position on this matter. In the message he reiterated the House request for information—"to cause to be furnished to that House an account of all payments made on President's certificates from the fund appropriated by law through the agency of the State Department, for the contingent expenses of foreign intercourse since the 4th of March 1841, until the retirement of Daniel Webster from the Department of State, with copies of all entries, receipts, letters, vouchers, memorandum or other evidence of such payment, to whom paid, for what and particularly all concerning the northeast boundary dispute with Great Britain."

Then Polk described the Act of 1 May 1810 which created the annual appropriation "for the contingent expenses of intercourse between the United States and foreign nations." He explained that the third section of the act provided: "That when any sum or sums of money shall be drawn from the treasury, under any law making appropriation for the contingent expenses of intercourse between the United States and foreign nations, the President shall be, and he is hereby, authorized to cause the same to be duly settled, annually, with the accounting officers of the treasury, in the manner following, that is to say: by causing the same to be accounted for, specially, in all instances wherein the expenditure thereof may, in his judgment be made public, and by making a certificate of the amount of such expenditures as he may think it advisable not to specify; and every such certificate shall be deemed a sufficient voucher for the sum or sums therein expressed to have been expended."

In Polk's opinion the president in office at the time of the expenditures is made by the law the sole judge of whether the expenditures should be public or private. Polk's immediate predecessor (John Tyler) for the time period requested gave certificates for $5,460, which President Tyler determined should not be made public.

Polk concluded that under the law he could not provide the information requested—"If Congress disapproves the policy of the law, they may repeal its provisions." This is just one of many examples of Polk fighting to keep the executive strong and its activities secret.[18]

What grave matters of state were considered important enough, in the judgment of presidents Tyler and Polk, to be kept from the people of the United States? When Secretary of State Daniel Webster was attempting to settle the northeast boundary question with the British, Maine resisted the compromise settlement. F. O. J. Smith, a Maine politician, offered his services as an unofficial agent to propagandize to Maine's leaders and citizens the virtue of compromise. For a small fee plus expenses, Smith would plant articles in newspapers, circulate petitions, and lobby at Augusta. Tyler gave Webster his authorization to use funds from the appropriation for the contingent expenses of intercourse between the United States and foreign nations for this purpose. While Smith used these secret funds to spread the word in Maine, Webster wrote the governor, senators, congressmen, and judges of Maine asking for their support on the compromise. A well-run covert operation was used to influence a foreign nation, but in this instance it was the state of Maine.

Polk debriefed John Slidell for about an hour on 8 May 1846. The meeting covered his mission and United States/Mexican relations. Slidell believed the only road open to the United States was prompt and energetic redress of wrongs and injuries from Mexico. Polk agreed with him, and told him it was only a matter of time.[19]

Secretary of the Navy Bancroft of 13 May 1846 (the same day Congress declared a war to exist between Mexico and the United States) wrote to Commodore David Conner: "Private and Confidential. If Santa Anna endeavors to enter the Mexican ports, you will allow him to pass freely."[20] Polk had taken the first step in a joint covert operation with Santa Anna to dismember Mexico and install Santa Anna as dictator.

The following day Secretary Buchanan wrote R. B. Campbell, United States consul at Havana. Buchanan informed him that the two Mexican steamers recently transferred to Havana were possibly sent there for the purpose of privateering against the United States. There was also reason to believe that an attempt would be made to fit out privateers bearing letters of Marque and Reprisal for this purpose in the ports of Cuba and Puerto Rico. Campbell was to exert the utmost vigilance in acquiring information on this subject, and he was to send any information he collected to Commodore Conner, commander of the Home Squadron. A copy of this letter was sent to the United States consuls at Matanzas, Trinidad, and St. Iago de Cuba, Cuba, and San Juan, Mayaguez, Ponce, and Guayama, Puerto Rico.[21]

While all this intrigue was spiraling around the Caribbean, Polk sent William Linn Brown to Havana to report on the intentions of Santa Anna. Consul Robert B. Campbell reported Brown's presence in Cuba on 25 May

1846, but he also admitted that the secret agent had not told him anything about his mission. Campbell protested the use of such a secret official, advising that in the future the consul should be used in negotiations with Santa Anna or any other officials.[22]

William Linn Brown wrote to Secretary Buchanan from Havana on the same day as Consul Campbell. In this letter he reported his contact with Santa Anna, and proposed a covert operation:

> Dear Sir
>
> On my leaving Washington you suggested that a few lines to you from me on passing events from here would be acceptable and I now have that pleasure.
>
> Since my arrival here the news from our Mexican frontier has directed much attention to Mexico and her affairs and from direct sources I learn the following plan is arranged and adopted, namely to erect a *Triumvirate government* for Mexico, on the part of Santa Anna, Herrara [sic] (who now in fact holds the power in Mexico) and Bustamente: Santa Anna to be the head. The principles upon which this government is to be based I have knowledge of, shewing clearly, that in the Main private ends and ambition are its root, and that the diseases of poor Mexico cannot be healed by it, but on the contrary, she will be the victim of abused power, and her tranquility destroyed.
>
> The last news from our frontier and the operations there will hasten this arrangement, and Santa Anna informs me he intends giving up his present residence, has in fact done so, near Serro and purposes moving farther up the Island.
>
> Now Sir I have good reason to believe that this is a pure "Ruse," and that he will leave the Island before he gets into his new residence.
>
> Now Sir I have reason to know that these Mexican Chiefs have but little patriotism, nor are they such true lovers of their country to be willing to lay down their lives for her, or even to sacrifice their pecuniary interests for her tranquility and happiness.
>
> What therefore can unhappy Mexico expect from such distribution of power? Not peace and prosperity for which she had struggled so long and suffered so much, but on the contrary it would twist her chains the tighter.
>
> It is true the best thing now for her would be for the United States now during a time of actual hostility with her, to push the war with vigor—conquer the power of the Country and then make a *magnanimous surrender* of it upon a sufficient *guarantee* of her peace and repose securing to her *settled tranquility* and *happy independence*. But will you do this? That you *can* is very certain.
>
> The next best thing would be to capture Santa Anna, and hold him as a hostage. How Sir! I will engage to do that. I mean what I say and have taken the necessary preliminary steps to do it if he leaves the island and he is met on the seas and the war continues. This is considered pretty certain unless he changes his contemplated route.
>
> The next question that presents itself to us is if he still remains on the Island and the War continues are we justified in doing so? I cannot think so! unless we have some assurance from the president that it

would not be displeasing to the Government or if it would in that case it will be immediately abandoned. If not displeasing and he will so signify in any form he choses and address it to me here to that effect on or before the first July (thus giving ample time) I will engage to deliver him the first week in July to the authorities at Key West, as if he or we can be spared the work of crossing the gulph in a small vessel and a man of war will cruise the Coast of Cuba during the *first week in July* between the span of Matanzas [Brown wrote "Mantanzas"] and the west end of Cuba within 20 miles of shore and I am informed of the fact I will engage to deliver him to the Commander in the Cabin of his vessel. I will also be responsible for the life of the General from personal assault or violence from any one under my command with my life.

Will you sir please hold this communication in strict confidence between yourself and the president and his cabinet advisers if you should include them, and please say to the president that no such enterprise would enter into my mind did I not believe it an honorable one, the means justifyable, and the end meritorious and serveable and, if he or yourself thinks it deficient in any such qualities and you signify as much it shall be instantly abandoned. If not and I receive the assurance asked, then Sir! I will pledge myself to perform it to the exact letter and Spirit of the instructions.

I will add in conclusion that no man shall be, or is enlisted in the enterprise who bears the least personal animosity to General Santa Anna.

> I remain with High Respect
> Your
> Wm Linn Brown

P.S. Address me under cover to the Consul if you see it right to do so. I will say for your information that Genl. Almonte is still here, and that the present Captain-General expects shortly to be relieved.[23]

Brown's plan was unacceptable. Polk wanted Santa Anna in Mexico not Key West. Brown's concern for a Mexico in chains was not shared by Polk, and a new man was sent to Cuba.

On 25 May 1846, the same day that Consul Campbell and William Linn Brown were writing their letters to Buchanan, President Polk was preparing a backup for his covert operation in Cuba. Commander Alexander Slidell Mackenzie was ordered to report to the Navy Department for special service.[24]

John Slidell had recommended to Polk his Spanish-speaking brother, Commander Alexander Slidell Mackenzie, for the mission to Santa Anna. John Slidell accompanied his brother to the White House where Commander Mackenzie received his verbal instructions directly from the president.[25]

Alexander Slidell added Mackenzie to his name by an act of the New

York legislature in either 1837 or 1838. He requested the legislature to allow him to assume his mother's maiden name of Mackenzie in addition to that of Slidell in order to qualify him to inherit property.[26]

Commander Mackenzie was born Alexander Slidell in New York City on 6 April 1803. He was appointed midshipman in the United States Navy on 1 January 1815. He served on various ships and made several cruises to the Mediterranean. At the age of 26 his first book, *A Year in Spain*, was published, and from that time on writing absorbed all his spare time. He wrote various books on his travels in Spain and England, and the lives of John Paul Jones and Oliver Hazard Perry.[27]

In 1842 when Commander Mackenzie was commanding officer of the United States Brig *Somers*, a training vessel for apprentices, he presided over an unusual affair which brought him into the limelight. The *Somers* was en route home from the west coast of Africa where it had been sent to deliver dispatches to the Africa Squadron, when Mackenzie discovered plans for a mutiny. A midshipman and two sailors were tried and hanged for their involvement. The midshipman was Philip Spencer, who happened to be a son of the secretary of war, John C. Spencer. When the *Somers* reached the United States, the hanging became an event of great notoriety. Commander Mackenzie was tried by a court-martial in the spring of 1843 on charges of murder, and was acquitted.[28]

On 6 June 1846 Secretary Bancroft sent a confidential letter to Commander Mackenzie. He was ordered to Norfolk where he would board the United States Brig *Truxtun* and proceed to Havana, Cuba. His mission was to ascertain if any vessels were being fitted out in Cuba as privateers. He was further directed to visit the different ports of the island and collect all the political and commercial information that he could, and to report his findings to the Navy Department. No reports of this kind from Mackenzie have ever been found.[29] Bancroft's written orders were cover for the real mission.

Commander Mackenzie's secret mission was to deliver a personal message to General Santa Anna from the president of the United States. Polk did not trust Colonel Atocha and would not use him as a go-between in this covert operation. Polk personally briefed Commander Mackenzie in Washington and purposely avoided giving him any written directions. Later Mackenzie had difficulty with Polk because he put Polk's verbal instructions in a written memorandum.[30]

Commander Mackenzie was provided excellent cover for his mission. Secretary Buchanan's letter of 14 May 1846 to Consul Campbell describing the United States's concern regarding privateers operating out of Cuba and Puerto Rico, made the appearance of a U.S. naval officer in Cuba quite feasible. The cover was good but security was not; even the secretive Polk could not stop the leaks in his administration.

Commander Mackenzie's cover did not last past the Cape Henry light: "The New York Journal of Commerce notes that Mackenzie sailed on June 14th from Norfolk in the United States brig *Truxton*, that he is bound for Havana charged, it is said, with a mission to Santa Anna" (*Philadelphia Ledger*, 23 June 1846).[31]

Commander Mackenzie reported the details of his covert operation in Cuba to Secretary Buchanan. Mackenzie arrived in Cuba on 5 July 1846. The next morning he delivered a letter from Buchanan to United States Consul Campbell. The consul, who considered Santa Anna intellectually feeble, took Mackenzie to Santa Anna's residence. Mackenzie went in full dress uniform, in an open carriage, through the principal streets of Havana at noon. He left his card, stating he had a message from President Polk. Not a good start for a secret agent entering into secret negotiations. After Mackenzie left, Santa Anna exclaimed to his secretary: "Why has the President sent me that fool?"[32] Mackenzie returned later to give Santa Anna a copy of Secretary Bancroft's orders to Commodore Conner, directing the commodore to allow Santa Anna to enter Mexico.[33]

Mackenzie spent three hours with Santa Anna on 8 July, and during this time he outlined Polk's position:

1. Polk would view with pleasure Santa Anna's restoration to power in Mexico.

2. To show good faith Polk had given orders to allow Santa Anna freely to return to his country.

3. When Santa Anna returned to power, Polk would suspend hostilities by land, send a minister at once, and offer Santa Anna liberal terms for the settlement of every existing difficulty.

4. Polk promised to pay liberally for the establishment of a permanent geographical boundary.

5. Polk wanted portions of the northern territory of Mexico but was prepared to act immediately to provide ample consideration in ready money.[34]

Mackenzie reported that Santa Anna seemed satisfied with Polk's concept of the covert operation and expressed his gratitude for permission to return to Mexico. However, there were some problems to be discussed and some strategy to be implemented for the covert operation to be successful.

Santa Anna had a problem with the Texas boundary. The Nueces River had always been the boundary of Texas, and he wanted to know by what authority the United States claimed territory now to the Rio Grande. Mackenzie succinctly explained the situation: Polk and the people of the United States wanted the Rio Grande to be the boundary. It did not matter what Santa Anna or the Mexican people thought on the subject. The United States would retain what it wanted for a permanent boundary, but from a sense of magnanimity it would pay for whatever it might retain. The United States was strong; Mexico was weak.[35]

Santa Anna got the message. Polk had the power, knew he had the power, and would not hesitate to use it; and now Santa Anna knew. Polk also knew the British would not be a factor in the dismembering of Mexico. On 6 June 1846, in an attempt to settle the Oregon question, Lord Aberdeen, the British foreign secretary, offered Polk the boundary along the 49th degree of latitude. A private visit from a British banker convinced Polk that if he would accept the compromise boundary in Oregon, the British would not use their influence in Mexico in opposition to the United States.[36]

Santa Anna told Mackenzie that rather than see Mexico ruled by a foreign prince (could he have meant Polk instead of the European variety?), he would negotiate a peace by means of a treaty of limits. If the United States would position its military forces as directed by Santa Anna so that Santa Anna's actions appeared the actions of a patriot, he agreed to respond positively to such a peace treaty as Mackenzie had described. But, first, he demanded the greatest secrecy concerning this covert operation. His countrymen might form a doubtful opinion of his patriotism if his treason was exposed.

Santa Anna displayed in these secret negotiations one of his most notable characteristics: his willingness to deal with friend or foe alike, simultaneously if need be, to further his own interests. For nearly a decade Santa Anna had denounced the United States for its failure to be neutral during the Mexican war with Texas. Now in exile Santa Anna showed he was not above dealing with the hated enemy, if such negotiations might aid him in returning to power in Mexico.[37]

To convince the Mexican people that their situation was desperate, Santa Anna advised Polk to take the following military actions: first, advance to Saltillo; second, take Veracruz and then attack Ulloa Castle; and third, occupy Tampico. It would then be Santa Anna's patriotic duty to save his country by negotiating a treaty of peace. In reality, it was a covert operation to make Santa Anna the rich dictator of Mexico and Polk the president of a whole new nation. Neither Polk nor Santa Anna apparently considered the loss of life or human suffering that they would cause with their secret arrangements.

Mackenzie considered Santa Anna's military recommendations so important that he proceeded at once to General Taylor's headquarters in Mexico, even though this was not in his instructions.[38]

Commander Mackenzie forwarded more information concerning his meeting with Santa Anna to Secretary Buchanan on 11 July 1846. He reported Santa Anna was on friendly terms with the French and British, but because the United States was at war with Mexico and so close to

Mexico, it did not matter who Santa Anna preferred as friends; reality and plain common sense forced him to come to terms with the United States. In Mackenzie's opinion, if the United States was going to use Santa Anna as a front to dismember Mexico, it would be necessary to produce some propaganda in the United States to play up Santa Anna as the best deal for Mexico.[39]

When Polk received Santa Anna's affirmative answer to the covert operation, he renewed his efforts to complete secret financial arrangements. Polk wanted a secret executive fund of $2 million to be used in negotiating a treaty with Mexico; the fund to be used, if necessary, as a payment before the Senate ratified the treaty. This money was needed to buy a treaty by underwriting the pay of the Mexican army to keep Santa Anna in power.[40]

Only one month after he was sent into exile in July 1845, Manuel Rejón, a loyal supporter of Santa Anna, suggested to Gómez Farías that the exiled federalist leader and Santa Anna should cooperate to overthrow the present government. Farías was told that Santa Anna was firm in his decision not to rule but only to act as a soldier. In March 1846 Santa Anna stepped up his campaign to return to Mexico as political conditions began to swing a little in his favor. He endorsed the ideas of federalism and popular government to gain support from that influential faction in order to achieve his primary goals — to return to Mexico to fight the invader, in this case the United States, and to regain power as a dictator.[41] Santa Anna created a variety of alliances, some false, some true, and some half and half, to provide the support and resources he needed to implement his plans.

On 3 August 1846 Vice President Bravo, Santa Anna's man in Mexico, overthrew President Paredes. Santa Anna departed Havana on the steamship *Arab* on 8 August, accompanied by Almonte, Rejón, and other supporters. On the same day in Washington, D.C., Polk asked Congress to appropriate $2 million to negotiate the expected peace settlement in Mexico.[42] Santa Anna's ship passed through the United States blockade off Veracruz on 16 August, under the arranged chaperonage of a British navy captain who reported to Commodore Conner that the ship carried no contraband. Now, Polk had his man in Mexico.[43]

Commodore Conner reported: "I have allowed him to enter without molestation, or even speaking to the vessel, as I was informed by the senior English naval officer here, Captain Lambert, she carried no cargo and would not be allowed to take any in return. I could easily have boarded the *Arab*, but I deemed it most proper not to do so, allowing it to appear as if he had entered without my concurrence."[44]

Colonel Atocha, who accompanied Santa Anna on his journey from Cuba to Mexico in August 1846,[45] returned to Washington, D.C., in

January 1847. Since Atocha's last visit, war had been declared and
American forces had claimed victories from Monterey to Santa Fe to
Monterrey. Secretary Buchanan at the 12 January cabinet meeting
reported he had talked to Atocha, and that Atocha was going to talk to
Senator Thomas Benton. Buchanan told the cabinet Atocha claimed to
possess letters from Generals Santa Anna, Almonte, and Rejón which
"professed to disclose to him the views and opinions of Santa Anna and
Almonte, in favor of peace between the two countries."[46]

Benton read the letters addressed to Atocha from Santa Anna and
Almonte. The letters expressed a desire for an honorable peace and gave
the impression that Atocha's visit to Washington was at their insistence.
They would cede California for $15 to $20 million and recognize the Rio
Grande as the boundary, but wanted to reserve territory between the Rio
Grande and Nueces River as a buffer zone between the two countries. To
implement these terms it was recommended that commissioners meet in
Havana. Benton translated these letters personally for Polk. Polk asked
Benton about New Mexico. Benton, who had talked to Atocha (Polk did
not talk to Atocha during these discussions), replied he had asked but
Atocha seemed to be uninformed on that point. Polk was now satisfied
that Atocha was an agent of Santa Anna and could be useful. As an addi-
tional proof to Polk, Santa Anna had told Atocha all the details of the visit
made to Santa Anna by Commander Mackenzie.[47]

Buchanan told the cabinet on 16 January 1847 of his talk with Senator
Benton concerning Colonel Atocha, and of his own conversation with
Atocha that morning. Buchanan believed Atocha had the confidence of
Santa Anna, Almonte, and other principle men of the Mexican government, and had no doubt Atocha had been sent to prepare the way for
peace. Polk told Buchanan he could not agree to the proposed neutral territory, and the United States must obtain a cession of New Mexico as well
as California for a consideration. Buchanan replied that he had so informed Atocha. Atocha would take the United States proposition for
peace to Mexico, and if Mexico accepted and appointed commissioners,
the blockade of Veracruz should be raised. Polk objected to raising the
blockade because Mexico might not be sincere, use the time to import
arms, and "subject the administration to the ridicule of the whole world
for its credulity and weakness." The cabinet agreed a letter should be sent
to the Mexican minister of foreign affairs by Secretary Buchanan, propos-
ing the appointment of commissioners to meet at Havana to negotiate for
peace, and Atocha should be the bearer of the letter.[48]

The next day Benton and Buchanan discussed the proposed letter
with Atocha. Colonel Atocha objected to the part of the letter which
declared the war would continue until the commissioners concluded a
peace. He wanted the commissioners to have the authority to raise the

blockade or to suspend hostilities. Benton and Buchanan agreed with Atocha, and went to see if they could convince Polk. The president, who had been completely against this concept, did a 180-degree turn and agreed. Buchanan rewrote the letter to the Mexican minister of foreign affairs and took it to Polk for his approval. Polk approved the modified letter and authorized the secretary of the treasury to provide transportation for Atocha. That night Buchanan, Benton, and Atocha met again at Benton's house to discuss the arrangements.[49]

It would appear that the covert operation agreed upon by Polk and Santa Anna was on track and on schedule. Santa Anna had been passed through the naval blockade, had taken control of the army, and was fighting the heroic battle for his country. Polk had put military pressure on Mexico as requested by Santa Anna, and had added a little of his own. By January 1847 not only was General Taylor in Monterrey and Tampico and General Scott on his way to Veracruz, but California and New Mexico were part of the United States by conquest. Polk wanted a quick, small war for political reasons. This type of war would not give birth to Whig military heroes to run against his Democratic Party, and would give the country a patriotic lift without asking for sacrifices. The covert operation was tailored to Polk's requirements.

On 19 January 1847 Buchanan informed the cabinet that Colonel Atocha had the letter for the Mexican minister of foreign affairs. Secretary of the Treasury Walker reported he had ordered the Revenue Cutter *Bibb* to transport Atocha from New Orleans to Veracruz and return him to the United States when he had an answer from the Mexican government. Atocha would leave for New Orleans that night. These arrangements were made by Walker, Benton, Buchanan, and Atocha during another long meeting at Benton's house.[50]

Buchanan had written a short letter to Mr. Black, late United States consul at Mexico City, and also a letter to Mr. Beach of the New York *Sun*, who was on a secret mission for Polk in Mexico City. Polk read the letters and sent them on their way, via Colonel Atocha.[51] A strange situation, Santa Anna's secret agent delivering letters to a man who would have a price put on his head by Santa Anna.

At the 20 March 1847 cabinet meeting Buchanan announced Atocha's return from Mexico with a letter from the Mexican government. Mexico would reopen negotiations only if the United States Navy withdraw from the Mexican coast and the United States Army from Mexican territories. Polk would not accept these conditions.[52] The quick, small war now assumed the potential of becoming the long, costly war.

On 28 August 1847 Polk received an intelligence report dated 15 August describing the return of General Paredes to Mexico. The ex-dictator arrived 14 August at Veracruz on the British mail steamer.

Disguised and using an assumed name, he slipped through the United States military forces stationed there. Polk thought that Paredes's return to Mexico could prolong the war.[53]

The cabinet at their 8 January 1848 meeting discussed the request of the House of Representatives for information relating to the return of Santa Anna to Mexico in August 1846 and of Paredes in August 1847. The cabinet's concern was the domestic and international reactions if the information contained in Commander Mackenzie's reports were made public. Polk told the cabinet that he sent Mackenzie as a confidential agent to ascertain whether any Mexican privateers had been commissioned to cruise against American commerce. However, he did authorize Mackenzie to see in a prudent way what Santa Anna's views were. If Santa Anna was for peace, Mackenzie was to inform him that he was free to enter Mexico. Polk distanced himself from this covert operation by stating that Mackenzie exceeded his instructions. Polk said he had provided Mackenzie with no written instructions, but Mackenzie *read* to Santa Anna what he purported to be a message from Polk. Very few people, if any, ever received written instructions from Polk when he was conducting a covert operation. After his meeting with Polk, Mackenzie set down Polk's oral instructions in detail, in order that he could carry out his mission exactly as Polk had instructed. Buchanan concisely summed up the situation — if the Mackenzie reports were made public, "no government would ever again trust us." All present at the meeting agreed not to send to the House of Representatives the communications received from Commander Mackenzie.[54]

The House of Representatives received a presidential message on 13 January 1848. In this message Polk set forth the request of the House — "any instructions which may have been given to any of the officers of the army or navy of the United States, or other persons, in regard to the return of President General López de Santa Anna, or any other Mexican, to the republic of Mexico, prior or subsequent to the order of the President or Secretary of War, issued in January 1846, for the march of the army from the Nueces river, across 'the stupendous deserts' which intervene to the Rio Grande; that the date of all such instructions, orders and correspondence, be set forth, together with the instructions and orders issued to Mr. Slidell at any time prior or subsequent to his departure for Mexico as Minister Plenipotentiary of the United States to that republic"; and also to "communicate all the orders and correspondence of the government in relation to the return of General Paredes to Mexico."[55]

Polk's message transmitted reports concerning the return of Santa Anna and Paredes from the secretaries of state, war and the navy; "which contain all the information in the possession of the executive, which it is deemed compatable with the public interests to communicate." There was nothing in these reports concerning Commander Mackenzie, Colonel Atocha, or William Linn Brown. In fact, many of the documents submitted to the House in this report had nothing to do with Santa Anna or Paredes. Bancroft's letter of 13 May 1846 to Commodore Conner, ordering him to allow Santa Anna to pass freely into Mexico, was included. The facts and considerations which induced the order of the secretary of the navy to Commodore Conner were provided in Polk's annual message to Congress, dated 8 December 1846, and Polk referred the House to that message.

Polk provided all the documentation concerning Paredes. He had arrived at Veracruz on the *Tevoit,* traveling under the assumed name of M. Martinez. He was landed before the ship was cleared, went to the house of José G. Zamora, a businessman, and presented a letter of introduction from Paris. His request for horses for himself and his servant was immediately fullfilled, and ten minutes after his landing he passed through one of the gates of the city on his way to the interior.[56]

As far as the request for Slidell's instructions, Polk went back in history to defend his position. He pointed out that an earlier Congress had requested "a copy of the instructions to the minister of the United States, who negotiated the treaty with the King of Great Britain," and President Washington in his message to the House, dated 30 March 1796, declined to comply. Washington believed that foreign negotiations required caution and secrecy. The Constitution reflected this belief by designating the president to make treaties and the Senate with its small membership to advise and consent. The larger House was not in the process.

Polk wrote, "I have heretofore, communicated to Congress all the correspondence of the minister of the United States to Mexico, which, in the existing state of our relations with that republic, can, in my judgement, be at this time communicated, without serious injury to the public interest."

Polk ended his message stressing executive privilege, "I regard it to be my consitutional right and solemn duty, under the circumstances of this case, to decline a compliance with the request of the House contained in their resolution."[57]

During his tenure in the White House, James Polk showed himself as a man of action. He would approve bold ideas and plans, but would demand the planning, preparation, and execution be meticulously implemented, and with such a secretiveness that his friends called him "the mole."[58]

On 7 February 1848 Buchanan received a letter from Atocha, dated 12 January 1848. Atocha suggested that he be furnished with money to bribe the Mexican Congress for a peace treaty. When Buchanan showed Polk the letter, Polk called Atocha, "a great scoundrel."[59]

The "great scoundrel" appeared before the Senate Select Committee on Mexican Claims on 9 June 1852. The committee was formed to see how much of the $3.25 million provided by the 1848 treaty was paid on spurious, fraudulent, and fictitious claims.

Atocha's claim had been rejected by the "Commissioners on Claims against Mexico" in 1849, and it was his position that other claims based on "precisely the identical ground" were allowed.

He was asked by the Select Committee "in which cases was an improper award made to other parties." Atocha referred to the more prominent ones—"Hargous, Gardiner, John Belden, William S. Parrott and Elisha Saulnier."[60]

Notes to Chapter 4

1. The Historic New Orleans Collection, personal letter.
2. Jones, *Santa Anna*, p. 101.
3. Rives, *United States and Mexico*, 2:119.
4. Jones, *Santa Anna*, p. 97.
5. Louisiana State Museum, personal letter.
6. Quaife, *Polk Diary*, 1:223.
7. Ibid., 1:226.
8. Ibid., 1:227–229.
9. Ibid., 1:230.
10. Ibid.
11. Ibid., 1:233–234.
12. Ibid., 1:238.
13. Ibid., 1:305–306.
14. Ibid., 1:308.
15. Ibid., 1:319.
16. Ibid., 1:328.
17. Ibid., 1:331–333.
18. U.S. Congress, House, *Presidential Message*, H. Ex. Doc. 187, 29th Cong., 1st sess., 1846.
19. Quaife, *Polk Diary*, 1:382.
20. Reeves, *Tyler and Polk*, p. 298.
21. Moore, *Buchanan*, 6:488.
22. Jones, *Santa Anna*, p. 104.
23. National Archives, Miscellaneous Letters of the Department of State (RG 59).
24. Department of the Navy, Naval Historical Center, personal letter.
25. Sellers, *Polk, Continentalist*, p. 430.
26. Department of the Navy, Naval Historical Center, personal letter.
27. *Dictionary of American Biography*, 1981 index, s.v. "Mackenzie, Alexander Slidell."
28. Rives, *United States and Mexico*, 2:232.
29. Department of the Navy, Naval Historical Center, personal letter.
30. Jones, *Santa Anna*, p. 104.

31. McMasters, *United States*, 7:447.

32. Alfred Hoyt Bill, *Rehearsal for Conflict* (New York: Alfred A. Knopf, 1947), p. 108.

33. Reeves, *Tyler and Polk*, pp. 299–301.

34. Ibid., pp. 299–302.

35. Ibid., pp. 302–304.

36. Dumas Malone and Basil Rauch, *Empire for Liberty* (New York: Appleton-Century-Crofts, 1960), 1:552.

37. Jones, *Santa Anna*, p. 101.

38. Reeves, *Tyler and Polk*, pp. 304–307.

39. Wilfred Hardy Callcott, *Santa Anna* (Norman: University of Oklahoma Press, 1936; reprint ed., Hamden, Conn.: Anchor Books, 1964), pp. 232–234.

40. Ibid., p. 239.

41. Jones, *Santa Anna*, pp. 100–101.

42. Ibid., p. 106.

43. Bernard DeVoto, *The Year of Decision, 1846* (Boston: Little, Brown, 1943), p. 287.

44. Jones, *Santa Anna*, p. 107.

45. John Edward Weems, *To Conquer a Peace* (Garden City: N.Y.: Doubleday, 1974), p. 196.

46. Quaife, *Polk Diary*, 2:322.

47. Ibid., 2:325.

48. Ibid., 2:331–332.

49. Ibid., 2:336.

50. Ibid., 2:339.

51. Ibid., 2:339–340.

52. Ibid., 2:432.

53. Ibid., 3:152.

54. Ibid., 3:290–291.

55. U.S. Congress, House, *Presidential Message*, H. Ex. Doc. 25, 30th Cong., 1st sess., 1848.

56. Ibid.

57. Ibid.

58. Malone and Rauch, *Empire for Liberty*, 1:549.

59. Quaife, *Polk Diary*, 3:329.

60. U.S. Congress, Senate, *Select Committee on Mexican Claims*, S. Rep. Com. 182, 33rd Cong., 1st sess., 1852.

Chapter 5

Covert Operations in the Northern Mexico Campaign

At the time of the arrival of the first United States troops in 1845, Corpus Christi was a small Mexican village of less than 100 people. Henry Lawrence Kinney and his partner owned and operated a trading post in the village where they sold goods, especially tobacco, to Mexican smugglers.[1] Kinney appears to have organized a government of his own at Corpus Christi, and as the man in charge, was alternately the friend and foe of Mexicans, Texans, Americans, and Indians living in this vast frontier area.[2] Owing to the nature of his business, he established an efficient network of spies to keep him informed of Mexican, Texan, American, and Indian activities. Kinney knew the political and military leaders of Mexico, and acted as an unofficial negotiator, most notably between President Anson B. Jones of Texas and General Arista of Mexico, in events preceding the Mexican War.[3]

Henry Lawrence Kinney is considered the founder of Corpus Christi. He was born in Bradford County, Pennsylvania, in 1814. As a young man he served in the army during the Black Hawk Indian campaign. Kinney had a pleasing personality and was a good soldier. In addition, his father, a lawyer, had connections in the army. This combination provided young Kinney with the opportunity to meet and become friendly with such men as Abraham Lincoln, Zachary Taylor, Winfield Scott, Albert Sidney Johnston, and Jefferson Davis.[4]

In 1839 Kinney and his partner William Aubrey opened a trading post at Corpus Christi. Texans were authorized to trade with Mexicans, but the duties were high, and Corpus Christi was a convenient place for exchanging contraband. The Mexicans traded horses, mules, saddles, bridles, blankets, and silver for cloth, tobacco, wines, and other high duty items. The smugglers were able to avoid paying customs due to the great expanse of the frontier and the confusion and lawlessness caused by the dispute over the area by Mexico and Texas. They were also able to make immense profits with minimum risk.[5]

Aubrey ran the trading post while Kinney roamed far and wide, making friends and political and business contacts. Kinney operated in an area claimed by both Mexico and Texas, and the lack of respect for custom duties reflected the turmoil throughout the region. The Mexican government established custom houses along the coast of the disputed area. This increased the amount of goods smuggled through Corpus Christi. American schooners from New Orleans brought the contraband to Corpus Christi where it was transferred to mule pack trains bound for the Rio Grande.[6]

Kinney's public relations trips were very successful. One trip was to Matamoras where Kinney met General Mariano Arista, commander of the northern army of Mexico. It is not known what arrangements were made, but Corpus Christi was not disturbed by Mexican authorities after that meeting. Kinney was well suited for the frontier. He had a knack for languages and not only spoke fluent Spanish, but was able to converse with ease among the different Indian tribes. He was an excellent horseman, and his reputation as an Indian fighter earned him the name "Diablo" from the Mexicans.[7] In a few years Kinney had accumulated enough wealth to enable him to control most of the trade from Mexico and from all the towns of any importance along the Rio Grande.[8]

Most of Kinney's land was south of the Nueces River in the disputed area. To protect this investment Kinney waged a campaign to interest politicians in the area. For months prior to annexation, Kinney and Andrew Jackson Donelson, the United States minister to Texas, joined in a secret alliance. Through Donelson, Kinney's ideas reached Washington, D.C., in a steady flow. Kinney wanted to impress the administration with the importance of making the Rio Grande not the Nueces River the boundary with Mexico. Even though Kinney had made many business arrangements with Mexicans in Mexico and in the disputed area, he believed that he would lose his vast landholdings if the disputed area was conceded to Mexico.

In June 1845 Brevet Brigadier General Zachary Taylor was ordered to the western frontier of Texas in anticipation of annexation. Taylor had been instructed to keep in contact with Donelson. When Kinney heard of Taylor's orders to move, he urged Donelson to recommend Corpus Christi as the best site for Taylor's camp. Donelson did recommend Corpus Christi to Taylor: "Corpus Christi would be a likely point at which to establish a base for operations against Mexico, as it [is] the most westerly point now occupied in Texas." Taylor made it his base.[9] The Army of Occupation made Corpus Christi a boom town, and Kinney realized huge profits.[10]

Brigadier General Taylor landed at Corpus Christi on 31 July 1845, as commander of the troops sent to Texas by President Polk when Texas

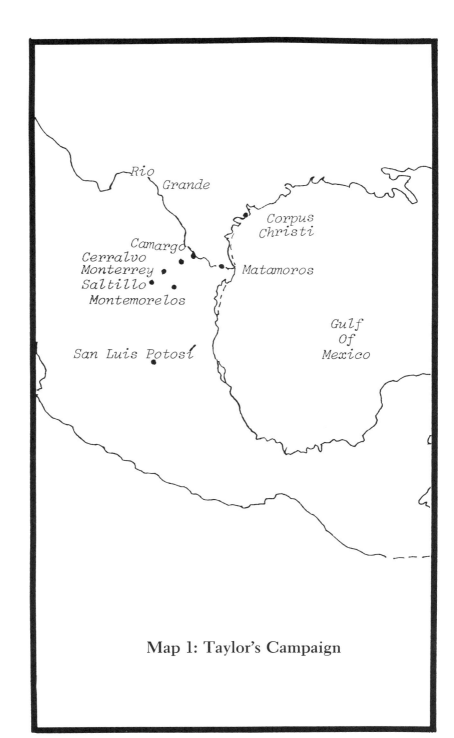

Map 1: Taylor's Campaign

became part of the Union. His command would grow to an aggregate of 3,922, be called the Army of Occupation and would remain encamped at Corpus Christi from August 1845 to March 1846.[11] (See Map 1.)

Zachary Taylor at 60 years old had been in the army for 37 years. He was appointed first lieutenant in 1808 and promoted to colonel in 1832. In July 1837 he took command of the field force in Florida, and was made brevet brigadier general after a battle at Lake Okeechobee on 25 December 1837. After two years of frustration in Florida he requested to be relieved and was sent to the southwestern frontier. Taylor's youth was spent working the plantation with his father in Kentucky, and his only formal education was provided by a tutor on the plantation. Taylor's military career consisted mainly of frontier duty.[12]

While at Corpus Christi, Taylor received reports of the Mexican military movements in and around Matamoros through Kinney. Although war had not been declared officially, Taylor's army was camped in disputed territory, and the Mexican government had stated it considered annexation of Texas tantamount to a declaration of war.[13] A continuous flow of information concerning the potential enemy was vital.

Chapita Sandoval, one of Kinney's Mexican agents and a loyal confederate who had assisted Kinney in an escape from a Mexican prison, returned from Matamoros on 12 August with important information. He had covered approximately 158 miles in 24 hours to report General Arista was en route to Matamoros with 1,000 infantry and 500 cavalry.[14]

Taylor incorporated Kinney and his spy network into the Army of Occupation. Kinney acted as quartermaster to the army in 1845, became division quartermaster, and was cited for bravery at Monterrey in 1846. Chapita was on the payroll as Taylor's guide.[15]

In his report to the adjutant general, Taylor, "wearing" his intelligence staff officer hat, evaluated the information collected by Chapita Sandoval as "authentic," and stated, "I shall not fail to communicate promptly to the department all such intelligence upon which I think reliance can be placed."[16]

In his next report to the adjutant general, Taylor praised his covert intelligence collection organization. He wrote, "We have no news from the Rio Grande. Idle stories are brought in from that quarter, but with the means of accurate information which we now possess, I do not deem it necessary to repeat them."[17]

On 6 September 1845 Taylor reported to the adjutant general that there were no extraordinary preparations for war and no increase in troops in Matamoros. His source was judged intelligent and reliable. During this mission the confidential agent was told by the United States consul in Matamoros that in his opinion there would be no declaration of war.[18]

Colonel Ethan Allen Hitchcock and General Taylor called on Kinney on 6 September. As Colonel Hitchcock was leaving he met Chapita, whom he identified as Kinney's spy. Chapita had just returned from the Rio Grande.[19] Captain William Seaton Henry noted that the spy, Chapita, returned from Matamoros on 6 September.[20] Chapita was the confidential agent whom Taylor judged intelligent and reliable.

Lieutenant George G. Meade did not trust the likes of Henry Kinney. Meade lamented the fact that with almost 4,000 troops in Corpus Christi there was not one who could speak Spanish, and therefore obtain information from a Mexican. As a result, the United States Army had to depend upon (in Meade's words) "worthless characters," who, just by living on the frontier, had picked up a little knowledge of the language. Meade questioned the validity of the information received, when these "worthless characters" were used as middlemen between the United States Army and Mexican spies.[21]

During the fall and winter at Corpus Christi, reports and rumors of all descriptions poured into the camp. Unfortunately, no one knew enough Spanish to evaluate and analyze the facts they might contain.[22] Lieutenant John C. Peck complained of seeing Mexican spies in the camp every day.[23] Without the language capability all intelligence functions were impaired.

On 8 March 1846 the Army of Occupation began the march south to the Rio Grande, and from the Rio Grande conflicting reports and rumors concerning the intentions of the Mexicans marched north. The Mexicans had either concentrated north of the Rio Grande to meet the American advance or retreated to the south bank of the river to avoid the United States troops.[24]

The orders to move Taylor's army were based on information provided by Major General Winfield Scott in Washington, D.C., not General Taylor. Scott, in a long report, showed the Rio Grande site to be far superior for the purposes of the United States government. He explained that the Rio Grande site was healthier, had better water, better grazing, and a better port. From a tactical viewpoint, Scott felt the enemy could be pursued faster and his line of retreat cut quickly from this site.[25] This report reflected a considerable amount of intelligence work on the part of Scott, and was a precursor of his outstanding ability to manage the functions of intelligence. Much of his information was obtained from Colonel Anthony Butler and General J. T. Mason, both of whom had traveled extensively in northern and central Mexico.[26]

The move from Corpus Christi to the Rio Grande required large numbers of mules and horses which the Army of the Occupation did not have, so American traders in Corpus Christi and Mexican smugglers came to the army's assistance. The Mexican smugglers used wild horses and mules to ply the barren reaches of this vast area. The American traders contracted with the army to provide mules and horses, and then paid the Mexican smugglers to capture the animals.[27] Kinney was the purchasing agent for the army and chief of the mule corps on the march.[28]

The army delayed at Colorado Creek for a few days, awaiting the arrival of the supply train. Here Taylor received word of Mexican troops occupying Point Isabel, and General Ampudia arriving at Matamoros with 5,000 men.[29] Based on this information, Taylor changed his plans and marched directly to Point Isabel instead of Matamoros. The information was incorrect. Point Isabel was not occupied by the Mexicans, so then Taylor marched his troops to Matamoros.[30]

The army arrived at its new campsite opposite Matamoros on 29 March. It was now deep in territory largely inhabited by Mexicans. The only sources of information were the local inhabitants. Again, the language barrier made effective covert intelligence collection operations difficult. Mexicans who supplied information to the Americans could have been bearers of disinformation or collectors of information for the Mexican military. Lieutenant Peck wrote that the situation in camp opposite Matamoros was the same as it had been at Corpus Christi: "Our camp is full of spies."[31] In spite of all the difficulties, covert intelligence collection operations were conducted.

Information began flowing across the river as soon as the American troops arrived. Chapita, his relatives, friends, and others bridged the river with information. During the first week at the new camp Captain Philip N. Barbour recorded in his journal the following:

> [29 March] . . . Duncan's Battery, under mask, has been put in position so as to batter Mejia's quarters and the wall of the fort near them. These have been pointed out by Chipita, our guide, who having lived a long time in Matamoras knows their position.
>
> [30 March] About tattoo last night we received notice that 600 of the enemy's cavalry had crossed the river, and [we] were ordered to sleep on our arms.
>
> A boy swam the river today from Matamoras bringing the General a note from some person there but who it was and what it contained we have not learned. This boy says there are 2800 regular troops in Matamoras and that Ampudia, with 3000 more, will be there in a few days.
>
> [31 March] General Canales is reported to have joined Mejia with about 600 Cavalry [Militia].
>
> [1 April] It is reported today, that the Mexican force has been reenforced, making 3300 regular troops.
>
> [5 April] . . . On our return found the camp considerably excited by the report of a soldier of the 8th sent over to Matamoras yesterday by General Worth as a spy. He played his part well—pretended to be a deserter and was permitted to go at large in the city which enabled him

> to gather a good deal of valuable information. He reports their strength at about 3500−1000 of which is cavalry. They have two mortars and about 25 field pieces, none of them larger than 9 pounds. Ampudia is expected tomorrow with 3500 men which will make their force 7000 strong.[32]

Covert intelligence collection operations of all types continued while the Army of Occupation was encamped opposite Matamoros. A spy sent over to the Mexican side on 7 April reported a Mexican force of about three thousand.[33] A source in Matamoros, known only as a friend of General Taylor's, warned an attempt might be made to cut the line of communication to Point Isabel. On the same day, 11 April, General Ampudia arrived at Matamoros to assume command, accompanied by cavalry and followed, as the Americans understood, by two or three thousand more troops.[34]

An informant, identified only as a Mexican from Matamoros, swam the Rio Grande on 15 April to deliver information to Taylor. The informant reported that General Arista had been ordered to relieve General Ampudia, and all operations against the United States were to cease until 1 June. Chapita authenticated this information.[35] Regardless, Lieutenant Meade believed the Mexicans were lying. Whatever General Taylor's thoughts concerning these matters, he did not allow any information to deter him from making preparations for war.[36]

Only General Ampudia was in favor of war at a military meeting in Matamoros on 17 April. After the meeting he departed Matamoros. The only identification of the source of this report was a Mexican from Matamoros.[37]

Major General Arista did arrive at Matamoros as predicted in the intelligence reports. However, he was bearing orders to attack the Americans immediately, not orders to cease all operations until 1 June. Arista took command on 23 April, and ordered his 1,600 cavalrymen to cross the Rio Grande above Matamoros.[38]

Taylor, notified of the Mexican crossing,[39] sent Captain Seth B. Thornton, with a squadron of dragoons and Chapita as their guide, to reconnoiter. Chapita returned to camp the next day, reporting Thornton had been ambushed by a large body of Mexicans, and the dragoons had been either cut to pieces or taken prisoner. Captain Hardee, who escaped from the ambush, related that prior to the engagement Chapita refused to guide the dragoons any farther because of the danger of an ambush — the enemy was close and their position was unknown. Captain Thornton, however, decided to push on and advanced into the ambush.[40]

The Mexican crossing put Taylor in a precarious situation because of the exposed position of his supply base at Point Isabel. While maneuvering to protect this base he fought the Mexican army at Palo Alto and Resaca de la Palma on 8 May and 9 May respectively. Taylor did not use covert intelligence collection operations to provide advance information. He wrote, "If the enemy opposes my march, in whatever force, I shall fight him," and he did and he won.[41] The Army of Occupation crossed the Rio Grande, occupied Matamoros, and, in the words of Lieutenant Ulysses S. Grant, became the "Army of Invasion."[42]

Reports arrived at Matamoros claiming the retreating Mexican army, which had halted at Linares, was reduced from 4,000 to 1,000 men by disease and desertion. Meade, always the skeptic, did not know what confidence to place in these reports.[43]

President Polk and Secretary of War Marcy wanted action and information from Taylor. They wanted to know what avenues into the interior of Mexico were available to an invading army and which of these avenues, now Major General Taylor, the man on the scene and the hero of the hour, recommended. They were frustrated and confused by Taylor's lack of response and lack of action. Frustration and confusion were increased by the slowness of communications. It took three to four weeks to deliver a dispatch from Washington to Matamoros. President Polk usually heard of developments from the British Embassy before reports came through from the army.[44]

Polk needed this information because he insisted on running the war. It was his intention to be knowledgeable of each and every move of his subordinates. Polk established for all succeeding presidents the authority of the president as commander-in-chief. When the adjutant general attempted to withhold information from Polk, he expressed his determination to be commander-in-chief in the clearest possible terms:

> His presumption in with-holding the information which I had requested from me, and in attempting to control my actions, vexed me, & finally I spoke shortly to him. Among other things I remarked that as I was constituted by the Constitution commander in chief of the Army, I choose to order him to furnish the list of vacancies from the records of his office which I had desired. I repeated to him that he must regard what I said as a military order & that I would expect it to be promptly obeyed.[45]

Back in Mexico, Taylor knew he needed information, but the questions were how to collect and evaluate it. General Scott advised Taylor to employ a large force of secret agents in order to have many reports to compare — providing a means to separate the wheat from the chaff. Many people in northern Mexico were dissatisfied with their national government and could have been used for this purpose.[46] Instead, Captain Ben McCulloch and 40 Texas Rangers checked out two possible routes to Monterrey and returned to Taylor's headquarters.[47]

On 24 July 1846 at Point Isabel Lieutenant Grant met "Captain A. Slidell McKenzie," who had arrived in a navy ship direct from Havana. Mackenzie was with General Taylor for several hours, and then departed for Washington, D.C.[48]

Reports from Monterrey which reached Matamoros on 30 July 1846 provided the following information: the Mexicans had not been reinforced at Monterrey; only the remains of the army that had retreated from Matamoros were there; but, however, these men were operosely engaged in fortifying the city.[49]

The first contingent of United States troops departed Matamoros for Monterrey on 6 July. The route was to Camargo via the Rio Grande and San Juan Rivers, and then over land to Monterrey. Taylor arrived at Camargo on 8 August. His letter to the adjutant general, dated 25 August, stated that a confidential messenger from Monterrey reported 2,000 to 2,500 troops in the city, and that there was some attempt to fortify the city by the erection of batteries to command the approaches.[50] This information had arrived at Matamoros on 30 July. The confidential messenger was not identified.

Troops under General William J. Worth started the march to Monterrey from Camargo in the middle of August. At Cerralvo (approximately three days's march from Monterrey), the information which Worth's spies carried from Monterrey was not encouraging.[51]

General Worth wrote to Major William W. S. Bliss (key officer on Taylor's staff) from Cerralvo on 3 September. He reported the arrival at Monterrey in late August of 2,000 troops with four pieces of field artillery. This was in addition to the ten guns which had previously been put in position. In preparation for the attack, his principal engineer, Lieutenant George Meade, was trying to get an accurate plan of the city, showing the approaches and projected points of interest.[52]

General Worth used covert intelligence collection operations to provide advance information. Captain William S. Henry wrote, "General Worth, through means of spies, has received information on which he relies. Ampudia certainly arrived at Monterrey on the 31st of August and assumed command."[53]

Major General Taylor detached the Texas Ranger companies of Captains McCulloch and Gillespie from regimental headquarters, and employed them under his immediate command as "Spy Companies."[54] These west Texas men had been in direct conflict with Mexicans for years. The Texas Ranger companies comprised of east Texas men of were used for escort duty.[55]

On 11 September a spy from Monterrey reported to General Worth with far more detailed information concerning the number of troops and the strength of the fortifications than any previously received. The information was so vivid that many of the officers did not believe it. When Lieutenant Meade drew the batteries on a map, they appeared to cover every approach to the city with direct, cross, and enfilading fire.[56]

In the middle of September Polk was still exasperated by the lack of information from Taylor. He wanted reliable information on the topography, resources, and defenses of the country in order to direct the movement of United States troops into the interior of Mexico. Taylor had not established the covert intelligence collection network to provide a continuous flow of information to fulfill these requirements. In addition, the communication problems were still not solved.[57]

Monterrey fell, but at a high cost. The battle was a series of vigorous skirmishes, heroic assaults, and grave errors. Taylor, with little knowledge of military science or the use of artillery, resolved to take a fortified town by bayonet assault, which caused considerable slaughter of his own men.[58] American losses were 120 killed, 368 wounded, and 43 missing, or 8.5 percent of the 6,220 effectives.[59]

Taylor's tactics were described by officers under his command as "rash," "injudicious," and "headlong." His second-in-command said the troops at Monterrey had been "murdered." Lieutenant Meade commented that Taylor had shown "perfect inability to make any use of the information" given him. Major Bliss agreed that Taylor had "no conception" of the Mexican preparations. General Worth evaluated Taylor's force as "literally a huge body without a head."[60]

After the fall of Monterrey reports from various sources concerning the activities of General Santa Anna flooded into the city. However, there was still little effort put forth to project extensive covert intelligence collection operations into the interior, or to evaluate, analyze, and disseminate the information which was already available.[61]

General Worth was in command of the troops at Saltillo and this meant false alarms. Worth was a good soldier in battle, but when the battle was over, every report and every rumor was taken at face value. His troops were always standing to arms because General Worth was always about to be attacked.

In December 1846 Worth sent an express rider to Taylor at Montemorelos. The rider arrived 18 December and delivered this message: "Santa Anna was advancing on Saltillo." General Taylor was loath to believe this intelligence, but he did move his troops to support Worth.[62] Santa Anna had decided to advance upon Worth's force at Saltillo and was scheduled to commence the movement around 24 December. When Santa Anna discovered Taylor's movement, he countermanded his orders. As Santa Anna was not marching but planning to advance on Saltillo, Worth's call to arms in this case was a half alarm.[63]

Santa Anna did not move until February 1847. He had in his possession a captured letter from General Winfield Scott to General Taylor describing the transfer of troops from Taylor to Scott for the Veracruz landing, and Scott's recommendation to Taylor to go on the defensive at Monterrey. Taylor, with an army composed almost entirely of volunteers who had not been in battle, was not on the defensive in Monterrey, but in an exposed position south of Saltillo.[64]

Santa Anna's forces were reported within two days' march of Taylor's camp at Aqua Nuevo on 20 February 1847. This information caused Taylor to order a reconnaissance in force far beyond the reach of his pickets. Three hundred dragoons and the now Major McCulloch's Texas Ranger company were deployed to search for the enemy.[65]

McCulloch's company was sent to the hacienda of Encarnación, thirty miles from Aqua Nuevo on the road to San Luis Potosí, and reported a cavalry force of unknown strength at that place. Disguised as "rancheros," Major McCulloch and a small party of Texas Rangers went back to the Mexican camp. They passed through the enemy lines at dark and from the dimensions of the camp calculated the size of the force. McCulloch sent six men back to Taylor with this information. He and another ranger remained in the camp to see what daylight would reveal, and then, covered by the woodsmoke of the camp fires, rode slowly and deliberately out of the camp between the Mexican pickets.[66]

Major McCulloch reported to Taylor and his staff that Santa Anna had a force of 20,000 men. Owing to this intelligence, Taylor decided to leave the plains of Aqua Nuevo for a better defensive position, eight miles south of Saltillo. Here at Buena Vista the last battle of Taylor's campaign was fought and won.[67] American losses were 272 killed, 387 wounded, and 6 missing, 14 percent of the 4,594 effectives.[68]

United States military covert intelligence collection operations in the northern Mexico campaign reflected the fighting style, experience, and education of Taylor. While the Army of Occupation was camped at Corpus Christi, Kinney's spies provided all the necessary information concerning Mexican military movements in and around Matamoros.

When the United States forces moved to camp opposite Matamoros, Chapita, his friends, relatives, and others provided a continuous flow of information. The engagements at Palo Alto and Resaca de la Palma were fought in Taylor's style. Intelligence was not necessary because he was going to march from Point A to Point B, and if the enemy opposed him, he would attack head on — no feints, no flanking movements, and no intelligence needed. And he won.

President Polk was not happy with his military commander in northern Mexico. He could not pry information out of Taylor, and when he did, it took three to four weeks for the question to travel from Washington to Taylor in the field, and the same amount of time to return

to Polk. When Taylor decided on the route to Monterrey and started moving troops and supplies in that direction, he had not established the covert
intelligence collection network needed to penetrate deep into Mexico to
provide information for the battle or battles after Monterrey. There were
no covert intelligence collection operations set up to ensure a continuous
flow of information from Monterrey, but both Taylor and Worth did send
spies into Monterrey to gather intelligence. These activities did not satisfy
the intelligence collection requirements of Polk.

Taylor took 6,640 men from Camargo to attack the fortified town of
Monterrey. His decision was not based on the strength of the enemy
forces or fortifications but on his transportation problems, his supply
problems, and his opinion of volunteer troops. He had problems, but
there were solutions and alternatives which could have increased his force
and its firepower. Thousands of troops were moved from Matamoros to
Camargo and left there while a relatively small force with limited supplies
and artillery attacked Monterrey and won.

Prior to the battle of Buena Vista, Santa Anna was able to advance
from San Luis Potosí to within 30 miles of Taylor's position before he
was discovered. Worth, even with his false alarms, had put spies into the
field to provide him with advance information, but he had been transferred to Scott's command. Taylor's small army lacked the long vision provided by covert intelligence collection operations, but he won nonetheless.

United States military covert intelligence collection operations did
provide significant inputs to the decisionmaking process at two critical
junctures on this front. At Monterrey, based on the information gathered
by covert intelligence collection operations, Taylor made an unconventional decision. He split his force and attacked Monterrey at two widely
dispersed points. If Taylor had committed his total force in a concentrated frontal bayonet attack, the possibility of a successful Mexican
defense and or unacceptable American losses would have been sig-
nificantly increased. At Aqua Nuevo a Texas Ranger covert intelligence
collection operation provided Taylor with an accurate enemy force
estimate. Using this information Taylor made the decision to move his
small force to a more advantageous position. Without this movement, the
large Mexican force would have had a greater opportunity to win the
battle.

In the northern Mexico campaign, covert intelligence collection
operations were limited. The Americans, in Taylor's style, basically
pounded the Mexicans into submission. Taylor won every battle, but his
casualty list was very long. Any study of the campaign must keep in
perspective the Mexican soldier. The Mexican army of that day was
hardly an organization. The private soldier was picked up from the lower

class of the inhabitants when wanted—his consent was not asked.[69] The majority of the Mexican rank and file were ignorant Indian conscripts, half-trained, half-starved, poorly clothed, and seldom paid.[70]

Notes to Chapter 5

1. Ulysses S. Grant, *Personal Memoirs of U. S. Grant* (New York: Charles L. Webster, 1885), 1:64.

2. Ethan Allen Hitchcock, *Fifty Years in Camp and Field* (New York: G. P. Putnam's Sons, 1909), pp. 196–197.

3. Coleman McCampbell, *Texas Seaport* (New York: Exposition, 1952), pp. 28–29.

4. Warner E. Gettys, *Corpus Christi—A History and Guide* (Corpus Christi: Caller Times, 1942), p. 45.

5. Ibid., p. 52.

6. Ibid., p. 53.

7. Ibid., pp. 54–55.

8. Ibid., p. 45.

9. Ibid., p. 65.

10. Ibid., p. 72.

11. Holman Hamilton, *Zachary Taylor* (New York: Bobbs-Merrill, 1941), p. 163.

12. *Dictionary of American Biography*, 1981 index, s.v. "Taylor, Zachary," by Wendell H. Stephenson.

13. Hamilton, *Taylor*, p. 166.

14. William Seaton Henry, *Campaign Sketches of the War with Mexico* (New York: Harper and Brothers, 1847; reprint ed., New York: Arno, 1973), p. 28.

15. McCampbell, *Texas Seaport*, pp. 28–29.

16. U.S. Congress, House, *Hostilities by Mexico*. H. Doc. 196, 29th Cong., 1st sess., 1846, p. 85.

17. U.S. Congress, House, *Mexican War Correspondence*, H. Ex. Doc. 60, 30th Cong., 1st sess., 1848, pp. 105–106.

18. Ibid.

19. Hitchcock, *Fifty Years*, p. 199.

20. Henry, *Campaign Sketches*, p. 35.

21. George G. Meade, *The Life and Letters of George Gordon Meade* (New York: Charles Scribner's Sons, 1913), 1:31.

22. Bill, *Rehearsal*, p. 84.

23. John James Peck, *The Sign of the Eagle* (San Diego: Union-Tribune, 1970), p. 6.

24. Meade, *Life and Letters*, 1:50.

25. Smith, *Mexico*, 1:153–154.

26. Rives, *United States and Mexico*, 2:195.

27. Grant, *Memoirs*, 1:69.

28. John Reese Kenly, *Memoirs of a Maryland Volunteer* (Philadelphia: J. B. Lippincott, 1873), p. 95.

29. Bill, *Rehearsal*, p. 89.

30. Meade, *Life and Letters*, 1:52.

31. Peck, *Sign of the Eagle*, p. 18.

32. Rhoda Doubleday, ed., *Journals of P. N. Barbour and His Wife M. I. H. Barbour* (New York: G. P. Putnam's Sons, 1936), pp. 21–30.

33. Meade, *Life and Letters*, 1:53.

34. Smith, *Mexico*, 1:161.

35. Doubleday, *P. N. Barbour*, p. 37.

36. Meade, *Life and Letters*, 1:57.

37. Doubleday, *P. N. Barbour*, p. 39.

38. Smith, *Mexico*, 1:149.

39. Meade, *Life and Letters*, 1:73.

40. Henry, *Campaign Sketches*, pp. 82–83.

41. Brainerd Dyer, *Zachary Taylor* (Baton Rouge: Louisiana State University, 1946), p. 172.

42. Grant, *Memoirs*, 1:99.

43. Meade, *Life and Letters*, 1:96.

44. DeVoto, *Year of Decision*, p. 287.

45. McCoy, *Polk*, p. 141.

46. Smith, *Mexico*, 1:226–227.

47. Hamilton, *Zachary Taylor*, p. 196.

48. Meade, *Life and Letters*, 1:116.

49. Ibid., 1:119.

50. U.S. Congress, House, *Mexican War Correspondence*, H. Ex. Doc. 60, 30th Cong., 1st sess., 1848, p. 412.

51. Edward S. Wallace, *General William Jenkins Worth* (Dallas: Southern Methodist University Press, 1953), pp. 81–82.

52. Rives, *United States and Mexico*, 2:255.

53. Henry, *Campaign Sketches*, p. 178.

54. U.S. Congress, House, *Mexican War Correspondence*, H. Ex. Doc. 60, 30th Cong., 1st sess., 1848, pp. 322–323.

55. Walter Prescott Webb, *The Texas Rangers* (Boston: Houghton Mifflin, 1935), p. 101.

56. Nathan Covington Brooks, *A Complete History of the Mexican War* (Philadelphia: Grigg, Elliot, Baltimore, Hutchinson and Seebold, 1849; reprint ed. Chicago: Rio Grande, 1965), p. 168.

57. Quaife, *Polk Diary*, 2:139.

58. *Encyclopaedia Britannica*, 1956 ed., s.v. "Taylor, Zachary."

59. K. Jack Bauer, *The Mexican War 1846–1848* (New York: Macmillan, 1974), p. 100.

60. Otis A. Singletary, *The Mexican War* (Chicago: University of Chicago Press, 1960), p. 133.

61. Meade, *Life and Letters*, 1:147.

62. Ibid., 1:170.

63. Wallace, *General Worth*, p. 111.

64. Grant, *Memoirs*, 1:123.

65. Samuel E. Chamberlain, *My Confession* (New York: Harper and Brothers, 1856), p. 106.

66. Webb, *Texas Rangers*, p. 112.

67. Benjamin F. Scribner, *Camp Life of a Volunteer* (Philadelphia: Grigg, Elliot, 1847; reprint ed., Austin: Jenkins, 1975), pp. 58–59.

68. Bauer, *Mexican War*, p. 217.

69. Grant, *Memoirs*, 1:168.

70. Hamilton, *Zachary Taylor*, p. 182.

Chapter 6

Covert Operations in the New Mexico Campaign

On 13 May 1846 Congress declared the United States in a state of war with Mexico. On the same day Secretary of War William L. Marcy issued orders to Colonel Stephen W. Kearny to organize and lead an expedition over the Santa Fe trail to invade and seize New Mexico (see Map 2). George T. Howard of Texas was dispatched by the secretary of war with these orders. After delivery of them to Kearny, he was to overtake a caravan of traders who had recently left Independence, Missouri, for Santa Fe, New Mexico, notify them that a state of war existed between the United States and Mexico, and instruct them to wait for the army.[1]

Marcy also sent a confidential letter to Kearny informing him of Howard's covert mission and Kearny's responsibility to provide Howard with a detachment of dragoons of sufficient strength to ensure his safety, not just to the caravan but to the Mexican border.[2]

Kearny's dragoons escorted Howard to the caravan and then to the Mexican boundary, where he was on his own to perform his primary mission — a covert intelligence collection operation for the secretary of war. Howard was a prominent Santa Fe trader who was given a twofold mission — one, collect information on the capabilities and intentions of the Mexican people and government in the area, and two, attempt to convince the Mexicans not to oppose the invading American forces.[3]

Senator Thomas H. Benton sent word to Independence, Missouri, for James Wiley Magoffin to come to Washington by the fastest means.[4] Magoffin was a citizen of the United States who had been a long-time resident in New Mexico, and Benton wanted him to assist the Army of the West with his exceptional knowledge of the people and the terrain in that area of Mexico.[5]

James Magoffin was a man of wealth, with unlimited capacity for drinking wine and making friends, fluent in the Spanish language, and on friendly terms with most of the leading men in New Mexico and Chihuahua. He had been profitably engaged in the Santa Fe trade for over

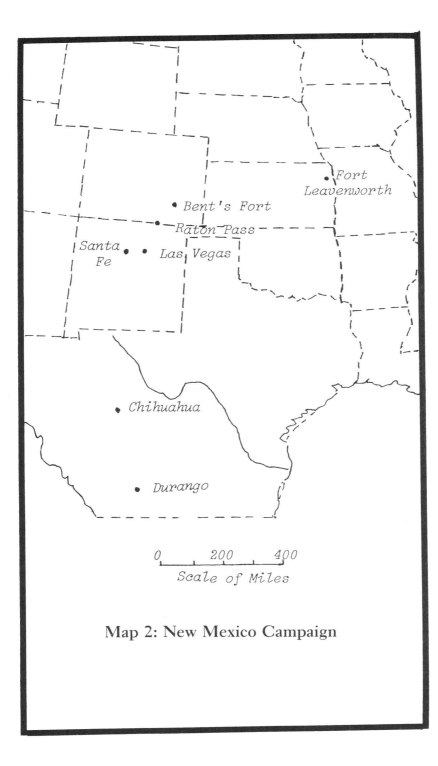

Fort
Leavenworth

Bent's Fort

Raton Pass

Santa
Fe

Las Vegas

Chihuahua

Durango

0   200   400
Scale of Miles

Map 2: New Mexico Campaign

twenty years. He married a daughter of the native gentry with rich properties in Chihuahua and Durango. She died in 1844 and he moved to Independence, but he was still active in the trade.[6]

On 25 May 1846 Magoffin had just returned to Independence,
Missouri, from Chihuahua. When he received Benton's message, he immediately set out for the capitol. By 30 May he was in St. Louis, and on
15 June he was introduced to President Polk by Benton at the White
House.[7] President Polk talked to Magoffin for an hour. He described him
in his diary as an intelligent merchant and trader with good information
on the northern provinces of Mexico.[8]

On 17 June 1846 Polk, Marcy, and Magoffin had a long conversation
concerning the forthcoming invasion of Mexico. Again Polk was impressed with Magoffin's intelligence and knowledge of Mexico. Magoffin
offered to provide supplies for the army and to conciliate the people of
the northern provinces of Mexico to the United States. Marcy gave him
letters to Colonel Kearny and to General John E. Wool, the commander
of the Chihuahua expedition, requesting them to avail themselves to
Magoffin's services.[9] What Polk said to Magoffin, and Magoffin to Polk is
not known. "When the President had a secret he kept it even from his
diary."[10]

Marcy, in his letter, informed Kearny of the several meetings Polk
had had with Magoffin, and how favorably impressed the president was
with him. The president believed Magoffin could render important services to Kearny in his invasion of New Mexico, such as providing important information and abundant supplies for the troops. Then came the
real orders: Magoffin, after he caught up with Kearny and they had their
private meeting, was to proceed immediately to Santa Fe.[11]

With this letter and other communications for Colonel Kearny,
Magoffin headed west. He traveled light and fast with the latest sleeping
bags and the best wines and cigars.[12] His secret mission was the same as
Howard's: covert intelligence collection and covert action to persuade
resident Americans, Mexican traders, government officials, and most
especially the governor of New Mexico, not to fight the invading United
States forces.[13]

Fort Leavenworth was the place of outfit and departure for the Army
of the West. This army was less than 1,700 men with about 200 regular
troops and the rest Missouri volunteers. Under the command of Colonel
Kearny, the army commenced its march on 26 June 1846.[14]

George Howard, returning from his mission in Santa Fe, met Kearny
on the trail to Bent's Fort on 19 July. He reported the common people of
New Mexico were inclined to accept Kearny's terms. Those terms included surrender of the Mexicans to the American forces and an oath of
allegiance to the United States. In return, the Mexicans would become

American citizens. However, the Mexican leaders rejected these terms, and were making preparations for war. Howard believed there was one unit of 2,300 men planning to defend Santa Fe, and another detachment of unknown size around Taos.[15] Howard's report produced quite a sensation in camp. It was now expected that Santa Fe would be vigorously defended.[16]

Howard only partially completed his mission, but he was reimbursed for his services. He was paid $1,659.19 on 24 October 1846 for expenses incurred on his special mission to New Mexico. The expenses included hotels, railroad fares, stagecoach fares, steamboat fares, horses, mules, camp equipment, medicines, and the services of 12 men. He received an additional $1,270.19 on 2 November 1846. All of these funds were provided from the "Contingent expenses — military account."[17]

Just ten days after meeting Howard, Colonel Kearny received a message from Bent's Fort — the information came from Santa Fe. Governor Manuel Armijo was deciding on the best means to defend the town. Every report made it more likely that the Army of the West would be opposed.[18]

Bent's Fort was a small outpost on the north bank of the Arkansas River, 650 miles west of Fort Leavenworth. Here the caravan of Santa Fe traders awaited the arrival of the Army of the West. For the rest of the journey the caravan would move under the protection of the army. The caravan consisted of 414 wagons which were heavily laden with dry goods for the markets of Santa Fe and Chihuahua, and valued at over $1 million.[19]

Samuel Magoffin drove his wagon into Bent's Fort on 27 July 1846. With him was his 19-year-old wife, Susan, one of the few white women on the trail that summer. Samuel and Susan had been married for eight months. She was pregnant, in poor physical condition, and suffered a miscarriage at Bent's Fort.[20]

James and Samuel Magoffin were brothers and partners. Once and sometimes twice a year the brothers took large caravans into Mexico. The year 1846 would be different. James was not with a wagon train as usual. Another brother, William, was in charge of the one that he would ordinarily have commanded.[21]

Kearny and James Magoffin met at Bent's Fort on 31 July. Magoffin explained how he hoped to induce Governor Armijo and his officers by persuasion or bribery, or both, to submit peacefully.[22] Kearny said he hoped New Mexico would not be defended, but he desperately needed a wide variety of information if it was going to be defended. Kearny had serious transportation, supply, and communication problems, and added to these was the fact that on the march to Santa Fe he could be attacked anywhere at anytime. With the caravan in tow, he was a large, slow-moving target, immersed in enemy territory. Kearny told Magoffin that he wanted him on the trail to Santa Fe as soon as possible.[23]

Magoffin had a confidential letter dated 3 June 1846 for Kearny from Secretary of War Marcy. The letter instructed Kearny, after taking Santa Fe, to head west and take possession of California. This letter changed Kearny's original instructions, which were to take all of New Mexico east of the Rio Grande in accordance with the claim of Texas. There is no reason to believe that Polk, Marcy, or Kearny informed Magoffin of the change in plans. Involved as he was in a covert intelligence operation, there was every reason to keep him ignorant of the change.[24]

Captain Philip St. George Cooke and his troop of dragoons joined the Army of the West on 31 July 1846 at Bent's Fort. Colonel Kearny sent for him immediately and gave him a surprise mission. Cooke was to set out in advance of the army with a flag of truce to Santa Fe, a distance of 300 miles. He was to take 12 dragoons and two traders, James Magoffin and José Gonzales of Chihuahua.[25] Cooke had a letter to deliver to Governor Armijo from Kearny. The letter notified Armijo that the United States was annexing all of New Mexico east of the Rio Grande in accordance with the claim Texas made to that river as its western boundary. Kearny was definitely keeping his change of orders to himself.[26]

During the time the army was camped at Bent's Fort, three Mexicans, posing as supporters of the United States but actually spies, were caught. Kearny showed them around the camp to impress them with his strength and let them go.[27]

On 2 August Captain Cooke and his party departed for Santa Fe. On the same day, Mr. Liffendorfer, a trader, was sent in the direction of Taos to feel the pulse of the Pueblo Indians and the Mexican people in that area. William Bent and six others were sent in advance to scout the mountain passes. The army split into sections for the march and left on 1 and 2 August.[28] The caravan which followed the invading army carried over $1 million in goods, was protected by the United States Army, and was there for the express purpose of trading with the enemy.

Bent's scouts, on 10 August, captured five Mexicans trying to spy on the invading army. On the same day, an American citizen, Mr. Towle, escaped from Taos and informed Kearny that Governor Armijo had declared martial law and called the citizens to arms. He had assembled all the Pueblo Indians (2,000) and all citizens capable of bearing arms. In addition, 300 Mexican dragoons had arrived in Santa Fe and 1,200 more were expected hourly.[29]

The Army of the West marched over the mountains into New Mexico at Raton Pass. Bent's scouts brought in various Mexicans, and other Mexicans came to see the Americans for themselves. Kearny considered them all spies, showed them around camp, and sent them home, hopefully to report he was unbeatable. The Mexicans coming into camp brought notice of trouble ahead. There were reports of 2,000, 5,000, 8,000, and 12,000 troops assembling to resist the invading army. Kearny prepared for the worst. He closed up the interval of his infantry units, posted more guards, and kept on marching. The daily captives provided by Bent's scouts told conflicting stories — either no preparations to resist or the whole province was standing to arms to stop the invaders. Americans from Santa Fe arrived and reported that Armijo would make his stand at Apache Canyon which was 15 miles from Santa Fe.[30] Kearny needed intelligence. He had scouts out and he had spies out. His hope was that Magoffin would collect all the needed information, and Cooke would deliver it in time.

Meanwhile, Cooke and his group were proceeding to Santa Fe in an alcoholic haze. Magoffin kept the entire party laughing, well fed, and cheerful on a seemingly inexhaustible supply of claret. At Las Vegas, a village on the road to Santa Fe, Magoffin visited the home of Don Juan de Dios Maes, the alcalde (mayor), and his friend. The party was entertained with Taos whiskey and dinner, during which Magoffin hinted at their mission. Their host arranged for the alcalde of the next village to have their horses guarded against theft, and he also sent a messenger to Governor Armijo. Thereafter the progress of the party was somewhat akin to an impromptu procession, the inhabitants coming out to greet them respectfully as they passed through Tecolote and on 10 August, San Miguel.[31]

Captain Cooke reached Santa Fe on 12 August. He was taken to the governor to whom he presented his credentials and was questioned concerning the strength of Kearny's force. Armijo put an apartment at the disposal of Cooke and Gonzales, where a number of American merchants visited them.[32]

Magoffin and Armijo conferred privately for several hours. Apparently they had come to an understanding when they entered Cooke's apartment accompanied by Colonel Diego Archuleta, the lieutenant governor. Armijo told Cooke he had decided not to defend Apache Pass. Colonel Archuleta was offended by this cowardly decision until Magoffin pointed out to this ambitious officer that the annexation by the United States would proceed only to the Rio Grande and this could be a grand opportunity for the right man. Armijo's defection would make Archuleta himself the logical man to negotiate the status of the important territory west of the Rio Grande. Archuleta became very quiet and withdrew from the conversation, while Governor Armijo and Magoffin settled the final details. Santa Fe was to be evacuated of troops and a commissioner, Dr. Henry Connelly, was to be sent to Kearny. Armijo and Magoffin shook hands over the bargain.[33]

The next day, Captain Cooke and Dr. Connelly set out to rejoin Kearny. Connelly was an American by birth who had lived in Chihuahua for many years where he imported goods from the United States. Kearny learned from Cooke and Connelly of the all-important night session Magoffin and Cooke had with Armijo and Archuleta on 12 August. Not even Cooke was certain that Magoffin had bribed Armijo with gold, though he certainly suspected it. There was strong circumstantial evidence that bribery was used, and Armijo's previous record of venality supported the suspicion.[34]

Armijo did not stay and fight, and the Army of the West passed through New Mexico and entered Santa Fe unopposed. The caravan immediately followed the army. James Magoffin had a dinner of oysters and champagne waiting for his family. At the dinner on 31 August, he entertained with stories and funny anecdotes. Nonetheless, his sister-in-law Susan had had a very difficult trip.[35]

Under the direction of the now General Kearny, Magoffin left Santa Fe on 1 September to perform the same services for General Wool at Chihuahua. Secretary of War Marcy had given Magoffin two letters of introduction, one to Kearny and one to the commander of the Chihuahua expedition. There were two problems developing at the time which would affect Magoffin's future operations. Wool's orders were changed and he did not go to Chihuahua as planned, which meant the Mexicans in Chihuahua would not be under the immediate threat of attack; no United States forces at the gates, no deals. The second problem was just a chance happening. Two prominent Mexicans from Chihuahua were in New Mexico at the time of the approach of the American troops. They understood that it was the positive intention of Armijo and particularly Archuleta to defend the province. These men reported to the officials in Chihuahua that Magoffin had been the cause of the nonresistance at Santa Fe and that he had bribed both Governor Armijo and Colonel Archuleta.[36]

Magoffin, Gonzales, and three other traders arrived in Chihuahua and were arrested. Gonzales and the others were put under house arrest.[37] Magoffin was imprisoned and was to be tried as a spy because of his dealings with Armijo in Santa Fe and his possession of a letter from the United States secretary of war introducing him to General Wool.[38] When Colonel Alexander Doniphan took possession of Chihuahua on 1 March 1847, all the American residents and merchants in the city (about 30) were liberated except for James Magoffin. The Mexicans sent him to Durango in order to retain him as a prisoner, and there he stayed until the end of the war.[39]

As a prisoner Magoffin entertained freely. Philip St. George Cooke calculated there were 3,392 bottles of champagne consumed by Magoffin and his guests during the time of his incarceration.[40] Champagne cost $50 for one dozen bottles and claret cost $36 a dozen. Magoffin became a great favorite with the Mexican officers, and this saved his life.

Kearny had written to Magoffin acknowledging his services in New Mexico. The delivery of the letter was entrusted to Dr. Connelly, who lived in Chihuahua. Connelly was arrested on his journey near El Paso, and the letter was sent to Chihuahua by Mexican officials. The Mexican military judge advocate took the sealed letter to Magoffin and told him to destroy it if there was anything in the letter that would incriminate him. The Mexican officer did not want anything to happen to a gentleman who had entertained him so generously. Magoffin looked at the letter and put it into the fire, as the letter in the hands of the Mexicans was his death warrant.[41]

After the war was over, Magoffin was released from prison in Durango. He traveled to Washington and arrived there in the last days of the Polk administration. Magoffin had arranged no terms for compensation prior to his mission; he had used his own money and received nothing in advance. He expected remuneration, but the Polk administration had no money set aside for this contingency.[42]

Senator Benton, who got Magoffin involved in the first place, took his case to a secret session of the Senate and obtained an appropriation of $50,000 for secret service rendered during the war. The money was granted on the last night of the outgoing administration, so the execution of the appropriation was the responsibility of the incoming administration. Benton went with Magoffin to see President Zachary Taylor. He told Magoffin he could have used his services in the war, and gave orders to his secretary of war to attend to the case as if there had been no change of administration. Instead, Secretary of War Crawford required statements to be filed, almost in the nature of an account and finally proposed a $30,000 payment. Benton said this barely covered expenses and losses, but Magoffin did not want to argue, and accepted.[43]

When Magoffin submitted his account for expenses, he included the following statement: "The Above [statement of Account] is submitted, not as an account against the United States, but as data to assist in forming an opinion of the amount that ought to be paid me for my services by showing what they cost me; as for the services themselves, they cannot be valued in money." As an example of this, one item in his account with no amount provided was, "Nine months imprisonment at Chihuahua and Durango, (can't be estimated)."[44]

On the other side of the ledger, when Secretary of War Crawford pointed out to Magoffin that $10,000 was a very large item for wine, Magoffin responded, "Yes, but, Mr. Secretary, champagne at $37.50 a basket counts up very fast."[45]

Benton hinted that Magoffin was authorized $50,000 by Polk to bribe Armijo. There was "general belief that the same means which had heretofore purchased favors for the Santa Fe traders enabled Magoffin to convince General Armijo that it was best for him to abandon the idea of making any defense at the Apache Pass."[46] Money for the bribe could have come from the War Department, from the Santa Fe traders, or from a padded claim.

Magoffin submitted an itemized claim for $37,780.96 to Secretary Crawford on 4 April 1849. Items included were $10,000 for wine, $2,000 for entertainment, and $4,300 for bribes to unidentified persons. One may safely conclude that Armijo was a bribable man, that Magoffin admitted using bribery during his mission, and that to the Santa Fe traders bribery was a way of life in Mexico.[47]

Kearny was able to enter Santa Fe with his army of 1,700 men and take possession of all of New Mexico without firing a shot or spilling a drop of blood. Armijo had 3,000 troops to stop Kearny at the narrow mountain passes, but he did not attempt to do this. Archuleta could have made a strong defense in eastern or western New Mexico, but he did not.[48]

Philip Cooke wrote the following letter to Magoffin on 21 February 1849:

> I am strongly impressed with the skill you exhibited not to com-promise your old influence over the Mexican General, by an ap-pearance of your real connection with myself. At night, however, you accompanied Genl. Armijo to my quarters when, by your aid, we had a secret conference. I then understood the Mexican Governor's real disinclination to active resistance, to which, I believe, according to your instructions, you gave important encouragement particularly in neu-tralizing the contrary influence of the young Colonel Archuleta, by sug-gesting to his ambition the part of bringing about a pronunciamento of Western New Mexico in favor of annexation.[49]

James Magoffin was an excellent selection to carry out the covert in-telligence collection and or action operation planned by Polk and Marcy. Magoffin had the uncanny ability to be liked and trusted by others. Ben-ton, Kearny, Cooke, Armijo, Archuleta, and many others were impressed and influenced by this man. His business was in Mexico, he spoke Spanish fluently, he had married into a distinguished Mexican family, he knew the character of the Mexican people, and understood how business was con-ducted in Mexico.

Magoffin used all of these assets to influence the decision-making process of Governor Armijo and Colonel Archuleta. Prior to Magoffin's ar-rival at Santa Fe, there was every reason to believe the Mexican officials would organize resistance to the American invasion. Owing to the mountainous nature of the terrain and the logistic problems of the Americans, a stout resistance by the Mexicans could have been a disaster for the Americans. The success of Magoffin's covert intelligence collection/action operation was crucial to the success of the Army of the West.

Notes to Chapter 6

1. Quaife, *Polk Diary*, 1:395–396.

2. U.S. Congress, Senate, *Secretary of War Marcy, Letter to Colonel S. W. Kearny*, S. Ex. Doc. 18, 31st Cong., 1st sess., 1849, p. 233.

3. Dwight L. Clarke, *Stephen Watts Kearny, Soldier of the West* (Norman: University of Oklahoma Press, 1961), p. 106.

4. DeVoto, *Year of Decision*, p. 255.

5. Thomas Hart Benton, *Thirty Years View* (New York: D. Appleton, 1857), 2:683.

6. DeVoto, *Year of Decision*, p. 255.

7. Stella M. Drumm, ed., *Down the Santa Fe Trail, The Diary of Susan Shelby Magoffin* (New Haven, Conn.: Yale University Press, 1926), p. xviii.

8. Quaife, *Polk Diary*, 1:472.

9. Ibid., 1:474–475.

10. DeVoto, *Year of Decision*, p. 256.

11. Drumm, *Susan Magoffin*, p. xii.

12. DeVoto, *Year of Decision*, p. 256.

13. Ibid.

14. John T. Hughes, *Doniphan's Expedition* (Cincinnati: U. P. James, 1847), p. 17.

15. Clarke, *Kearny*, p. 121.

16. Hughes, *Doniphan*, pp. 50–51.

17. U.S. Congress, Senate, *Expenditures from the Appropriations for the Contingent Expenses of the Military Establishment for the Year 1846*, S. Doc. 143, 29th Cong., 2nd sess., 1846, p. 4.

18. Hughes, *Doniphan*, p. 32.

19. Ibid., p. 33.

20. Clark, *Kearny*, p. 126.

21. Drumm, *Susan Magoffin*, p. xi.

22. Clark, *Kearny*, p. 126.

23. DeVoto, Year of Decision, p. 269.

24. U.S. Congress, House, *Secretary of War Marcy Letter to Colonel Kearny*, H. Ex. Doc. 60, 30th Cong., 1st sess., 1847, pp. 153–155.

25. Philip St. George Cooke, *The Conquest of New Mexico and California* (New York: G. P. Putnam's Sons, 1878; reprint ed., New York: Arno, 1976), pp. 5–6.

26. Clark, *Kearny*, p. 127.

27. Brooks, *Mexican War*, p. 229.

28. W. H. Emory, *Lieutenant Emory Reports* (Albuquerque: University of New Mexico Press, 1951), p. 36.

29. Ibid., p. 42.

30. DeVoto, *Year of Decision*, p. 273.

31. Otis E. Young, *The West of Philip St. George Cooke 1809–1895* (Glendale, Calif.: Arthur H. Clark, 1955), p. 178.

32. Cooke, *Conquest*, pp. 26–30.
33. Young, *Philip Cooke*, p. 180.
34. Clark, *Kearny*, p. 136.
35. Drumm, *Susan Magoffin*, p. 107.
36. Ibid., pp. xv–xvi.
37. Cooke, *Conquest*, p. 44.
38. Drumm, *Susan Magoffin*, p. 169.
39. Hughes, *Doniphan*, p. 163.
40. Cooke, *Conquest*, p. 44.
41. Benton, *Thirty Years*, 2:683.
42. Ibid., 2:684.
43. Ibid.
44. Drumm, *Susan Magoffin*, p. xvii.
45. Cooke, *Conquest*, p. 44.
46. Young, *Philip Cooke*, p. 176.
47. Ibid.
48. Drumm, *Susan Magoffin*, pp. xii–xiii.
49. Ibid., pp. 264–265.

Chapter 7

Covert Operations in the Mexican Province of California

George Bancroft of Massachusetts was an educator, historian, poet, and from 1837–1844 Collector of the Port of Boston. He was an advocate for the annexation of Texas, and for the extension of the "area of freedom."[1] Bancroft belonged to the expansionist wing of the Democratic Party which not only wanted Texas, but believed the acquisition of California equally feasible and desirable.

While most Massachusetts Democrats backed off from the Texas issue, Bancroft came out for immediate annexation. At the party state convention in 1844 he argued for it to be included in the platform.[2]

At the Democratic National Convention in Baltimore, Bancroft switched from Martin Van Buren to James K. Polk over the Texas issue, and assisted Gideon Pillow of the Tennessee delegation to gain the support of Ohio and New York for Polk. Bancroft promised Polk his whole-hearted support in the campaign, and even ran for governor on the Democratic ticket in Massachusetts. Bancroft lost, but Polk won.[3]

In February 1845, at the request of Polk, Bancroft was in Washington, D.C. Prior to his inauguration, Polk was as secretive about his appointments as he was about his covert operations after the inauguration. So on 15 February 1845 when Bancroft wrote to his wife, he did not know what his position would be in the Polk administration. He described a visit to the home of Senator Thomas Benton where he met "his most interesting son-in-law Lieutenant Frémont." During the visit Bancroft was impressed with explorer John Charles Frémont's description of Oregon. Bancroft had very definite views concerning this region: "destined you may be sure to be filled by Yankees, and whether under our government or not to be peopled by men who have no notion of owing allegiance to any power but of their own selection."[4]

Bancroft did not know until 2 March 1845 of his selection as secretary of the navy. Polk's concept of the future demanded a strong, effective navy, and he did not believe the navy of 1845 fit that description. Bancroft was given his sailing orders; rehabilitate the naval department, raise its standards and morale, and improve the service in every possible way.

Polk had picked the right man. Secretary Bancroft proceeded to "titivate ship." He outlawed the casual flogging of seamen by officers and stopped promotion by seniority only. From 1845 the criteria for promotion would include the fitness of the officer. This was one of Bancroft's most important reforms, and was liked or disliked depending on each individual's situation.[5]

The strong, effective navy envisioned by Polk needed a supply of intelligent and well-trained officers. The United States Navy of 1845 did not have a system to fulfill that need because Congress had twice voted down appropriations for a naval academy. When Bancroft in his annual report presented Congress with a fully organized naval academy in smooth and efficient operation, created from existing resources, Congress acquiesced and appropriated nearly $30,000 for its continuance.[6]

During the first weeks of the administration Polk told Bancroft of his goal to acquire California from Mexico.[7] California was on the minds of other people of influence. At the end of May 1845 news of the Californians's revolt against Governor Micheltorena caused expansionist editor Moses Yale Beach of the New York *Sun* to burst out in new warning against British seizure of the province.[8]

In the spring of 1845 Bancroft discussed a covert operation with Senator Benton. Bancroft wanted to extend John Frémont's third "exploratory" expedition beyond the Rocky Mountains into California and Oregon. If there was a war with Mexico, Frémont, leading a well-armed and carefully selected body of men, would be either "exploring" in California or poised near the border in Oregon. The cover story for the expedition was feasible. Immigration to the area was heavy, and such an expedition would provide valuable information for the settlers. Benton and Frémont understood the real reason for an armed force in northern California. Frémont credited the secretary of the navy as the originator of the plan: "His mind was alive to the bearing of actual conditions, and he knew how sometimes skill and bold action determine the advantage of a political situation."[9]

George Bancroft was an intelligent and imaginative man of action. To him the United States of America and her people were special, and it was her destiny to rule from sea to shining sea. He did not see Mexico or any other nation blocking this vision of expansion. In a letter dated 25 August 1845 to William Sturgis, he presented his views on geopolitics as they pertained to Oregon. Bancroft believed the present and future colonists of Oregon would prefer to join a free government rather than keep an authoritarian government. Thus, if all Oregon was ceded to Britain, she could not keep it. In this case Britain's naval superiority was not a factor. The British fleet could enter the harbor but, it was Bancroft's contention, they could not occupy it. America was in the process of an aggressive geographical, ideological, and political expansion, and no one was going to stop her.[10] Bancroft assisted President Polk in every way possible to make this vision come true, but in later life felt he had never received enough credit for his part in adding California to the Union.[11]

John Charles Frémont did not look the part of a mountain man. He was approximately five feet two inches tall with a pale complexion and the manners of a gentleman.[12] His first expedition followed the Oregon Trail which was not in need of exploration in 1842. Senator Benton and a small group of like-thinking senators pushed the expedition's modest appropriations through Congress. Benton and his group had some idea of meddling in Oregon, a territory still held jointly with Britain, and Frémont was to collect intelligence for them. Frémont and Benton had their own secret objectives for this expedition, and in the field Frémont extended his journey beyond South Pass. It is unclear if Colonel Abert, head of the Topographical Department, knew of Benton's intentions, and it is doubtful if Senator Benton included President Tyler or Secretary of War John C. Spencer in his secret dealings with Frémont.[13]

Frémont's second expedition was also extended by a secret arrangement with Senator Benton, which caused some confusion with Colonel Abert. Frémont requested a twelve-pound howitzer for the expedition. Colonel Abert ordered Frémont to return to Washington, D.C., to explain why he needed artillery on a scientific expedition to the Rocky Mountains. Jessie Benton Frémont intercepted the message, and sent her husband on his way, cannon and all, without knowledge of the orders. Senator Benton took responsibility for his daughter's action, and at the same time condemned the reprimand implied in Colonel Abert's instructions. Colonel Abert replied to Senator Benton:

> Now as the equipment of his party contemplated a serious change in the character of the expedition under his command, one that might involve the Government in Indian hostility, I have no doubt you will admit it to have been a negligence deserving some reproach that he did not seek the advice and orders of the Department. The Department might, under such anticipations, have prohibited the expedition, or it might have made it adequate successfully to have encountered the contemplated emergency.[14]

Frémont not only took a twelve-pound howitzer on this expedition, but he exceeded his instructions. In response to the wishes of an expansionist group of western senators, led by Senator Benton, Frémont did not return from the Columbia River by the Oregon Trail as ordered. Instead, he headed south, and by a reckless and extremely difficult crossing of the

Sierra Nevada mountains in midwinter, entered California. He spent the winter near Sutter's Fort on the Sacramento River, and returned by a route of his own choosing.[15] Thousands of copies of his report of this expedition were printed. Frémont had a way with words and a certain style that made him a hero.

Frémont returned from this expedition fascinated with California — "I determined to make there a home."[16] On 31 July 1844 at General Scott's recommendation Second Lieutenant Frémont received the double brevet of first lieutenant and captain — "for gallant and highly meritorious service in two expeditions to the Rocky Mountains."[17]

Supported by Senator Benton, chairman of the Senate Military Committee, and by Secretary Bancroft, who was the "active principle" of the administration in all plans relating to California, Brevet Captain John Frémont obtained approval of the War Department for a third exploratory expedition.[18] This was officially an expedition to the Rocky Mountains. There is no evidence to suggest that Colonel Abert contemplated sending a transcontinental expedition to California — "As in his two previous excursions the true purpose of this one was known only to himself and Senator Benton, and the Pathfinder again felt free to depart at will from Colonel Abert's orders."[19]

Secretary Bancroft and Senator Benton were mainly responsible for the secret decision that the expedition would carry Frémont far into Mexican territory (see Map 3). Frémont was to lead his expedition to that section of the Rocky Mountains which gave rise to the Arkansas, Rio Grande, and Colorado rivers; then to the Great Salt Lake; and then to the Cascade and Sierra Nevada mountain ranges, "to ascertain the lines of communication through the mountains to the ocean in that latitude." The proposed geographical surveys to be made were in greater part in Mexican territory. Frémont understood this. He wrote, "And in arranging this expedition the eventualities of war were taken into consideration."[20]

Frémont's third and final government expedition was larger, better financed, and better armed than his previous expeditions. This expedition included 60 well-armed men, and was seen as either so important or so exciting by Kit Carson that he sold his ranch at a loss to join.[21] Frémont's expedition was the only real indication of Polk's interest in California at the beginning of his administration.[22] The expedition would be on the frontiers of Oregon and California at a time expected to be critical in Mexican-American affairs; "and if there seems to be a certain convenience in having an army officer and sixty armed men on hand there, let it stand."[23]

At the same time Frémont was heading west Commodore John Drake Sloat, United States Navy, commander of the Pacific Squadron, was issued orders by Secretary Bancroft to occupy San Francisco and to

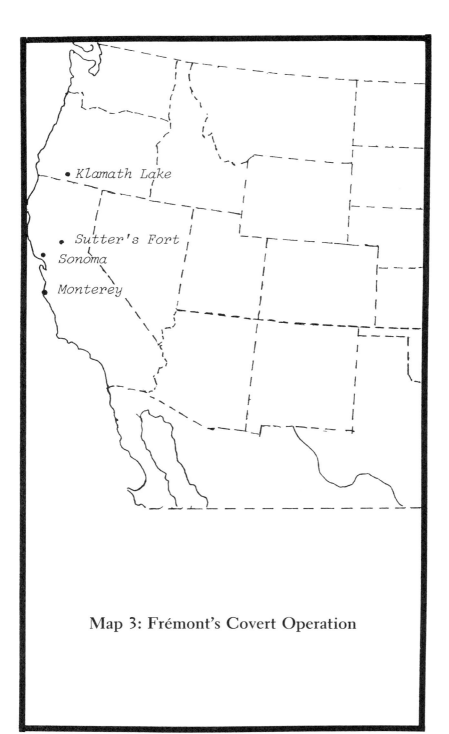

Klamath Lake

Sutter's Fort
Sonoma

Monterey

Map 3: Frémont's Covert Operation

occupy or blockade such other ports as he could, if Mexico declared war.[24] Bancroft was preparing for war.

Theodore Talbot, who accompanied Frémont on his second expedition, was in St. Louis in June 1845, handling the logistics for the third expedition. He wrote his sister on 4 June, "As far as I have heard we will winter in California," and on 9 June, "Our howitzer has not yet arrived from Memphis so it will probably be under my escort."[25]

Brevet Captain Frémont's party departed St. Louis on the steamboat *Henry Bry* to Westport (now Kansas City, Missouri), and then to a camp on Boone's Fork where the expedition was organized.[26] Theodore Talbot wrote his mother on 15 June and described his traveling companions: "All of us told, we amount to seventy men and we most certainly present a very formidable appearance and one calculated to strike awe into the bosoms of any evil disposed marauders we may chance to encounter."[27] Another member of the expedition wrote that they were "so large a body of armed men, sufficient to form a small army . . . wagons laden with, munitions, ammunition . . . 80 men or more, some 200 head of horses and mules."[28] Frémont explained, "ample means had been provided, and in view of uncertain conditions the force suitability increased." Because of this view Frémont had procured a dozen rifles, "the best that could be found" to use as prizes for the best marksman in contests during the journey.[29]

The expedition broke camp and started west on 23 June 1845. Frémont assembled all hands on 24 June and gave them his rules of the road. With the exception of Frémont no one would be allowed to keep a journal. The plans, routes, and objectives of the expedition were secret. The men were not to discuss this information with anyone. Finally, Frémont declared martial law to be the law of his camp. Ten or eleven men returned to Westport after Frémont's briefing. To raise morale Frémont distributed fifty pairs of horse pistols.[30]

The expedition arrived at Bent's Fort on 1 August 1845. From here the party split. Lieutenant James W. Abert, son of Colonel Abert, led a military reconnaissance southward and eastward along the Canadian River through the country of the Kiowa and the Comanche, ending at Fort Gibson. The chief scientific results were geographic, and Abert's information would be put to immediate use in the upcoming military campaigns in the southwest.[31] The departure of Lieutenant Abert and his party left Brevet Captain Frémont as the only representative of the United States government in his party. Frémont left Bent's Fort on 16 August 1845, "with a well-appointed compact party of sixty mostly experienced and self-reliant men, equal to any emergency likely to occur, and willing, to meet it."[32]

On 16 September 1845 President Polk and Senator Benton discussed Captain Frémont's expedition and his intention to visit California. At the same meeting they agreed that no new foreign nation could be permitted to colonize on any part of the North American continent.[33] Polk decided he needed more weapons in California to fend off foreign intervention and bring California into the Union, and another covert operation was developed. The objectives of this covert operation would be to persuade Californians to resist foreign influence and to build American influence, until California became independent of Mexico and applied for admission to the Union: in other words, to acquire California as Texas had just been acquired.[34] The United States consul at Monterey, Thomas O. Larkin, and Commodore Sloat, commander of the Pacific Squadron, were to be sent instructions to implement this covert operation.

The instructions were to be sent by ship and by special messenger across the continent. Lieutenant Archibald H. Gillespie, USMC, was selected to be the special messenger.

Secretary of State Buchanan's secret instructions dated 17 October 1845 to Thomas Larkin contained the following:

1. The United States would not tolerate the transfer of California to Britain or to any other European power.

2. If California became independent, the United States would consider her a "sister Republic."

3. Warn the government and people of California of the danger of British, French, and/or European domination, and excite their love of liberty and independence.

4. If California wanted to become a state, they would be received as brethren, if it could be done without affording Mexico just cause for complaint. (Just cause was not defined.)

5. Larkin was appointed a confidential agent to help implement the above policy and to collect all the information on California of use to the United States.

6. Lieutenant Gillespie was ordered to cooperate as a confidential agent with Larkin in carrying these instructions into effect.

7. Specific intelligence collection requirements included: population, military forces, disposition of Californians toward the United States, leaders, resources, trade, American settlements, American immigration, and routes used by immigrants.

Larkin was to receive $6 per day plus travel expenses, and other expenses incurred in his covert activities. He was to keep an accurate account and procure vouchers when possible.[35]

The same day Secretary Bancroft dispatched a similar note to Commodore Sloat, ordering him to keep in touch with Larkin, to assist him in inducing California to consider secession, and to ascertain the designs of France and Britain in regard to California.[36]

Also on 17 October Bancroft sent sealed orders to Commodore

Robert Stockton, commanding officer of the United States frigate *Congress*. Stockton was directed not to open his orders until the ship was "without the Capes of Virginia." The United States commissioner and the consul to Hawaii with their families were on board. Stockton was directed to sail from Norfolk to the Hawaiian Islands, offload his passengers, and then sail directly for Monterey. Stockton personally or "a perfectly trustworthy hand" was to deliver the enclosed letter to the United States consul at that place.[37]

Lieutenant Gillespie, who spoke fluent Spanish, was to carry a duplicate order to Commodore Sloat in cipher and memorize the dispatch to Larkin who had no cipher. Secretary Bancroft's business friends in Boston provided false identification papers for Gillespie, allowing him to cross Mexico from Veracruz to the Pacific Ocean, rather than take the time-consuming route through the Rocky Mountains. Gillespie did not leave for Veracruz until 16 November.[38] This could be explained by the change in mission. Originally, Gillespie's mission was to deliver a copy of instructions for a covert operation to Larkin and Sloat, but it was expanded to include finding Frémont. The ramifications of this last minute change could have set in motion the need for further coordination, planning, and decisionmaking, all of which took time. Gillespie was paid a total of $632 from the "Contingent expenses of the Navy" account.[39]

Polk wrote in his diary on 30 October 1845, "I held a confidential conversation with Lieut. Gillespie of the Marine Corps, about 8 o'clock P.M., on the subject of a secret mission on which he was about to go to California. His secret instructions & the letter to Mr. Larkin, U.S. Consul at Monterey, in the Department of State, will explain the object of his mission."[40] The secret instructions have never been found, and if Polk was following his normal operation procedures for briefing outgoing agents, there were no written secret instructions. Polk's diary, which includes some valuable information, must also be considered a source of misinformation because of what is missing from it. Polk was a secretive man by nature, and when it came to his covert operations he was a very secretive man.

Thomas O. Larkin was born in 1802 in Charleston, Massachusetts. In 1821 he went to North Carolina where he engaged in various business enterprises for the next nine years. He left North Carolina with little wealth and poor health. To recapture his wealth and health, Larkin sailed for the Pacific coast of Mexico and landed at Monterey on 13 April 1832. His original passport to California, dated 2 September 1831, contained the following information:

Age: 29 years
Height: 5 ft. 7½ in.

Complexion: Dark
Eyes: Dark
Hair: Dark[41]

The change of coasts and countries changed the fortune of Larkin. He acquired considerable wealth as owner of a wholesale and retail store in Monterey, trading at ports from Oregon to Hawaii and along the whole Pacific coast of Latin America. Larkin was a gracious host and a sincere promoter of goodwill between native Californians and the United States. His hospitality was always highly praised, and his house was the social headquarters of the Americans in California for some years prior to 1846.[42]

Larkin's new home, a frontier Mexican province, suffered uncommonly from the ills of political confusion spawned during the reign of General Santa Anna. Larkin was involved in a series of claims against the Mexican government for unwarranted imprisonment and loss of property based on the general roundup of foreigners in California on 7 April 1840. States' rights movements sought greater decentralization within Mexico, and a small handful of Mexicans with a group of newly arrived Americans looked forward to independence and possible annexation to the United States.[43]

Larkin was the most prominent American in northern California. "El Bostoño" declined to become a Mexican citizen and always celebrated 4 July in a lavish style; but he was also very influential with the Mexicans. The last two Mexican governors of California were in debt to him and, in fact, departed without satisfying those debts.[44] Larkin probably made money out of the situation. He was so calculating in business that he was sometimes accused of dishonesty. By 1846 Larkin not only had a very successful business, but he had acquired large property interest in California. Larkin's biographer, Ruben L. Underhill, described him as an "influential trader; prosperous merchant; first press agent; first real-estate agent, speculator and subdivider; reputedly the first millionaire" of his adopted land.[45]

Thomas Larkin was the first and only United States consul to serve in California. He served in the following United States appointed positions: United States consul, 1844–1848; confidential agent, 1846–1848; navy agent, 1847–1849; and naval storekeeper, 1847–1848.[46]

When Larkin received his letter of appointment as consul on 2 April 1844, he immediately handed over the bulk of his business to Talbot H. Green, who had been his clerk and now became his partner.[47] As United States consul, Larkin sent to the State Department numerous, detailed reports of the various aspects of the political and social life in California, on the growth of foreign influence, and the lack of support from Mexico

City and the consequent turmoil and instability inherent in the local government. Larkin provided detailed reports of the military situation, including equipment, personnel, and morale. In his enthusiasm he exaggerated the potential greatness of California, which advanced the expansionist view of bringing California into the Union.[48] In a letter to Secretary Buchanan dated 10 July 1845, Larkin reported the Mexican government was fitting out an expedition at Acapulco to throw out the Californians and reinstate Mexican authority. At the same time William S. Parrott in Mexico City was reporting on the same subject.[49]

While Larkin was reporting, Frémont was heading west, and by the end of October 1845 was camped in Mexican territory in what is now the western part of Nevada.[50] On 8 November 1845 the expedition split into two groups, the main body under Talbot to follow the Humboldt River and ten men under Frémont to set out directly west.[51] The two groups joined on 27 November at Walker Lake, located at the base of the Sierra Mountains, where Frémont again decided to take different routes. Talbot with the main body went south around the mountains into the San Joaquin Valley, and Frémont with 15 men swiftly marched west to cross the mountains before the snow blocked the passes to Sutter's Fort.[52]

If Frémont had been leading a purely explorative expedition it would have made more sense to spend the winter mapping the little known Great Basin rather than hurry on to the well-known coastal belt of California. As the leader of a covert operation Frémont's reasons for reaching California in a hurry were numerous and varied:

    1. To conduct a military reconnaissance;

    2. To be in California when the expected war with Mexico started, in order to stop the transfer of California to Britain;

    3. To give the American settlers on the Sacramento River assurance of aid;

    4. Finally, to do whatever was needed to accomplish Polk's goal, i.e., bring California into the Union.[53]

From the head of the Arkansas River the expedition had been continuously in Mexican territory. The United States government had no interest in covertly sending a large, well-armed force into a foreign country to do mapping, unless it was for military reconnaissance.[54]

By the end of 1845 about 800 American settlers—men, women, and children—were in California. Most lived in the Sacramento Valley, and their base was the fortified trading post (Sutter's Fort) at New Helvetia on the site of present day Sacramento.[55]

Frémont arrived at Sutter's Fort on 9 December. John A. Sutter was a Mexican magistrate, and Frémont obtained from him passports to Monterey for himself and eight of his men. They traveled to San Francisco where Frémont spent a few days with William Alexander Leidesdorff, the United States vice-consul.[56] Leidesdorff, a naturalized Mexican citizen, was appointed vice-consul by Larkin in October 1845. He migrated to California in 1841, and earned a reputation as a prominent businessman and real estate owner.[57]

On 26 January 1846 Frémont and Leidesdorff arrived in Monterey, and immediately went to Larkin's house. Frémont and Larkin paid calls on the Commandant General José Castro, the prefect, Manuel de Jesus Castro, the alcalde, Manuel Diaz, and Juan Bautista Alvarado who had been the revolutionary and then constitutional governor of California from 1836 to 1842.[58]

Brevet Captain Frémont presented himself not as a soldier, but as an engineer employed by the Topographical Bureau to survey the shortest route from the United States to the Pacific Ocean. He was in Monterey to obtain permission for his survey party to refit, obtain supplies, and winter over in California.[59] The commandant general was polite but plainly suspicious. Despite Frémont's explanation, the prefect sent a formal letter to Consul Larkin requesting the purpose for which American troops had entered California and their leader had come to Monterey. Larkins replied with Frémont's approval the following:

1. Frémont had come under the orders of his government to survey a route to the Pacific.

2. Frémont had left fifty civilians, not soldiers, on the frontier of California to rest.

3. Frémont came to Monterey to obtain clothing and money.

4. When his men were rested Frémont intended to continue his journey to Oregon.[60]

The authorities gave verbal or tacit permission for Frémont to winter in California with his party, provided he would agree to keep away from the coast; but they also reported the affair to Mexico City.[61] Frémont obtained information, funds, and supplies from Larkin, and departed Monterey on 29 January 1846. The splitting of his force as it entered California effectively hid Frémont's strike force as a real danger to the local authorities.

On 15 February the expedition was reunited at a vacant ranch about 13 miles south of the village of San Jose.[62] From here 60 well-armed and extremely tough foreigners commanded by a foreign army officer started their march. Instead of going to Oregon, Frémont marched at a leisurely pace to the shores of the Pacific near Santa Cruz. From there he continued south along the shore, and then up the Salinas Valley not far from Monterey. Frémont had no authority for his movements. In fact, they were contrary to his representations made to the Mexican authorities.[63] Frémont's reason for these movements was extraordinary—he was looking for real estate. He was impressed with California and wanted to live there. Frémont went to the coast because he had not yet seen the ocean, and wanted to experience "the invigorating salt breeze." Frémont was also looking for waterfront property because "This I wanted for my mother."[64]

On 3 March 1846 Brevet Captain Frémont and his men were camped 25 miles from Monterey. Two days later letters were delivered to the camp from the commandant general and the prefect, ordering Frémont and his party out of California and threating force if Frémont did not comply. Frémont expressed surprise and refused to comply "to an order insulting to my Government and myself."[65]

The commandant general wrote that he had been informed of Captain Frémont and his party entering the towns of the department, and this was prohibited by law. Therefore Frémont must "immediately retire beyond the limits of this same department such being the orders of the supreme Government and the subscriber is obligated to see them complied with."[66]

The prefect wrote Captain Frémont, "I have learnt with surprise that you against the laws of the authorities of Mexico have introduced yourself into the towns of this Departmental district under my charge with an armed force under a commission which must have been given you by your government only to survey its own proper lands." He ordered Frémont to immediately leave the limits of the department.[67]

On 5 March Frémont wrote Larkin of his reluctance to leave his party to visit Larkin in Monterey. He did not think it wise because his "little force might be disagreeable to the authorities."[68] On the same day Larkin sent Frémont translated copies of the letters from the Mexican authorities, and a copy of his answer which he would deliver the next day.[69]

Larkin's letter of 6 March to Commandant General Castro acknowledged receipt of the note to Frémont to leave the country immediately. Larkin cautioned Castro, "that you, as a Mexican officer and a patriot, are bound to take every step that may rebound to the integrity and interest of your country," but asked him to check out his information and discuss the matter with Frémont before it came "to some unhappy conclusion."[70]

In the meantime, Frémont moved his camp to a nearby hilltop. Here, there was water, grass for the animals, and excellent firing positions for the sharpshooters. Frémont raised the flag and waited.

Prefect Manuel Castro wrote Consul Larkin on 8 March: "The undersigned when he ordered Capt. Frémont to march back founded himself on repeted orders and decrees from the Supreme Government of the Mexican Republic which prohibits the introduction not only of troops belonging to any power but even that of Foreigners who do not come provided with legal Passports."[71]

On 8 March 1846 "The Citizen José Castro Lieut. Col. of the Mexican army and commander in chief of the Department of California" invited his fellow citizens to place themselves under his orders to "lance the ulcer" of a band of robbers commanded by Captain J. C. Frémont, United States Army.[72]

Larkin wrote Frémont on 8 March that General Castro was "on the plain last night with about sixty people." Larkin estimated there would be 200 men with Castro the next day. Larkin had no knowledge concerning Frémont's instructions from the United States government, but he had faith Frémont would follow them. If Frémont had no orders to enter "this country," Larkin believed the authorities were correct in saying he could not remain with a company of armed men. Larkin made sure Frémont understood the situation; "You are officially ordered to leave the Country." He informed Frémont the "Natives" would probably attack him because he was camped too close to Monterey. If Frémont moved away from Monterey, Larkin could probably arrange a truce, if for some unknown reason he could not leave California. He informed Frémont that the conflict "may cause trouble hereafter to Resident Americans."[73]

Frémont wrote Larkin on 9 March of his determination to fight to the death, "trusting to our country to avenge our death." With his field glasses Frémont could see the troops gathering and the cannons being prepared. He wrote, "and if we are hemmed in and assaulted, we will die every man of us, under the Flag of our country."[74]

Larkin's courier to the camp reported Frémont's 62 well-armed men could defend their position against 2,000 men. This was good news to Larkin, and he wrote Frémont on 10 March, "It took from me a weight of uneasiness respecting your situation."[75] Frémont remained on the hilltop with flag flying for three days, receiving information from Larkin and others of the events taking place concerning him. General Castro's volunteers gathered, but did not attack. On the third day of this Mexican/American standoff the pole bearing the American flag fell down and Frémont decided to move out—"Besides, I kept always in mind the object of the Government to obtain possession of California and would not let a proceeding which was mostly personal put obstacles in the way."[76]

General Castro saw Frémont's departure as a victory. His proclamation of 13 March stated, "Compatriots, the act of unfurling the American flag on the hills, the insults and threats offered to the authorities, are worthy of execration and hatred from Mexicans."[77]

Larkin reported to Secretary Buchanan, "Captain Frémont received verbal applications from English and Americans to join his party, and could have mustered as many men as the natives."[78]

Larkin sent word to Commodore Sloat at Mazatlán of the Frémont affair. Mrs. Isaac T. Mott, wife of the Mazatlán representative of the merchant house of Mott and Talbot described Commodore Sloat as "a nice rosy-faced old gentleman fond of talking." The old gentleman reacted to Larkin's letter. On 1 April 1846 Sloat ordered Commander John B. Montgomery, USN, as follows:

> You will proceed with the U.S. Ship Portsmouth under your command to Monterey Coast of California where you will afford countenance and all proper protection to our citizens and their interests in that country, you will also visit the Bay of San Francisco and any ports on that Coast you may judge necessary for the same objects.
>
> When on that coast you will communicate frequently with our consul at Monterrey and will ascertain as exactly as you can the nature of the designs of the English and French in that region, the temper of the inhabitants — their disposition toward the U. States and their relations toward the central Government of Mexico. You will do every thing that is proper to conciliate towards our country the most friendly regard of the people of California.
>
> When at Monterrey and San Francisco you will distribute the accompanying constitutions of the State of Texas printed in Spanish.
>
> Should you meet Commo Stockton at Monterrey you will deliver to him the accompanying letters. Should he not have arrived you will leave one with the U.S. Consul at that place — the other you will leave at St Francisco should he not have been there: but in case he has been on that Coast and you can ascertain that he has gone South you will retain both letters.
>
> In addition to the above you will be governed in your general course by the instructions you have heretofore received.[79]

Montgomery was sent on a many pronged mission; protect United States citizens, collect intelligence, conciliate Californians, distribute propaganda (Texas constitution), and find Stockton.

Larkin's thirty-ninth report went to Buchanan on 2 April 1846. In it he explained Brevet Captain Frémont's reception; "The arrival of Captain Frémont has revived the excitment in California respecting the Emigration, and the fears of the Californians of losing their country."[80]

When Frémont was in Monterey in January 1846, he arranged with Larkin to have supplies for him and his party sent by ship to Santa Barbara. Larkin also reported this on 2 April to Buchanan, "'tis supposed he [Frémont] has gone to Santa Barbara where an American Vessel was sent by the undersigned in February with funds and provisions for his use."[81]

Lieutenant Gillespie, in the guise of a British agent of MacDougal Distilleries, Ltd. of Edinburgh, Scotland, reached Mexico City in December 1845, where he was delayed by the overthrow of President Herrera by General Paredes. On 9 February he rode into Mazatlán, delivered his message to Sloat, and requested transportation to Monterey—all without divulging his mission. Sloat sent him by way of the Hawaiian Islands. At Honolulu Gillespie was received by the king, and his military rank was printed in the Honolulu *Polynesian* of 14 March 1846. He had previously visited Honolulu and was well known there.[82] Gillespie arrived at Monterey on 17 April 1846, six months after the date of the instructions with which he was charged to convey to Larkin.[83]

Gillespie's memory proved to be excellent. His reproduction of Buchanan's instructions to Larkin was accurate except in one or two wholly unimportant aspects.[84] Buchanan informed Larkin: "the President has thought proper to appoint you a confidential agent in California; Lieutenant Archibald H. Gillespie of the Marine Corps.... He is a gentleman in whom the President reposes entire confidence ... will cooperate as a confidential agent with you."[85]

Larkin answered Buchanan on the same day. In report number 42 Larkin accepted "with unfeigned satisfaction the appointment now offered." It was Larkin's opinion those in power would soon be prepared to separate from Mexico, and if the number of immigrants into California continued in 1847 as they had in 1846, the destiny of California was decided.[86]

Larkin presented Gillespie to the Monterey community as a merchant traveling for his health (Gillespie had traveled across Mexico in the guise of a merchant in search of health and amusement). This story did not cover the energetic Gillespie, but it was to have a short life span.[87]

In Buchanan's letter of 17 October 1845 Gillespie was to cooperate as a confidential agent with Larkin. Apparently Gillespie's mission changed in the time between Buchanan writing the instructions and Gillespie's departure. Gillespie delivered the instructions and immediately departed Monterey to search for Frémont. Prior to Gillespie's departure, Larkin consulted with him and gave him a letter of introduction to William Leidesdorff, the vice-consul at Yerba Buena, who facilitated Gillespie's efforts to overtake Frémont.

The *Portsmouth* anchored in Monterey on 23 April 1846. Commander Montgomery told Larkin the Mexican authorities at Mazatlán were daily expecting war with the United States. Larkin sent this information to Gillespie, and added, "I have [as my opinion] said to Generals Castro, Carrillo, and Vallejo that our flag may fly here in thirty days." This letter reached Gillespie at Yerba Buena. (Yerba Buena became San Francisco in January 1847.)[88]

On the same day Larkin wrote William Leidesdorff, "Our Minister has been refused in Mexico.... And in all likelihood the States have declared War against M. to bring her to peace in proper time." Leidesdorff and Gillespie acknowledged receipt of their letters on 25 April.[89]

Secret Agent Larkin went to work immediately to implement Buchanan's secret instructions to bring California into the Union, but conditions were not altogether favorable for sweet-talking the Californians. The Frémont incident, much talk of an uprising by American settlers, and rumors of a war between the United States and Mexico generated mistrust of the United States and its representatives. Mexico reflected this mistrust in a new law, announced by General Castro in April 1846. The law declared the purchase or acquisition of land by foreigners who had not become naturalized as Mexicans "will be null and void, and they will be subject (if they do not retire voluntarily from the country) to be expelled whenever the country may find it convenient."[90] Very few Americans had obtained grants of land and most were considered squatters.

In his favor, Larkin, as a general rule, was on exceptionally good terms with the Californians. He was very close to former Governor Micheltorena. Larkin also agreed wholeheartedly with Buchanan's plan, and believed there were other prominent Americans and Californians who would help him carry out the proposed plan. Finally, Larkin was attuned to the Californian expectation that some kind of a change was coming very soon in the political status of the country.[91]

Larkin had worked full-time without pay as consul, so the appointment as confidential agent meant a pleasing change in his relationship with the Department of State. "The only practical difference in his status was that he now received the ample remuneration which he had repeatedly requested of the Department."[92]

On 27 April 1846 Secret Agent Larkin started his covert operation to have California secede from Mexico. He wrote three American-Mexicans, Jacob P. Leese of Sonoma, Abel Stearns of Los Angeles, and John Warner of San Diego. These three prominent men were natives of the United States and naturalized citizens of Mexico. Larkin believed the profit motive and attachment to their native land would provide the incentives to involve these men in a covert operation to overthrow their adopted land. In the letter Larkin made the following points:

1. There was going to be a change in California;

2. The change would happen whether there was or was not war between the United States and Mexico;

3. Some Californians looked toward Europe for the change. It would not happen because President Polk would not let it happen; and

4. As lovers of freedom and independence, Californians should look only to the United States.

Larkin warned his potential conspirators to keep this communication secret, and asked to be kept informed of the desires of the government and the people concerning change.[93]

Abel Stearns answered promptly on 14 May. He was the only one who committed himself to any considerable degree to become involved. Jacob Leese replied briefly, after much delay, and did not commit himself. John Warner informed Larkin of a growing feeling that separation from Mexico must come, and if war broke out, all would be glad to be under the protection of the United States.[94]

Larkin offered Stearns an appointment as confidential agent. Stearns accepted, and reported a majority of government officials and businessmen in the south would favor any change that would secure a stable and permanent government for California.[95]

Larkin used misinformation in an attempt to influence the Mexicans. He drew up a document purporting to be his own views concerning the future of California, but it was really the administration's plan for the acquisition of California. This he translated into Spanish and disseminated to the authorities as his opinions. He sent a copy to Abel Stearns for him to use in the same manner.[96]

As Larkin initiated covert operations to seduce the province of California from Mexico, Commodore Sloat received word on 17 May 1846 in Mazatlán from acting United States Consul James R. Bolton of the attack by Mexicans on a small American force north of the Rio Grande.[97]

Frémont during this period was leisurely making his way north to Oregon. He stayed at Peter Lassen's ranch in northern California for 19 days. But his letters to his wife and father-in-law painted the picture of a dedicated scientist, diligently working to complete his assigned task in order that he would be able to rush home to his loved ones.

Gillespie was making his way north in the manner of a man with a mission. He arrived at Sutter's Fort on 28 April, secured men and horses, and continued after Frémont. Gillespie received much help from Peter Lassen and others in the upper Sacramento Valley, and on 9 May overtook Frémont at Klamath Lake which was just over the Oregon border.[98]

Gillespie not only traveled 600 miles from Monterey to find Frémont, but the latter part of the journey was at great personal risk owing to the Indian threat and the roughness of the terrain.

When they met, Gillespie informed Frémont, "that he had left Washington under orders from the President and the Secretary of the Navy." This helps to explain Gillespie's unexplainable actions. Frémont said of Gillespie, "He was directed to find me wherever I might be, and was informed that I would probably be found on the Sacramento River."[99]

Gillespie delivered a letter of introduction from Secretary of State Buchanan, a duplicate of the dispatch for Larkin, and letters from Frémont's family, including his father-in-law, Senator Benton. It does not seem probable that Gillespie traveled all those miles in pursuit of Frémont just to deliver these items.[100] Theodore Talbot in a letter to his mother dated 24 July 1846 described the event: "reached the Klamet Lake when Lt. Gillespie of the U.S. Marines overtook us with orders directly from the United States for us to return to California."[101]

Prior to his departure from Washington, D.C., in November 1845, Gillespie was briefed by the president, the secretary of state, and the secretary of the navy. If the written material Gillespie delivered to Frémont did not justify the effort, then the verbal communications must be considered. Gillespie's long and dangerous journey was not undertaken for the purpose of delivering unimportant instructions to an explorer in the wilds of northern California.[102] What were Gillespie's verbal instructions? We do not know, but we do know what action Frémont took after talking to Gillespie.

Frémont turned his party south to illegally reenter California. When the manner of his departure is considered, this return, if it was a private act, makes Frémont a filibuster, and if it was a public act, it was an act of war. At this point Frémont's mission became a covert operation. He was to do whatever was necessary to acquire California, but if he was caught, he had no written orders. The United States government would have been able to deny any involvement.

Many years after the event Frémont wrote of his meeting with Gillespie. His exact words to justify his actions are interesting in how closely his explanation parallels others in recent times who have been caught up in covert operations and had those covert operations exposed to the public.

> Mr. Gillespie informed me that he had left Washington under orders from the President and the Secretary of the Navy, and was directed to reach California by the shortest route through Mexico to Mazatlán. He was directed to find me wherever I might be, and was informed that I would probably be found on the Sacramento River. In pursuance of his instructions he had accordingly started from Monterey to look for me on the Sacramento. Learning upon his arrival at Sutter's Fort that I had gone up the valley, he made up a small party at Neal's rancho and, guided by him, followed my trail and had traveled six hundred miles to overtake me, the latter part of the way through great dangers.
>
> The mission on which I had been originally sent to the West was a peaceful one, and Mr. Bancroft had sent Mr. Gillespie to give me warning of the new state of affairs and the designs of the President. Mr. Gillespie had been given charge of despatches from the Secretary of the Navy to Commodore Sloat, and had been purposely made acquainted with their import. Known to Mr. Bancroft as an able and thoroughly trustworthy officer, he had been well instructed in the designs of the Department and with the purposes of the Administration, so far as they related to California. Through him I now became acquainted with the actual state of affairs and the purposes of the Government. The information through Gillespie had absolved me

from my duty as an explorer, and I was left to my duty as an officer of the American Army, with the further authoritative knowledge that the Government intended to take California. I was warned by my Government of the new danger against which I was bound to defend myself; and it had been made known to me now on the authority of the Secretary of the Navy that to obtain possession of California was the chief object of the President.

He brought me also a letter of introduction from the Secretary of State, Mr. Buchanan, and letters and papers from Senator Benton and family. The letter from the Secretary was directed to me in my private or citizen capacity, and though importing nothing beyond the introduction, it accredited the bearer to me as coming from the Secretary of State, and in connection with the circumstances and place of delivery it indicated a purpose in sending it. From the letter itself I learned nothing, but it was intelligently explained to me by the accompanying letter from Senator Benton and by communications from Lieutenant Gillespie.

This officer informed me that he had been directed by the Secretary of State to acquaint me with his instructions, which had for their principal objects to ascertain the disposition of the California people, to conciliate their feelings in favor of the United States; and to find out, with a view to counteracting, the designs of the British Government upon that country. The letter from Senator Benton, while apparently of friendship and family details, contained passages and suggestions which, read by the light of many conversations and discussions with himself and others at Washington, clearly indicated to me that I was required by the Government to find out any foreign schemes in relation to California and, so far as might be in my power, to counteract them.

Neal had much to talk over with his old companions and pleasurable excitement kept us up late; but before eleven o'clock all were wrapped in their blankets and soundly asleep except myself. I sat by the fire in fancied security, going over again the home letters. These threw their own light upon the communication from Mr. Gillespie, and made the expected signal. In substance, their effect was: The time has come. England must not get a foothold. We must be first. Act — discreetly, but positively.

Looking back over the contingencies which had been foreseen in the discussions at Washington, I saw that the important one which carried with it the hopes of Senator Benton and the wishes of the Government was in the act of occurring, and it was with thorough satisfaction I now found myself required to do what I could to promote this object of the President. Viewed by the light of these deliberations in Washington, I was prepared to comprehend fully the communications brought to me by Mr. Gillespie. Now it was officially made known to me that my country was at war, and it was so made known expressly to guide my conduct. I had learned with certainty from the Secretary of the Navy that the President's plan of war included the taking possession of California, and under his confidential instructions I had my warrant. Mr. Gillespie was directed to act in concert with me. Great vigilance and activity were expected of us both, for it was desired that possession should be had of California before the presence in her ports of any foreign vessel of war might make inconvenient.

I had about thought out the situation when I was startled by a sudden movement among the animals. Lieutenant Gillespie had told me that there were no Indians on his trail, and I knew there were none on mine. This night was one of two when I failed to put men on guard in an Indian country—this night and one spent on an island in the Great Salt Lake. The animals were near the shore of the lake, barely a hundred yards away. Drawing a revolver I went down among them. A mule is a good sentinel, and when he quits eating and stands with his ears stuck straight out taking notice, it is best to see what is the matter. The mules knew that Indians were around, but nothing seemed stirring, and my presence quieting the animals I returned to the fire and my letters.

I saw the way opening clear before me. War with Mexico was inevitable; and a grand opportunity now presented itself to realize in their fullest extent the farsighted views of Senator Benton, and make the Pacific Ocean the western boundary of the United States. I resolved to move forward on the opportunity and return forthwith to the Sacramento Valley in order to bring to bear all the influences I could command. Except myself, then and for nine months afterward, there was no other officer of the Army in California. The citizen party under my command was made up of picked men, and although small in number, constituted a formidable nucleus for frontier warfare, and many of its members commanded the confidence of the emigration.

This decision was the first step in the conquest of California.[103]

That night Indians killed three of Frémont's men before anyone in the camp knew what was happening. Frémont and his party spent the next two days killing as many Indians as they could. Then they headed south.

As Frémont marched to California, war was declared to exist between the United States and Mexico on 13 May 1846. Frémont was not forgotten in Washington. He was the only regular officer appointed to the new Regiment of Rifles which was created to provide officer billets for selected individuals from civilian life, basically deserving Democrats. This would also mean a promotion to lieutenant colonel for Frémont.[104]

In California rumors of Mexican and Indian attacks against Americans were flying through the American settlements. The American settlers were confused, angry, and leaderless, and then Frémont returned. He and his armed party camped on 29 May among the American settlers in the Sacramento Valley near the junction of the Bear and Feather rivers, below the present town of Marysville.[105]

Frémont's returning to California was an illegal act. He had been ordered to leave by competent authority, and he had not requested nor received permission to return, but he was there, and at the head of a trained, experienced strike force of 60 well-armed men. With this force,

Frémont decided to attack the Indians in order to establish his leadership position with the American settlers. He led his strike force against the Indian villages along the banks of the Sacramento River. The Indians apparently were not ready to attack anyone, and men, women, and children were easily murdered by Frémont's sharpshooters.[106] This decisive action and display of firepower rallied the American settlers around Frémont.

Gillespie was sent to the *Portsmouth,* which was anchored in San Francisco Bay, with a requisition for the following supplies: one keg of powder; 300 pounds of rifle lead; 8,000 percussion caps; food; medicines; soap; and tobacco.[107] The *Portsmouth* had sailed from Monterey on 1 June and anchored in San Francisco Bay on 3 June to be near the probable scene of action and to provide "aid and comfort" to Captain Frémont.[108] Commander Montgomery sent several officers to Frémont for liaison.[109] Frémont did not have written orders, but he did have logistic support.

On 1 June Thomas Larkin sent report number 44 to Secretary Buchanan. He described Gillespie's journey to find Frémont, the return of the whole party to the Sacramento Valley, and Frémont's intention to start immediately for the United States. Larkin praised Gillespie as a very capable person who could not pose as a merchant, and was known at once in Monterey to be an officer. Larkin reported he was planting the seeds of discontent among the Californians in accordance with Buchanan's instructions, but it would take time for the ideas to grow and bloom.[110]

Commander Montgomery wrote Frémont on 3 June. He described Frémont's activities in a very vague manner—"to the enterprise in which you are so actively engaged"; and "in the successful prosecution and issue of the Public interests committed to your direction"—and informed Frémont he required no information concerning his activities, other than what Frémont deemed necessary to tell him to enable Montgomery to aid and facilitate Frémont's operations. Commander Montgomery was ready to serve Frémont "in any manner consistent with other duties." Montgomery was extremely excited over one of two activities—Frémont leading a survey party or Frémont leading a revolution to bring California into the Union.[111] What Gillespie told Commander Montgomery when they met on the *Portsmouth* is unknown, but Montgomery's letters and his unquestioned support for an army brevet captain and his lethal party illegally in a foreign country speak volumes.

On 6 June Frémont decided he was ready, "and immediately concerted my operations with the foreigners inhabiting the Sacramento valley." General Castro provided Frémont with his first target. Castro needed horses to move his troops, and so he sent a small party to General Vallejo at Sonoma to get the horses. About 6 June the party departed from

Sonoma with 170 to 200 horses. They planned to drive the herd south to Santa Clara, via New Helvetia.[112]

Commander Montgomery wrote Frémont on 10 June. He had been informed by Gillespie that Frémont would proceed south to Santa Barbara, and would like a vessel of war at Santa Barbara during his stay. During this whole period Frémont and Gillespie apparently conducted an extensive disinformation operation, understanding that any communication, sent by any means, had an excellent chance of being intercepted by the Mexicans. Frémont wrote his wife and Senator Benton that he was coming home, Gillespie wrote Larkin that Frémont was heading east while telling Montgomery Frémont was heading south, and on it went.

In his letter Montgomery stated he was at liberty to visit any or all ports on the coast, "should the Public interest require it." If Frémont believed the presence "of a Ship of War at Santa Barbara may prove serviceable to you in carrying out the views of our Government," then, Montgomery wrote, "I will not fail [Providence permitting] to meet you there with the Portsmouth."

Montgomery was "gratified" to have it in his power to send Frémont the money ($1500) he wanted, and to have most of the supplies "required to meet the demand of your urgent necessities; regretting only, my inability to furnish the whole."[113]

By 10 June Frémont had developed covert operations which were designed to spark a revolution in California. He proposed to the American settlers to attack the most important targets in northern California; the government horses and the government officials at Sonoma.[114]

On the same day a party of 12 men led by Ezekiel Merritt rode out of Frémont's camp. Merritt regarded Frémont with enormous respect, and Frémont called him his field lieutenant. About 17 miles south of Sutter's Fort on 11 June this group surprised a Mexican lieutenant and his 12 men. They stole the horses, but allowed the soldiers to go free.[115]

Frémont's camp was humming with activity, as men, horses, and supplies were coming and going. Twenty armed men left the camp on 11 June to attack the small military post of Sonoma, the only Mexican settlement of any consequence in the region north of the San Francisco Bay. A surprise attack made in the middle of the night caused Sonoma to fall without opposition on 14 June 1846. The Americans captured eight field pieces, 200 firearms, powder, and Mexican officials. Frémont took over Sutter's Fort, and installed General Vallejo and others as prisoners there.[116] Mariano Guadalupe Vallejo was very influential. He was a colonel in the Mexican Army, but was called "General" because of his former service as commandant general. Vallejo was also Sonoma County's first commercial winegrower.[117] Sutter did not want General Vallejo imprisoned on his property. He argued with Frémont that Vallejo was one of the prime movers for California to secede from Mexico. Sutter, a German, was a naturalized Mexican citizen. In 1838 he was given a grant of 49,000 acres of land on the Sacramento River by the Mexican governor on condition that he would fortify and develop it into a strong Mexican outpost. He was appointed "Commissioner of Justice and Representative of the Government on the Frontier of the Rio del Sacramento."

Frémont told Sutter to go and join the Mexicans if he did not agree with the American revolution. If Sutter did not cooperate, he would lose his property. With or without Sutter, Frémont now had two good bases for controlling all northern California — Sonoma and Sutter's Fort.[118] At Sonoma on 14 June a group of about 30 American settlers declared California an independent republic.

During this time a launch from the *Portsmouth* reached New Helvetia. It brought flour, pork, soap, tobacco, candles, stockings, 100 blue flannel shirts, salt, 50 pounds of lead, 400 percussion caps, canvas and duck cloth, medical supplies, and 500 pounds of iron.[119]

With the two covert operations successfully completed, Frémont proceeded to the American settlements on the Sacramento and American rivers to recruit more men.[120] When the Mexicans reacted to the American revolution, Frémont wanted to be ready with an American army. As Frémont was gathering his army to fight Mexico for ownership of California, Jessie Frémont was writing to inform him of his promotion — eight years from an unknown second lieutenant to lieutenant colonel. She wrote that there was no pressure on the president to make this promotion. It was entirely a freewill gesture of the president which showed his respect, admiration, and faith in Frémont.[121]

When the news of the American revolution reached Monterey, Larkin's covert operation to gently push California into the Union came to a sudden stop, and in fact, Larkin was under suspicion as being involved. Larkin assured General José Castro and Prefect Manuel Castro that he would do anything in his power to assist in the recovery of the horses if citizens of the United States were implicated in the theft. A rumor that Larkin had knowledge of the affair grew until Larkin believed he might be seized as a prisoner of war.

This did not deter the secret agent from his intelligence collection duties. Buchanan had sent Larkin a list of specific intelligence collection requirements, and Larkin had been busy collecting this information. On 15 June 1846 Larkin sent to Buchanan report number 45 containing 65 pages on the past, present and future of California. The report covered the following areas:

1. Physical description of California;

2. List of towns and other settlements;

3. History of the Missions;

4. Class structure of the people;

5. Industries;

6. Naturalization procedures;

7. Land grants;

8. Indian depredations;

9. Amount of immigration in various years;

10. Immigrant routes;

11. Sutter's establishment;

12. Supplies which immigrants should have on leaving Independence, Missouri; their settlement and possible vocations in California;

13. Climate;

14. Political history;

15. Revolutions;

16. Potential military strength;

17. Contemporaneous politics;

18. Instability of the government;

19. Attitudes of various classes toward change;

20. Agriculture;

21. Minerals;

22. Fishing;

23. Potential of the San Francisco Bay region;

24. Education;

25. Commerce;

26. Description of the coastal trade;

27. Division of revenue by the civil and military departments;

28. Coins, weights, and measures;

29. List of the leading men;

30. Public debt;

31. Tabulated information about the army, custom house, and civil officers; giving names, age, by whom appointed, monthly pay, and arrears due on salaries as of 1 January 1846.[122]

On 16 June 1846 Frémont sent Commander Montgomery another confusing letter. It must be taken into account that Gillespie was moving back and forth between these two men, and his verbal communications would have to be considered very important. Frémont wrote that the people had taken actions to establish a new government, and because everyone believed Frémont was involved, he expected General Castro to attack him at any hour. Frémont wanted to start for home immediately, but lack of supplies and horses would keep him at New Helvetia until 1 July. On the other hand, if General Castro made a hostile move, Frémont "will most assuredly meet or anticipate them." To that end he "urgently" requested the *Portsmouth* remain in San Francisco Bay as a backup. He wanted Montgomery to set up a line of communications with his boats, and provide one of his ship's surgeons "in case of accident here."[123]

Larkin sent report number 48 on 18 June 1846. He had heard in June from Gillespie who was in San Francisco at the time. Frémont was two days's ride from New Helvetia on his way to the United States. Larkin expected Gillespie in Monterey the next week. He reported the stealing of the horses and the taking of Sonoma, and the suspected involvement of Gillespie and Frémont by the Californians. Vice-Consul Leidesdorff informed Larkin of foreigners in the Sacramento Valley calling the action a "popular movement." Larkin wrote Buchanan that he could only suppose the foreigners in the Sacramento Valley were determined to overthrow the government with the aid of the expected immigrants in September.[124]

The USS *Cyane* anchored in Monterey Bay on 19 June 1846. The ship carried a letter dated 18 May 1846 from Commodore Sloat to Consul Larkin: "It is my intention to visit your place immediately, and from the instructions I have received from my government, I am to hope that you will be prepared to put me in possession of the necessary information, and to consult and advise with me on the course of operations I may be disposed to make on the coast of California."[125]

Frémont received word that Sonoma was threatened by General Castro. He gathered his strike force together, and left camp for Sonoma on 23 June. Prior to riding to Sonoma Frémont drafted his resignation from the United States Army. It was to be sent to Senator Benton who would transmit it to the War Department if it became necessary to disavow Frémont.[126]

The same day Frémont was riding to engage General Castro, Secretary Bancroft was writing to Louis McLane concerning the California situation. Bancroft hoped the USS *Levant* was in Monterey and the USS *Warren* at San Francisco. The names were wrong, but United States ships were there, as the administration had hoped. This hope led to conviction, "Our people consider California and New Mexico as ours."[127] Apparently Frémont and Bancroft were on the same frequency.

The *Portsmouth* moved from Sausalito to San Francisco on 23 June at the request of Vice-Consul Leidesdorff to protect the vice-consul's property and other American citizens from "the probable outrages of the Californians." On the same day Montgomery wrote Frémont. He assured him communications would be kept open with his camp "by means of my boats." Montgomery also sent Frémont all the information he could collect on the military strength and intentions of General Castro, and the movements of the ships of the United States Navy. A ship's surgeon accompanied the letter.[128] While doing this Montgomery was proclaiming his strict neutrality to all who would listen. The Americans who captured Sonoma sent a representative to Montgomery for supplies. Montgomery stated he could not, as an officer of the United States Navy, give aid in any form, regardless of any sympathy he might have. From Monterey James H. Gleason wrote to his uncle, "The U.S. Ship Portsmouth ... supplies in a secret manner Ide's party with provisions and ammunition."[129]

Frémont with a force of 160 men reached Sonoma on 25 June. Before his arrival, 20 American settlers, fighting under the banner of their new republic, met a Mexican force of 70 men. In a brief fight the Americans stopped the Mexicans, and as a result General Castro retreated to Santa Clara. Frémont pursued the Mexicans without success, but he now controlled the whole area north and west of San Francisco Bay.[130] Montgomery believed the small group of revolutionists stopping a force of 70 "Californians" was a victory which, though small, would give a "favorable impulse to the operation of the insurgents, and attract at once, numbers of the Foreign residents to their aid."[131]

Commodore Sloat received word on 31 May 1846 of the engagements at Palo Alto and Resaca de la Palma. He arrived at Monterey on 2 July in his flagship USS *Savannah*. Sloat had orders to seize the port if war was declared between Mexico and the United States, but at this juncture he was not certain that war had been declared. For all Sloat knew the two engagements could have been the catalysts for peace talks.

Commodore Sloat had been ordered by the secretary of the navy to keep in touch with Consul Larkin. When Sloat arrived in Monterey, he found the consul was dismayed by the Bear Flag rebellion, and unable to comprehend that the orders to conciliate the Californians had been overtaken by events. Larkin passionately attempted to persuade Sloat to press on with conciliation.[132] Sloat sailed to Monterey for clarification, but anchored in confusion. His decision was not to make a decision.

On 4 July at Sonoma the American settlers organized the California Battalion. The battalion consisted of Frémont's men and volunteers from the settlers—a total of 234 men. Captain Frémont, USA, was elected commander and Lieutenant Gillespie, USMC, a major in the battalion.[133] The American settlers at Sonoma were called together by Frémont, and they unanimously adopted Frémont's recommendations—"California was declared independent; the country put under martial law, the force organized and officers elected." All of this was placed under Frémont's direction.[134] In a letter from Sonoma on 5 July Frémont informed Montgomery a "force under arms was yesterday made at this place." More men were needed to fight the Mexicans, so Frémont was headed for Sutter's Fort to recruit the American immigrants who were on their way to Oregon. While Frémont was involved with recruiting, he would need current intelligence on the enemy, and he wrote Montgomery, "I trust that, in case anything of moment should occur, you will not find it inconsistent with your convenience and the strict neutrality of your position to give me some information."[135]

Commodore Sloat received word from Commander Montgomery on 5 July indicating Captain J. C. Frémont, USA, had openly joined the Bear Flag revolt. Sloat assumed Frémont had official written orders from the United States government to take California; i.e., to make war on Mexico. Having orders to take no action prior to a declaration of war, Sloat, based on his readings of Frémont's actions, decided the United States must be at war, and raised the United States flag over Monterey on 7 July 1846.[136] Frémont received word from Montgomery on 10 July of Sloat raising the flag over Monterey, and "accordingly I directed the flag to be hoisted with a salute the next morning."[137]

The United States frigate *Congress* anchored in Monterey Bay on 15 July 1846. Commodore Robert Stockton had taken nearly nine months to sail from Norfolk to Monterey. The brig *Pilgrim* took five months to sail from Boston to Santa Barbara (14 August 1834 to 14 January 1835). The *Congress* spent 23 days in port in Rio de Janeiro, 12 days at Valparaiso, 42 days at Callo, and 14 days at Honolulu. Apparently Bancroft who had been in Norfolk to see the *Congress* get underway did not implant in Stockton a sense of urgency.[138]

Commodore Sloat had been ordered when war was declared to occupy California's ports, proclaim the occupation a deliverance from tyranny, and invite the consent of the natives. Frémont's covert operations and the creation of the Bear Flag Republic had made these orders obsolete, but Larkin still believed his own covert operation could succeed. He considered the action of the American settlers illegal and unjust to the Californians. He wanted to get Frémont under control, as did Commodore Sloat, but Sloat also hoped Frémont was acting under orders. If Frémont was not, Sloat considered himself in deep trouble.[139]

On 19 July about 160 Americans rode into Monterey from the north, armed with long, heavy rifles and large knives. At their head rode Frémont in a buckskin tunic, leggings, moccasins, and a blue shirt.[140] The same day on board the flagship *Savannah* Sloat asked Frémont under what authority he was acting. Frémont answered that he had no official or written orders for his actions. Sloat was astonished. He declined to muster Frémont's battalion into the service of the United States or cooperate with Frémont in his proposed operations.[141]

Commodore Stockton, who quickly relieved Sloat, mustered Frémont's men into the naval service as the Navy Battalion of Mounted Horsemen. Frémont was made major in command with Gillespie as captain.[142] The covert operation was over.

Secretary Bancroft wrote Commodore Sloat on 12 July 1846 concerning the exact procedures to be followed in preparing California for statehood. In this letter Bancroft provided the reason behind the covert operations in Texas to have that republic enter the Union at war with Mexico. Bancroft wrote, "The object of the United States is, under its right as a belligerent nation, to possess itself entirely of Upper California."[143]

Larkin sent report number 54 to Buchanan on 20 July 1846. He enclosed duplicate copies of report numbers 42, 43, 44, 48, 52, and 53. He was hard at work implementing his initial instructions, and anticipated bringing them to a successful conclusion in the latter part of 1847 through the will and voice of the Californians. To do this Larkin had confidential agents throughout the country who would aid him in convincing those in authority to join the Union. Larkin was making progress, as shown in his last conversation with "the General and a few other principal men, the General drew up in writing a short history of his plan of declaring California independent in 1847 or 1848 soon as the Country had sufficient numbers of people from abroad, to carry out the intentions." Larkin complained to Buchanan of obstacles being put in the way of his work to conciliate the Californians into the Union. He had had no expectation that Gillespie would commence covert operations of any kind in California without his knowledge. Gillespie and Frémont had raised 200 men by 17 July, and had taken New Helvetia and Sonoma. They raised the Bear flag, and issued two proclamations, all of which during the month of June was conducted under the name of William B. Ide. Larkin did not understand what Gillespie and Frémont were up to.[144]

In his letter of 25 July 1846 to Senator Benton, Frémont described his actions from meeting Gillespie in Oregon to his raising of the United States flag. The letter stressed the following:

1. Frémont was acting on his own initiative, and did not have orders from his government;

2. Snow, mountains, lack of supplies, and poor animals were his reasons to "retrace" his steps from Oregon;

3. General Castro harassed him whenever he entered California, and it became a matter of personal honor to stand and fight;

4. And with all things considered Gillespie did it.

Gillespie was mentioned seven times in the letter: Gillespie overtook Frémont in Oregon; Frémont sent Gillespie to the *Portsmouth* for supplies; Gillespie told Frémont that it was the opinion of the officers of the Pacific Squadron that Frémont could not retreat again and keep any military reputation; Gillespie's visit to the *Portsmouth* produced more help and enthusiasm for Frémont's operations than could have ever been expected; Gillespie accompanied Frémont from the camp on the American Fork on 23 June; describing Gillespie's role in the revolution Frémont wrote, "In all these proceedings, Mr. Gillespie has acted with me"; and Commodore Stockton approved "entirely of the course pursued by myself and Mr. Gillespie, who, I repeat, has been hand-in-hand with me in this business."[145] The letter disassociated the United States government from any of Frémont's actions with the exception of the messenger. The messenger's presence was repeated over and over in order that Benton and everyone else would understand that the messenger was the key. Frémont would stand alone for his actions, but the presence of the messenger showed he was not a "loose Cannon" or a filibuster, but a hidden weapon of the United States government.

On 27 August 1846 Larkin sent report number 60. The conquest was completed, and Larkin's official capacity as United States consul expired, but he hoped to continue as a confidential agent.[146]

Secretary Buchanan answered Larkin's letter on 13 January 1847. Larkin was to continue as "Confidential Agent, in the Californias." Buchanan paid a draft for $200 in favor of William M. Rogers, but elaborated, "I have known no instance in which Clerk hire has been allowed to a Confidential Agent, though I do not say this may not be done to a limited amount, under special circumstances; nor can I consistently with the rules of the Department allow you, out of the contingent fund for foreign intercourse, the expense of Couriers properly chargeable to the Navy Department." In regards to another draft sent to the State Department by Larkin, Buchanan responded, "as soon as your account shall be filed, with vouchers in support of it, where these can be obtained in accordance with your instructions, the remaining draft will be honored."[147]

Larkin remained a confidential agent until 30 May 1848, and his per diem allowance continued until that date; but his only official activity during 1847 and 1848 consisted of an occasional report to the State Department on political and general conditions in California. Secretary Buchanan informed Larkin of the formal discontinuance "of your Special Agency and of your consular functions," in a dispatch dated 23 June 1848.[148] For his services Larkin was paid $6,107.61.[149]

At the 21 March 1848 cabinet meeting a request by the Senate for a letter sent in October 1845 from the secretary of state to Thomas Larkin, United States consul at Monterey, was discussed. It was agreed that the opposition was hoping to find the letter contained instructions to produce a revolution in California "before Mexico commenced the War against the U.S.," and that Colonel Frémont had the authority to make the revolution. Polk believed publication of the letter would prove the falsehood of such an inference, and released the letter to the Senate, but not without some national security editing.[150]

Frémont was paid for "Military and geographical surveys west of the Mississippi" in fiscal years 1846 and 1847 a total of $47,085.58.[151]

The commissioners on claims against Mexico under the act of 3 March 1849 awarded Thomas O. Larkin $16,474.23, and Thomas O. Larkin and Talbot H. Green $4,608.52 on 15 April 1851.

Notes to Chapter 7

1. M. A. De Wolfe Howe, *The Life and Letters of George Bancroft* (New York: Charles Scribner's Sons, 1908), 1:287.

2. Russel B. Nye, *George Bancroft, Brahmin Rebel* (New York: Alfred A. Knopf, 1945), p. 146.

3. Ibid., pp. 130–132.

4. Howe, *Bancroft*, 1:259–260.

5. Nye, *Brahmin Rebel*, pp. 142–143.

6. Ibid., p. 143.

7. Ibid., p. 137.

8. Pletcher, *Diplomacy*, p. 263.

9. Nye, *Brahmin Rebel*, p. 152.

10. Howe, *Bancroft*, 1:279.

11. Ibid., 1:291.

12. Mary Lee Spence and Donald Jackson, eds., *The Expeditions of John Charles Frémont* (Urbana: University of Illinois Press, 1973), 2:x.

13. François des Montaignes, *The Plains*, ed. Nancy Alpert Mower and Don Russell (Norman: University of Oklahoma Press, 1972), p. xii.

14. Ibid.

15. John Charles Frémont, *Narratives of Exploration and Adventure*, ed. Allan Nevins (New York: Longmans, Green, 1956), pp. v–vi.

16. Ibid., p. 433.

17. Montaignes, *The Plains*, p. 4.

18. Allan Nevins, *Frémont* (New York: Harper and Brothers, 1928), 1:234.

19. William H. Goetzman, *Army Exploration in the American West, 1803–1863* (New Haven, Conn.: Yale University Press, 1959), 4:111.

20. John Charles Frémont, *Memoirs of My Life* (Chicago: Belford, Clarke, 1886), p. 422.

21. Nevins, *Frémont*, 1:237.

22. Pletcher, *Diplomacy*, p. 263.

23. DeVoto, *Year of Decision*, p. 21.

24. Smith, *Mexico*, 1:333.

25. Robert V. Hine and Savoie Lottinville eds., *Soldier in the West — Letters of Theodore Talbot* (Norman: University of Oklahoma Press, 1972), p. 13.

26. Montaignes, *The Plains*, p. xvi.

27. Hine and Lottinville, *Theodore Talbot*, p. 18.

28. Montaignes, *The Plains*, p. 25.

29. Frémont, *Narratives*, p. 436.

30. Montaignes, *The Plains*, pp. 22–23.

31. Goetzman, *Army Exploration*, 4:123–127.

32. Frémont, *Narratives*, p. 440.

33. Quaife, *Polk Diary*, 1:71.

34. Rayner W. Kelsey, "The United States Consulate in California," *Academy of Pacific Coast History* 1, no. 5 (1910): 60.

35. Moore, *James Buchanan*, 6:275–278.

36. Nye, *Brahmin Rebel*, p. 153.

37. Rives, *United States and Mexico*, 2:166.

38. Pletcher, *Diplomacy*, p. 284.

39. U.S. Congress, House, *Receipts and Expenditures of the Government—Ending 30 June 1846*, H. Doc. 10. 29th Cong., 2nd sess., 1846, p. 216.

40. Quaife, *Polk Diary*, 1:83.

41. Kelsey, "U.S. Consulate," p. 87.

42. Josiah Royce, *California* (Boston: Houghton, Mifflin, 1886), p. 38.

43. Hine and Lottinville, *Theodore Talbot*, p. 34.

44. Pletcher, *Diplomacy*, p. 92.

45. Frémont, *Narratives*, p. 474.

46. Kelsey, "U.S. Consulate," p. 7.

47. John A. Hawgood, ed., *First and Last Consul—A Selection of Letters* (San Marino, Calif.: Huntington Library, 1962), p. 17.

48. Kelsey, "U.S. Consulate," p. 48.

49. Manning, *Correspondence*, 8:735.

50. Rives, *United States and Mexico*, 2:171.

51. Frémont, *Narratives*, p. 449.

52. Ibid., p. 455.

53. Nevins, *Frémont*, 1:243.

54. Frémont, *Narratives*, p. 443.

55. Smith, *Mexico*, 1:318.

56. Frémont, *Narratives*, pp. 464–465.

57. Spence and Jackson, *Expeditions of Frémont*, 2:46.

58. Ibid., 2:67.

59. Manning, *Correspondence*, 8:834.

60. Rives, *United States and Mexico*, 2:172.

61. Goodwin, *John Charles Frémont*, pp. 94–95.

62. Frémont, *Narratives*, pp. 466–467.

63. Rives, *United States and Mexico*, 2:173.

64. Frémont, *Narratives*, pp. 468–470.

65. Ibid., p. 471.

66. Spence and Jackson, *Expeditions of Frémont*, 2:74.

67. Ibid., 2:75.

68. Kelsey, "U.S. Consulate," p. 53.

69. Spence and Jackson, *Expeditions of Frémont*, 2:74.

70. Ibid., 2:76.

71. Ibid., 2:77.

72. Ibid., 2:81.

73. Ibid., 2:78.

74. Ibid., 2:81.

75. Ibid., 2:83.

76. Frémont, *Narratives*, p. 472.

77. Spence and Jackson, *Expeditions of Frémont*, 2:85.

78. Nevins, *Frémont*, 1:267.

79. Fred Blackburn Rogers, *Montgomery and the Portsmouth* (San Francisco: John Howell—Books, 1958), pp. 19–20.

80. Manning, *Correspondence*, 8:839.

81. Kelsey, "U.S. Consulate," p. 96.

82. Rogers, *Montgomery*, p. 17.

83. Rives, *United States and Mexico*, 2:178.
84. Royce, *California*, p. 133.
85. Goodwin, *John Charles Frémont*, p. 98.
86. Manning, *Correspondence*, 8:842.
87. DeVoto, *Year of Decision*, p. 129.
88. K. Jack Bauer, *Surfboats and Horsemarines* (Annapolis, Md.: United States Naval Institute, 1969), p. 143.
89. Hawgood, *First and Last Consul*, p. 55.
90. Rogers, *Montgomery*, p. 29.
91. Kelsey, "U.S. Consulate," p. 64.
92. Ibid., p. 65.
93. Ibid., p. 66.
94. Ibid., p. 67.
95. Ibid., p. 68.
96. Ibid., p. 69.
97. Rogers, *Montgomery*, p. 48.
98. Rives, *United States and Mexico*, 2:179.
99. Frémont, *Narratives*, p. 497.
100. Benton, *Thirty Years View*, 2:688.
101. Hine and Lottinville, *Theodore Talbot*, p. 42.
102. Robert McNutt McElroy, *The Winning of the Far West* (New York: G. P. Putnam's Sons, 1914), p. 192.
103. Frémont, *Memoirs*, pp. 488–490.
104. Quaife, *Polk Diary*, 1:412.
105. Benton, *Thirty Years View*, 2:691.
106. Nevins, *Frémont*, 1:294–295.
107. DeVoto, *Year of Decision*, p. 201.
108. Joseph W. Revere, *A Tour of Duty in California* (New York: C. S. Francis, 1849), p. 50.
109. Pletcher, *Diplomacy*, p. 432.
110. Manning, *Correspondence*, 8:856.
111. Spence and Jackson, *Expeditions of Frémont*, 2:143.
112. Ibid., 2:181–185.
113. Ibid., 2:146.
114. Goodwin, *John Charles Frémont*, p. 104.
115. Nevins, *Frémont*, 1:302.
116. Rives, *United States and Mexico*, 2:186.
117. Rogers, *Montgomery*, p. 32.
118. Nevins, *Frémont*, 1:304–305.
119. Rogers, *Montgomery*, p. 25.
120. Spence and Jackson, *Expeditions of Frémont*, 2:181–185.
121. Nevins, *Frémont*, 1:339.
122. Kelsey, "U.S. Consulate," p. 72.
123. Spence and Jackson, *Expeditions of Frémont*, 2:151.
124. Manning, *Correspondence*, 8:866.
125. Kelsey, "U.S. Consulate," p. 76.
126. Nevins, *Frémont*, 1:310.
127. Howe, *Bancroft*, 1:286.
128. Spence and Jackson, *Expeditions of Frémont*, 2:155.
129. Ibid., 2:162.
130. Nevins, *Frémont*, 1:309–310.

131. Spence and Jackson, *Expeditions of Frémont*, 2:160.

132. DeVoto, *Year of Decision*, p. 261.

133. Nevins, *Frémont*, 1:314.

134. Spence and Jackson, *Expeditions of Frémont*, 2:181–185.

135. Ibid., 2:162.

136. Benton, *Thirty Years View*, 2:692.

137. Spence and Jackson, *Expeditions of Frémont*, 2:181–185.

138. Rives, *United States and Mexico*, 2:192.

139. DeVoto, *Year of Decision*, p. 279.

140. Smith, *Mexico*, 1:336.

141. DeVoto, *Year of Decision*, p. 280.

142. Ibid., p. 281.

143. Nye, *Brahmin Rebel*, p. 158.

144. Manning, *Correspondence*, 8:879.

145. Spence and Jackson, *Expeditions of Frémont*, 2:181–185.

146. Manning, *Correspondence*, 8:884.

147. Moore, *James Buchanan*, 7:195.

148. Kelsey, "U.S. Consulate," p. 13.

149. U.S. Congress, House, *Contingent Expenses of State Department*, H. Ex. Doc. 5, 30th Cong., 2nd sess., 1849, Schedule E, p. 18.

150. Quaife, *Polk Diary*, 3:395.

151. U.S. Congress, House, *Receipts and Expenditures of the Government—Ending 30 June 1846*, H. Doc. 10, 29th Cong., 2nd sess., 1846, p. 156.

Chapter 8

Beach and Storms: Secret Agents

In the early summer of 1846 Secretary of the Navy Bancroft received a long letter telling him how to reform the navy and fight the war with Mexico. The letter was signed "Storms." Bancroft asked Secretary of War Marcy if he knew "Storms." Marcy replied, "She is an outrageously smooth and keen writer for the newspapers in [New York]."[1]

Jane Maria Eliza McManus was born near Troy, New York, on 6 April 1807. Her father was a successful lawyer. Jane was baptized a Lutheran, but later converted to Roman Catholicism. A considerable part of her childhood was spent with her aunt, Mrs. Lemuel H. Sherman, of Brookfield, Connecticut, who was responsible for most of her education.[2]

In 1825 Jane McManus married William F. Storms. They had one son, but the marriage ended in divorce in 1831. At the same time, Jane's father was experiencing financial difficulties. In an attempt to recoup the family fortunes through land speculation, Mr. McManus, on the advice of Aaron Burr, became interested in Stephen F. Austin's colonization ventures in Texas. Mr. McManus, with other New York and New England investors including Aaron Burr, formed the Galveston Bay and Texas Land Company.

Jane and her brother, Robert O. W. McManus, were sent to Texas to secure land for this project. To assist Jane on the arduous journey Aaron Burr wrote a letter of introduction to a New Orleans friend. The trip was a success, and in 1833 father, daughter, and son accompanied a group of German settlers to Texas. The Germans did not like the land, and the deal fell through. Father and daughter departed Texas, but Robert remained, and eventually became a wealthy landowner and planter.[3]

Also in 1833 Aaron Burr, aged 77, married Eliza Bowen Jumel, a rich widow, aged 57. In 1834 Mrs. Burr sued her husband for a divorce, alleging various adulteries on Mr. Burr's part, specifically, one at his house in Jersey City with Jane McManus Storms in August 1833.[4]

Jane Storms returned to Texas in 1838. During this stay she acquired the firsthand knowledge to write a series entitled "The Presidents of Texas," which was published in the *Democratic Review*. She returned to New York in 1839, and continued writing for such periodicals as the New York *Sun*, the *Tribune*, the *Herald*, and the Washington *States*.[5] Mrs. Storms was a propagandist for proexpansionist issues, and wrote principally for Moses Yale Beach's popular New York *Sun*.[6] She was a close supporter of many Texas political leaders, including Sam Houston and Mirabeau B. Lamar. Jane Storms was a woman and a journalist, and women journalists were not plentiful in 1839. She signed much of her writing "J. M. Storms" or "Storms" so no one would know the female gender of the writer. Senator Benton knew her and complained of her "masculine stomach for war and politics."

During the 1840s Storms regularly visited Washington where she met President Polk on several occasions, and developed contacts with Secretaries Marcy and Buchanan, members of Congress and individuals within Polk's administration. She was an ardent observer of the political scene and active as a writer of political letters and essays. The Baltimore *Sun's* Washington correspondent considered her a very able writer, and the editor of the influential Louisville *Courier-Journal* heaped praise upon her; he wrote, "a braver, more intellectual woman never lived."[7]

In the late summer of 1846 a small group of Mexican aristocrats and ecclesiastics drew up terms of a possible compromise peace treaty, including cession of all territory north of 26 degrees latitude, in return for an indemnity of $3 million. This group was able to put their proposed peace treaty into the hands of officers in General Taylor's army.[8] William Leslie Cazneau and Mirabeau B. Lamar approached Moses Beach with this proposal. The information was also sent to Bishop John Hughes of New York.

In November 1846 Beach traveled to Washington to discuss this matter with Secretary of State Buchanan. The part played by Jane Storms is uncertain. It is certain that she knew Cazneau and Lamar from her visits to Texas and was well acquainted with Nicholas Trist, chief clerk of the Department of State.[9]

As the war continued and expectations for a small, quick war diminished, Polk's need for more detailed and reliable intelligence from Mexico grew. Consul Black's reports provided inconclusive evidence of what was happening in Mexico, or quite possibly did not fit Polk's perspective of what he thought should be happening. Therefore, when Beach presented himself as a volunteer to go to Mexico, Polk agreed. He had a man who was rich, influential, and as a newspaper man, the prerequisites to be an excellent intelligence collector. Polk sent him to observe conditions in Mexico and report on any chances for peace.[10]

Moses Beach, the prosperous publisher of the New York *Sun* and a champion of expansionist policies had several meetings with Buchanan and one meeting with Polk during his stay in Washington in November 1846. Buchanan laid out the terms of an acceptable peace treaty. Beach expressed the opinion that a treaty could be made, and inferred that he could make such a treaty. As Beach would be traveling under cover of private business, "it was deemed advisable to constitute him a secret agent to Mexico." In his diary Polk commented that Beach had no diplomatic powers, but if he made a treaty and it was a good one, Polk would accept it.[11] He was to report all useful information he collected to the State Department, and was to send very important intelligence through Consul Black to the United States Naval Commander off Veracruz.

The United States government would provide compensation of $6 per day from time of departure from the United States until his return. Beach would be reimbursed for his own travel expenses, and other necessary expenses during his absence. Receipts were required when these could be obtained without leading to discovery of the character in which he was employed.[12]

Moses Beach was an innovator in the gathering and dissemination of news, and his abilities as a newspaperman and businessman were reflected in his preparations for and execution of this covert mission. Beach returned to New York City where he collected letters of introduction from Bishop Hughes and others to influential people in Cuba and Mexico. Then, with his 26-year-old daughter, Drusilla, and Mrs. Storms, who spoke fluent Spanish, Beach left New York City in late November 1846. They sailed to Charleston, South Carolina, then by small schooner to Matanzas, Cuba, and then coastal steamer to Havana. F. M. Dimond, the former United States consul at Veracruz, was in Havana conducting a covert operation for General Winfield Scott when Beach arrived. However, Dimond knew nothing of Beach's mission.[13]

In Havana, Beach was warned not to enter Mexico without a passport of a nation at peace with Mexico. He went to work on the problem and arranged to have British passports. The British consul at Havana gave Beach a temporary appointment as "bearer of dispatches for the consul."[14]

Beach and his party remained in Cuba for about three weeks. During this time he met with the Catholic hierarchy in Havana and received from them letters of introduction to influential clergy in Mexico.[15]

His companion, Jane Storms, was a definite asset, as "she possessed infinite knowledge of Spanish-American affairs, looked like a Spanish woman, and wrote and spoke the Spanish language fluently." Jane Storms wrote a series of letters to the New York *Sun* during the stay in Havana. There were a total of 11 letters which appeared in the *Sun* on 12, 13,

14, 15, 16, 25, and 30 January; 8 February; and 17, 25, and 26 March 1847.
She also wrote letters that appeared in the New York *Tribune* on 14 and
18 January 1847.[16]

New Orleans newspaper correspondents in Havana covered Beach's
arrival and departure. It was reported in the New Orleans *Picayune.*

The Mexican consul at Havana reported to his government that
Beach and Storms were sent by the United States government "as apostles
of peace."[17]

A former Mexican consul general at New York met Beach and his
party on the ship from Havana to Veracruz, and accompanied them to
Mexico City, helping them over obstacles along the way. He wrote to a
friend that Beach's presence showed such eagerness for peace on the part
of the United States government as to encourage Mexicans to further
resistance.[18] Other letters were sent from Cuba to Santa Anna and to the
authorities at Veracruz denouncing Beach as an American agent.[19]

To finance the war the Mexican Congress on 11 January 1847 passed
legislation to collect 15 million pesos through the sale or mortgaging of
church property. The clergy refused to comply.[20]

During the second week of January Beach landed at Veracruz with
his daughter and Jane Storms. Beach was detained and questioned for
three days. He was released after giving a full description of his business
plans, including his proposals for a national bank and a canal across the
Isthmus of Tehuantepec.[21] While Beach was being questioned Storms in-
spected Veracruz, and reported her observations to the *Sun* on 13 January
1847. In the letter she criticized the United States Navy for inefficiency,
which she claimed added at least a year to the war. It was Storms' contention that Commodore Conner could have taken Veracruz seven months
earlier, rather than blockade it as he was doing.

During the two weeks it took to make their way to Mexico City, local
officials repeatedly called them in for questioning and or searched their
baggage.[22] They reached Mexico City on 24 January 1847. Beach, who
had many private and influential contacts, unlimited energy, and tempt-
ing proposals for business ventures, was on station and ready to operate
as a secret agent of the United States government.

On 22 January Santa Anna wrote a confidential note to the minister
of war. The note identified Beach as the editor of the New York *Sun* and
an agent of the United States whose mission was to negotiate a peace
treaty. The minister was informed that Beach had no official commission
but had full powers to negotiate, and would not spare money to accomplish his mission. Santa Anna in San Luis Potosí had received this information from private sources in Havana. Santa Anna ended his note with,
"His mission so prejudicial to the interests and honor of the Nation."[23]

In Mexico City Beach presented his banking and canal projects to government officials and businessmen, and began talks with his pro-clerical contacts in the midst of their protest against the expropriation law of 11 January. Beach's letters of introduction gave him an immediate confidential standing in the highest church circles. He used Consul Black to arrange these interviews with influential Mexicans.[24] Meanwhile, Jane Storms was sending her observations and opinions to the New York *Sun.* In these letters she continued to stress one of her major beliefs — Mexico should "be transferred under the wing of the United States."[25]

Beach succeeded in establishing friendly relations with acting President Gómez Farías and the leading members of his party on the basis of his plan for a national bank.[26] He also started negotiations with the special friends of Santa Anna on the subject of the Atlantic-Pacific canal and or railroad across the Isthmus of Tehuantepec. Both Farías and Santa Anna supporters were anxious to continue the war, hoping it would strengthen their power, but they were also willing to discuss banks, canals, money, and peace.[27]

Beach saw himself as the middleman between the United States and Mexico, arranging a quick peace agreeable to all concerned, and as a broker's fee for his efforts being granted the transit rights across the Isthmus of Tehuantepec.[28]

There was a slight problem. The right of transit plus a lavish grant of land had already been given to José de Garaz by Santa Anna in 1842. A survey of the route had been made by an Italian engineer, Cayetana Moro, and an account of the project and the survey had been published in book form in several editions in London and in Mexico City from 1844 to 1846 in efforts to attract capital. The transit rights and land grant passed to Ewen C. Mackintosh, the British consul at Mexico City, in January 1847. The rights were actually held by a London banking house of which Mackintosh was the Mexican partner. Beach, taking all this into consideration, believed the transit rights could be transferred to him.[29] Both of Beach's business propositions — the bank and the canal — would profit and, in fact, could only be realized from an American-directed peace or an American occupation.

Beach viewed his mission as a prelude to peace. He was to prepare the way for a treaty of peace. He considered the clergy of Mexico as the important player in this peace preparation. Beach's gaining their confidence was greatly facilitated by the letters of introduction from leading prelates of the Catholic Church in the United States and Cuba to similar parties in Mexico City. It was for this reason that Beach passed through Charleston, Matanzas, and Havana on the way to Veracruz.[30]

Beach convinced the leading bishops of the danger of aiding Santa Anna. He promised protection of the Catholic Church in its freedom and property by the United States government. He persuaded influential bishops to refuse all aid, direct and indirect, for the war, and to persuade their friends in Congress to advocate peace at the right moment.[31]

The Mexican Congress passed legislation on 11 January and 4 February 1847 to raise money for the war by using church property. When acting President Farías implemented the laws, Beach urged the clericals to offer organized resistance against the government. Various groups pledged to take up arms in support of the church, and on 27 February the rebellion began in Mexico City and Puebla. After nine days of indecisive skirmishing, the rebellion was running out of steam. The clergy informed Beach that $40,000 would be required to continue the rebellion for another week. The money would be provided if the importance of the crisis justified the outlay. Since General Scott was in the process of landing his force at Veracruz, Beach decided "almost any outlay would be justified," and urged the clergy to continue, which they did. The revolution was an important diversion. It occupied 5,000 troops, war supplies, and means of government for 23 days, effectually preventing the Mexican government from assisting Veracruz or strengthening Puebla or the strongholds nearer the coast.[32]

On 10 March Beach "dispatched a messenger to Gen Scott apprising him of the good will of the clergy, and all the matters necessary for his information and guidance, as he approached the Capital." The messenger was Jane Storms who, traveling by stagecoach, reached the American lines on 20 March. Scott did not enjoy the presence of Jane Storms on his battlefield, but he met her and he listened. She provided him with very important firsthand information concerning the revolution, the peace possibilities, and the conditions on the Veracruz–Mexico City invasion route.[33]

Beach had discussed provisional peace terms with several members of the Mexican Congress. These terms included: a 26-degree north latitude boundary; cession of a transit strip across the Isthmus of Tehuantepec; United States payment of $15 million to build the canal; assumption by the United States of all American claims against Mexico; and payment of an additional sum of money to Mexico. Beach believed the negotiations had a decided probability of success, but the sudden appearance of Santa Anna in Mexico City closed down Beach's covert operation and Beach had to run for his life.[34]

Santa Anna's rapid march from San Luis Potosí and his sudden appearance in Mexico City on 23 March upset all of Beach's plans. Santa Anna's return sent people flying from the city and ended the church-sponsored revolution. The clergy had much reason to fear Santa Anna and had already suffered at his hands. They would not defy him to his face, but they would secretly work for his overthrow.[35]

Beach was watched for several days by the police before Consul Black convinced him that he would be arrested as a spy if he remained in Mexico. Beach and his daughter slipped out of the city undetected by paying for their lodgings for some time in advance, leaving a trunk there, taking a carriage late at night without baggage, and choosing a difficult and dangerous route through the mountains to make their way to the American forces at Tampico.

A reward of $1,000 was offered for him, dead or alive. Notices were posted denouncing as a traitor anyone possessing a copy of the New York *Sun*. Beach was accused of having tried to bring about a clerical revolution, and also of having tried to induce the states of Guanajuato, Querétaro, San Luis Potosí, and Jalisco to secede and declare for the United States.[36]

On 29 March Jane Storms watched General Scott's troops occupy Veracruz. Her reporting from Veracruz contained a variety of observations and opinions:

1. The United States must accept various portions of Mexico into the Union;

2. Insure a right of way for the United States to build a canal or railroad across the Isthmus of Techuantepec;

3. Perote was the only strong point on the road to Mexico City;

4. Santa Anna would make his stand at Mexico City;

5. Recommended the United States make war on the Mexican military, not the people; and

6. (Openly critical of the navy) she called attention to such incidents as looting.[37]

Storms's letters from Mexico appeared in the New York *Sun* on 12 February; 15, 16, 19, 24, 28 and 30 April; and 3, 6, 7, 14, 21, 22 and 24 May 1847. She also wrote letters which were printed on the New York *Tribune* on 14 and 18 January; and 20 and 30 April 1847; and in the *Public Ledger* (Philadelphia) on 22 April 1847.[38]

The Mexican war was the first modern war to be covered by war correspondents. Jane Storms was the only woman correspondent to cover the war on a firsthand basis, and the only one of all the correspondents to report from behind the enemy lines.[39]

On 11 May 1847 President Polk wrote in his diary, "Mr. Moses Y. Beach, Editor of the N. York Sun, called and had a long conversation with me on Mexican affairs. He had recently returned from the City of Mexico, where he had gone several months ago in the character of a secret agent from the State Department. He gave me valuable information."[40]

Two days later Polk recorded in his diary: "Mrs. Storms of New York, who accompanied Moses Y. Beach, who was a secret agent of the Government, on his recent visit to the City of Mexico, called to-day." Storms spent an hour with Polk, giving him a detailed report on her trip to

Mexico. Polk considered Storms an intelligent woman, but was not enlightened by her information.[41]

On 13 May 1847 Moses Y. Beach received $2,609.05 for compensation and expenses from the State Department fund for contingent expenses of foreign intercourse.[42]

In 1850 Jane McManus Storms married General William Leslie Cazneau whom she had first met in Matagorda, Texas, in 1833. For the next 25 years they were involved in a number of unsuccessful projects to promote the American annexation of Santo Domingo and other Caribbean islands in a varied and colorful filibustering career.[43]

On 15 April 1851 the Commissioners on Claims against Mexico under the Act of Congress of 3 March 1849 awarded the Galveston Bay and Texas Land Company $50,000.

Mrs. Cazneau under the pen name Cora Montgomery wrote the following books: *The Queen of Islands and the King of Rivers* (1850); *Eagle Pass* (1852); *In the Tropics: By a Settler in Santo Domingo* (1863); *The Prince of Kashua: A West Indian Story* (1866); and *Our Winter Eden: Pen Pictures of the Tropics* (1878).[44]

Notes to Chapter 8

1. Thomas William Reilly, "Jane McManus Storms: Letters from the Mexican War, 1846–1848," *Southwestern Historical Quarterly* 90 (July 1981): 21.

2. Edward T. James, ed., *Notable American Women* (Cambridge, Mass.: Belknap Press of Harvard University Press, 1971), 1:315.

3. Ibid.

4. Edward S. Wallace, *Destiny and Glory* (New York: Coward-McCann, 1957), p. 253.

5. Webb, *Handbook of Texas*, 2:122.

6. James, *American Women*, 1:316.

7. Reilly, "Jane Storms: Letters," pp. 21–24.

8. Pletcher, *Diplomacy*, p. 77.

9. Anna Kasten Nelson, "Mission to Mexico—Moses Y. Beach, Secret Agent," *The New York Historical Society Quarterly* 59 (July 1975): 232–233.

10. Pletcher, *Diplomacy*, p. 476.

11. Quaife, *Polk Diary*, 2:476–477.

12. Moore, *Buchanan*, 7:119.

13. Pletcher, *Diplomacy*, p. 477.

14. Reilly, "Jane Storms: Letters," p. 27.

15. Nelson, "Beach, Secret Agent," p. 237.

16. Reilly, "Jane Storms: Letters," pp. 27–30.

17. Nelson, "Beach, Secret Agent," p. 237.

18. Pletcher, *Diplomacy*, p. 492.

19. Smith, *Mexico*, 2:11.

20. Nelson, "Beach, Secret Agent," p. 239.

21. Manning, *Correspondence*, 8:906–907.

22. Pletcher, *Diplomacy*, p. 491.

23. Justin H. Smith, ed., "Letters of General Antonio López de Santa Anna Relating to the War Between the United States and Mexico, 1846-1848," *Annual Report of the American Historical Association for the Year 1917* (1920), p. 409.

24. Pletcher, *Diplomacy*, p. 491.

25. Reilly, "Jane Storms: Letters," pp. 30–31.

26. Smith, *Mexico*, 2:12.

27. Manning, *Correspondence*, 8:906–907.

28. Reilly, "Jane Storms: Letters," p. 27.

29. Frederick Merk, *Manifest Destiny and Mission in American History* (New York: Alfred A. Knopf, 1963), pp. 131–132.

30. Manning, *Correspondence*, 8:906–907.

31. Ibid.

32. Ibid.

33. Ibid.

34. Ibid.

35. Smith, *Mexico*, 2:14.

36. Ibid., 2:332.

37. Reilly, "Jane Storms: Letters," pp. 35–36.

38. Ibid., p. 30.

39. Ballentine, *English Soldier*, p. xxxiii.

40. Quaife, *Polk Diary*, 3:22.

41. Ibid., 3:25.

42. U.S. Congress, House, *Contingent Expenses of State Department*. H. Ex. Doc. 3, 30th Cong., 1st sess., 1848, Schedule E, p. 30.

43. Reilly, "Jane Storms: Letters," p. 41.

44. James, *American Women*, 1:316.

Chapter 9

Central Mexico Campaign of Scott

Through the summer and early fall of 1846 President Polk and his advisers planned to win the war by winning battles in northern Mexico. Major General Winfield Scott had decided victory would require the capture of Mexico City. He did not see the American army threatening Mexico City from its present position in northern Mexico. The best way to win the war was to land at Veracruz and march to Mexico City from that point. Scott sent Secretary of War Marcy a memorandum on 7 October 1846 outlining his plan to "conquer a peace" by invasion of central Mexico from Veracruz.[1]

After much discussion within the administration Polk decided to shift the major military effort from northern Mexico to Veracruz. He selected General Scott to lead the Veracruz expedition, not because he had great confidence in Scott's ability or loyalty, but because Scott was the only man in the army "who by his rank could command Taylor." Polk regarded Taylor as a "narrow minded, bigotted partisan."[2]

Scott's relations with Polk were stormy for many reasons. General Scott was a national institution. When Polk was inaugurated in 1845, Scott had been almost 37 years in the army. He had served his country as a troop commander in the War of 1812, an Indian fighter, and a negotiator of boundary disputes and Indian matters. Polk had a profound distaste for the regular army of which General Scott was the epitome. Politically, the general was not only a Whig but had aspired to be the Whig presidential candidate. In addition, Scott had an overbearing personality, towering frame, and condescending manner that irritated the small and assertive Polk, who happened to be president.[3]

When Scott was appointed commander of the Veracruz invasion force in November 1846, he requested and received $30,000 for covert operations from the War Department.[4] He gave $1,200 to F. M. Dimond to finance covert operations in Cuba. Dimond, the former United States consul at Veracruz, went to Havana to recruit two spies to go into Mexico and report on conditions there. With the assistance of R. B. Campbell, the United States consul at Havana, Dimond prepared an agent for the covert intelligence collection mission, but he could not obtain a Mexican visa. Then Dimond selected a Frenchman and chartered a ship to take him to Mexico, and he completely disappeared. There had been no further trace of the spy or the project.[5]

Scott departed Washington, D.C., on 24 November 1846. He traveled to Veracruz via New York, New Orleans, Brazos Santiago, Tampico, and the Lobos Islands. On the way he gathered and trained his troops, worked on the plans and preparations for the amphibious landing, collected intelligence, and coordinated his logistic and shipping resources (see Map 4).

Scott was so sure he would meet serious opposition at Veracruz that he employed five or six spies to obtain information,[6] and directed Commodore Conner, commander of the Home Squadron, to use all his resources to provide him the enemy order of battle at Veracruz. While at Brazos Santiago Scott paid José — — — $450; Carl Kitchner $450; and Dupers $1,200 for their covert intelligence collection activities.[7]

Scott's force landed at Veracruz on 9 March 1847 and immediately laid siege to the city. Owing to the bombardment, the British, French, and Spanish consuls in Veracruz sent a letter requesting permission to leave the city. This prompted Scott to write to Secretary of War Marcy "that our batteries already had a terrible effect on the city (also known through other sources)."[8] The "other sources" reporting from inside the city were Carl Kitchner, who was paid $200, and an unidentified person paid a total of $1,600 on 29 March and 25 April.

Mrs. Jane Storms presented herself to General Scott at Veracruz on 20 March. She had important information from Moses Beach. Scott was indignant that a "petticoat" had been entrusted with such a mission.[9]

Petticoat or no petticoat, General Scott listened to Storms's report. From her he learned of the secret arrangements made by the church leaders to have Jalapa Enríquez, Perote, Puebla, and Mexico City refrain from opposing the Americans. In turn, Scott would respect Beach's guarantee to protect the property and religious freedom of the church.[10]

Veracruz fell on 29 March, and the American advance into the interior began on 8 April. Brigadier General David E. Twiggs led the advance and he was warned by Scott of a substantial army commanded by Santa Anna blocking the way. Scott had reports from his spies of Santa Anna preparing a defensive position below Jalapa Enríquez.[11] The battle at Cerro Gordo was fought and won on 18 April. Jalapa Enríquez, the next city on the road to Mexico City, was occupied the next day.

Prior to the battle at Cerro Gordo, the government in Mexico City started making plans for the defense of the city. The Catholic Church's

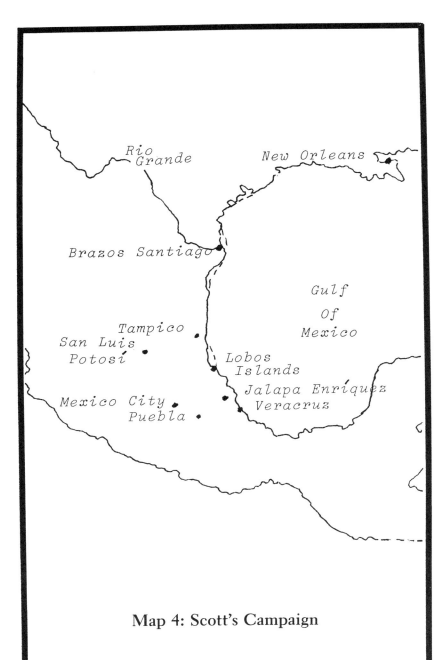

Map 4: Scott's Campaign

reaction to these preparations was naturally passive in view of the agreement with Moses Beach to let Scott enter the city unopposed. To counter
this passivity priests were forced into the streets by the civil authorities to preach religious fanaticism and rouse the public from their
apathy.[12]

Disbursements for covert operations in April in dollars were:

1 April	López	400.00
20 April	General Worth	1,000.00
21 April	Colonel Hitchcock	100.00
22 April	Colonel Hitchcock	200.00
23 April	Dr. Lawson	127.25
24 April	Colonel Hitchcock	150.00[13]

Colonel Hitchcock managed Scott's secret service. He paid the spies
and sent them on their missions. Many of Scott's disbursements for covert
operations were paid directly to Hitchcock. In these cases the names of
the actual recipients are not disclosed. Scott also disbursed money for
covert operations to his field commanders, such as the $1,000 to Worth.
The recipients of that money are not identified.

The fall of Veracruz was reported at the 10 April cabinet meeting.
This success raised the possibility of the Mexican government coming to
the negotiating table. It was agreed that someone should be in Mexico to
handle such eventualities. Secretary Buchanan recommended Nicholas
Philip Trist, chief clerk of the State Department. Trist could be deputed
secretly with plenipotentiary powers and sent secretly to Scott's headquarters in Mexico. After the meeting, Polk saw Trist and charged him
to keep the matter a "profound secret."[14]

Polk wanted Buchanan and Trist to prepare the necessary paperwork
themselves. The secretary of state and his chief clerk rebelled at this
security measure and asked for the services of Mr. Derrick, a clerk. Polk
relented but demanded Derrick be placed under strict injunctions of
"secrecy." Still Polk was not happy with these security measures. He had
Buchanan send Derrick to him and personally charged Derrick with
secrecy.[15]

At the 13 April cabinet meeting it was agreed to include in the proposed treaty the United States right of passage from the Gulf of Mexico
and the Pacific Ocean across the Isthmus of Tehuantepec.[16] (When Trist
finally got to the negotiating table, the Mexican representatives declared
they could not take the right to transit the isthmus from the British. Trist
dropped the subject.)

Trist was appointed peace commissioner to Mexico on 15 April. He
set out under an assumed name and arrived in Mexico in May.[17] Polk ob-
served in his diary on 16 April, "His mission has, as far as I have learned,

been kept a profound secret, and is known only to the cabinet."[18] On the same day Polk told Thomas Ritchie, editor of the party newspaper, all the details of the Trist mission. Polk wrote, "I did this in the strictest confidence, because it was necessary that he should know it in order to shape the course of his paper in reference to it."[19]

On 21 April the New York *Herald* published two letters which disclosed the departure of Trist on a mission to Mexico. The "profound secret" was leaked. President Polk blamed the clerk, Derrick.[20]

President Polk had his security leaks, but General Scott in the middle of Mexico, surrounded by the enemy, was having a personnel flood. His army was rapidly shrinking. On 6 and 7 May Scott released the volunteers whose contracts for active service terminated in June—a decision that left him with 7,113 men. This small force was then split in two. General Worth took 4,000 men and entered Puebla on 15 May. Scott was able to take this bold action because Moses Beach had made a secret deal with the leaders of the Catholic Church.[21]

Disbursements for covert operations in May in dollars were:

9 May	Colonel Hitchcock	200.00
14 May	— — — — — —	170.00
15 May	Azamendo	5.00
17 May	Colonel Hitchcock	153.00
18 May	Colonel Hitchcock	12.00
18 May	Colonel Hitchcock	150.00
19 May	L— — — O— — —	170.00
21 May	Colonel Hitchcock	20.00
21 May	Colonel Hitchcock	100.00
21 May	Lieutenant Blair, A.C.S.	800.00
22 May	Colonel Hitchcock	10.00
24 May	Colonel Wynkoop, commander at Perote	500.00
28 May	Colonel Hitchcock	10.00
30 May	Carl Kitchner	120.00
31 May	a Mexican officer	167.50[22]

From 15 May to 7 August, Scott's army waited at Puebla for reinforcements and supplies. The time was not wasted. The army was trained, and information was collected and analyzed. At Puebla, Scott directed Major William Turnbull, Topographical Corps, and Captain Robert E. Lee, Engineers, to make separate studies of the approaches to Mexico City. Lieutenant Ulysses S. Grant assisted in locating roads by quizzing teamsters, travelers, and native spies.[23] Scott examined the progress almost daily. He especially desired them to make a full investigation of the roads leading to Mexico City from the south, as it was soon apparent a direct advance on the city from the east by the main road, if not impracticable, would be very difficult.[24]

Scott's experience in the War of 1812 was bloody. In the battle at Lundy's Lane, Scott entered the fray with 1,300 men and ended it with 700. He was wounded twice and had to be carried off the field of battle. Frontal attacks and European military tactics meant long casualty lists. In Mexico Scott would use every means available to go around, outflank and or hit the weak spot of the enemy in order to inflict the heaviest punishment, while keeping his casualties as low as possible. This called for a commander who could manage the functions of intelligence. Information had to be collected, analyzed and effectively disseminated.

Scott's disbursements of secret service funds for June, July, and early August reflect a broad range of covert operations. Colonel Hitchcock, Scott's secret service manager, disbursed $1,546.30 to unidentified individuals and $1,534 to the Mexican Spy Company. Other United States Army officers disbursed $762 to unidentified persons to support covert operations. The following individuals also received secret service funds in dollars during this period:

2 June	Col. − − −, and aide-de-camp	201.00
4 June	an Irishman	32.00
12 June	a Frenchman	67.00
14 June	same Frenchman	33.50
15 June	messenger of the − − − consul	50.00
18 June	Mexican engineer	335.00
23 June	another Mexican engineer	502.00
30 June	− − − − − −, a courier, for a small map of Mexico City	10.00
12 July	a Mexican officer of rank	167.00
16 July	− − − and − − −	10,000.00
17 July	− − − − − −, courier	251.25
17 July	a Mexican officer	167.50[25]

When General William J. Worth arrived in Puebla, one of the town fathers pointed out Manuel Dominguez and identified him as a robber who should be in jail. Worth arrested the man and told him he was in jail because of the complaints of his own people. Worth offered Dominguez employment with the United States Army as a courier and Dominguez accepted. When Scott arrived at Puebla, Worth sent Dominguez with a note for Scott's staff recommending Dominguez as a safe bearer of dispatches.[26]

On 5 June 1847 Colonel Hitchcock hired Dominguez, whom he described as a celebrated captain of robbers. Hitchcock liked Dominguez's work and manner, even though there were complications. Mr. Spooner, an interpreter for Scott's army, recognized Dominguez as the man who had robbed him on the highway. Dominguez took $5 and gave Spooner a pass for protection from other robbers.

Americans were being robbed every day on the road from Veracruz to Puebla. Through Dominguez, Hitchcock arranged for the bands of robbers to let Americans pass for a monetary consideration. In addition, these professional robbers, for extra compensation, would furnish the Americans with guides, couriers, and spies.[27]

At the end of June Hitchcock hired five of Dominguez's men at $2 per day and sent them to collect information. Hitchcock immediately realized this was not nearly enough manpower to complete the enormous task confronting him. The informal arrangement with the highwaymen was not a proper resource. Hitchcock needed spies that only worked for him, could be trusted, and were on call 24 hours a day, seven days a week. This need created the Mexican Spy Company.[28]

The importance of Mexican spies to protect American forces moving from Veracruz to Puebla was highlighted in late June. Brigadier General George Cadwalader was fighting his way from Jalapa Enríquez to Perote. Colonel Wynkoop, the commander at Perote, had received information that a force had been collected to ambush Cadwalader's column. He sent Captain S. H. Walker and his Texas Ranger Company to destroy the ambush. Walker left Perote under cover of darkness and was guided by a Mexican spy to the camp of the enemy. The Texas Rangers routed a large force, and General Cadwalader's troops safely entered Perote. Colonel Wynkoop had received $500 from Scott for covert intelligence collection operations, and he had put these funds to good use.[29]

In Puebla, on 26 June, Hitchcock took 12 men out of prison to meet Dominguez. They were his friends and swore eternal fidelity to each other and to the United States. Hitchcock sent them back to prison promising he would ask General Scott to release them to work for the Americans. Scott released the prisoners, and Hitchcock distributed about $50 among them. He then arranged with Dominguez to recruit around 200 criminals. They were to be formed into companies, operate under the direct command of Scott, managed by Hitchcock, and designated the Mexican Spy Company. Each man would receive $20 a month.[30]

On 29 June Scott called together Generals Quitman, Twiggs, and Smith, and several colonels and majors, and briefed them on the details of the plan for employing the Mexican highwaymen. They were unanimously in favor of the Mexican Spy Company and discussed the implementation of the plan.[31]

At first only five companies were put on the payroll. They were employed in watching the towns adjacent to Puebla and constantly checking the highway, clear into Mexico City. At a time when everybody passing in and out of Mexico City underwent the most rigid examination, American spies entered the city as market people, selling apples, onions, etc.[32]

The Mexican Spy Company gave the American force an extra dimension. These highwaymen ranged from Veracruz to Mexico City as spies, couriers, guides, and soldiers. They kept General Scott accurately informed of Mexican military movements in his area. The ability of the American secret agents to penetrate Mexican security was clearly demonstrated by the delivery of letters from General Worth to an American prisoner in Mexico City.

When General Worth was at Saltillo, he warned Major John P. Gaines, Kentucky Volunteer Cavalry, to keep his troops constantly on the alert. After Worth's transfer to Scott's command, Major Gaines and his whole command of about 100 men were captured, asleep without sentries, by Santa Anna's cavalry. Gaines was imprisoned in Mexico City.[33]

At Perote on 27 April, Worth wrote Gaines, and the letter was delivered by a secret agent. At Puebla Worth wrote Gaines on 11 June, and 9 and 30 July, informing him of Scott's health, the possible date for attacking Mexico City, a prediction that Taylor would be elected president, and the arrival date at Puebla of General Pierce with 3,000 troops. All the letters were delivered by secret agents, and the subject matter reflected Worth's confidence in those agents. Major Gaines escaped and returned to the American lines at Puebla on 4 August.[34]

When General Worth entered Puebla in May 1847, the false alarms started ringing again. He envisioned the enemy in large numbers near the city, ready to attack him. He would shift the troops from place to place to combat these threats. Under Worth, the troops stood in formation all day waiting for an attack, while he galloped from one command to another proclaiming the coming of Santa Anna.[35] Such alarms came to be known as "Worth's scarecrows."

Captain Robert Anderson watched Worth at Puebla, and in his letters home wrote, "My opinion about reports taken even to Head Quarters is that they are frequently carried by men out of employment, who hope by their pretended assiduity and zeal to secure employment in some capacity with the army. Other reports are doubtless fabricated in the Mexican camp and sent out to produce an effect on their countrymen, or to attempt to deceive us."[36]

The arrival of Scott at Puebla ended the false alarms, and the troops returned to their regular training schedule. Nothing more was heard of Santa Anna and his myriads. The Mexican Spy Company investigated rumors and reports of hostile forces, and when they made contact, they fought.[37] On 3 August 1847 in the vicinity of Puebla there was a battle between the Mexican Spy Company and a party of guerrillas. The latter was defeated with a considerable loss.[38]

The success of the Mexican Spy Company created problems. The

Mexicans were furiously indignant at Scott's employment of natives in a spy company. When any of these spies and or traitors fell into the hands of their countrymen, they were executed.[39] When the Mexican government heard of the release of some Mexican prisoners, it suspected the prisoners would be used by the Americans. The government offered a free pardon for two of the principal men. Not knowing that Dominguez was in the pay of the enemy, the Mexicans asked him to deliver the letters to these men. Instead, the letters went to Colonel Hitchcock. Santa Anna tried a different tack. He sent a letter to all Poblanos (the men of the Spy Company were called this by the Mexicans because the company was raised in Puebla) in the service of the Americans, inviting them to return to their own people. He promised a pardon for all past crimes and a reward. Dominguez and the Mexican Spy Company did not accept.[40]

Through June, July, and the early days of August 1847 spies reported Santa Anna's numbers steadily mounting. With this information, the manager of Scott's secret service, Colonel Hitchcock, estimated Santa Anna's strength at 30,000 paid and well-fed men, of which 15,000 were trained soldiers.[41] It also became obvious that no effort was to be made by Santa Anna or any other Mexican to prevent the United States Army from entering the valley of Mexico. There were several points along the route over the mountains between Puebla and Mexico City where the roads could have been destroyed and a few hundred men could have held against thousands. It appeared as if agreements had been reached and money had changed hands.[42]

At Puebla in July 1847, Edward Thornton, a member of the British legation in Mexico, hinted to Nicholas Trist that the Mexicans could be bought. Trist approached Scott with this information. He told Scott that he could not take advantage of the situation because he had no authority to use funds for such a purpose.[43]

Scott considered it no worse to buy a politician than a spy, and he believed the use of a bribe could shorten the war. On 16 July Scott sent $10,000 to a certain English agent in Mexico City and earmarked $1 million more for the same purpose—to bribe Santa Anna to start peace negotiations.[44] Santa Anna did not begin peace negotiations as promised. Instead, he sent word to Trist that it was impossible owing to conditions in Mexico City for him to even mention peace negotiations at that time. But he would allow the United States Army to approach the city as far as Peñon, which was eight miles from Mexico City, and then endeavor to make a peace.[45]

On 7 August the advance from Puebla began, and Mexico City was occupied on 14 September. The following list of disbursements in dollars will identify the covert operations that were carried on during this period:

9 August	Colonel Hitchcock, Spy Company	500.00
12 August	Mexican officer	130.00
16 August	Colonel Hitchcock, Spy Company	500.00
19 August	to an Englishman for information	
	of Valencia, at Contreras	200.00
23 August	Colonel Hitchcock, Spy Company	500.00
27 August	a Mexican officer to watch that	
	the armistice was not violated	300.00
29 August	an Englishman, also to report	
	violations of the armistice	200.00
30 August	Colonel Hitchcock, Spy Company	500.00
5 Sept.	Same Englishman as above, for	
	his imprisonment and escape to	
	Scott	120.00
6 Sept.	Colonel Hitchcock, Spy Company	500.00[46]

Scott led his troops from Puebla to the outskirts of Mexico City, a distance of approximately 75 miles, without any opposition from the Mexicans. He established his headquarters at Ayotla, about 13 miles east of Mexico City, where four different roads communicated with the city. From this position he could reconnoiter most effectively and best deceive the enemy as to his ultimate line of approach. Much information was collected at headquarters from various persons of different nationalities. The information was then verified by actual reconnaissance, if it was to be used for routing the army. Ayotla was used as a headquarters for the express purpose of obtaining information, and its position in relation to the capital was important for that purpose.[47]

During this same period, Trist received a letter "from the intended recipient of the million," declaring that the covert operation was rapidly coming to a satisfactory conclusion. This was not to be. Other Mexican leaders, General Valencia for one, made it impossible for Santa Anna to openly propose peace even as a military necessity.[48] Scott did not pay the $1,000,000, and Santa Anna did not return the $10,000.

The army moved unopposed along the southern route, and then turned north to Mexico City, which was ten miles away. When the fighting started, the Mexican Spy Company was there. Lieutenant John J. Peck in a letter dated 17 August 1847 wrote, "a company of Mexicans, known as the Spy Service, in our service, participated with us" in a skirmish near San Augustin.[49]

On the night of 20 August, after the victories at Contreras and Churubusco, the British secretary of legation, the British consul general, and some American residents interested in Mexican finances visited Scott and Trist. They strongly recommended a ceasefire and a renewal of negotiations. They warned against further military actions which could drive away the government and indefinitely postpone peace negotiations.[50]

An armistice for the purpose of opening negotiations for a peace treaty was accepted by both sides, but Santa Anna and Trist could not come to terms. Santa Anna then broke his agreement with Scott and secretly started preparing to resume the war. Scott adhered to his pledges, but he was alert and his paid agents in the city reported the armistice violations. When the reports reached Scott, he requested an explanation from Santa Anna, received an unsatisfactory reply, and the armistice was at an end.[51] Mexico City was occupied on 14 September 1847.

Disbursements for covert operations from the occupation of Mexico City to the departure of Scott were many and varied, but showed a definite change in Scott's intelligence requirements. For thirteen weeks' service a "member of the municipality" was paid $1,612.50. A doctor, only identified as Dr. — — — — — —, was on the payroll for five weeks and received $725 for his services. The Mexican Spy Company was needed to keep open the communication/supply line to Veracruz and to collect information on possible threats to American forces. Colonel Hitchcock paid the Spy Company $11,362.50, and disbursed $229 to other unidentified persons. Other secret service funds in dollars were used as follows:

17 Sept.	a Frenchman, a deserter, servant of Santa Anna	150.00
19 Sept.	an M.C.	812.50
20 Sept.	fragment of letter book, belonging to the bureau of war	140.00
24 Sept.	— — — to visit Queretaro and to report	323.00
25 Sept.	a messenger to visit Toluca and to report	195.00
26 Sept.	Turned over to Gen. Quitman	2,000.00
28 Sept.	Placed in the hands of a committee of officers	2,000.00
3 Oct.	Mexican officer for information about powder works	100.00
12 Oct.	Advanced to Don — — —, M.C., and Gov. — — —	812.50
20 Oct.	in addition to payment of September 24, for the visit to Queretaro	162.50
31 Oct.	through Don — — — and Gov. — — —	3,250.00
28 Dec.	information about arms and an intended insurrection	150.00
31 Dec.	information about the guerrilla priest Jarauta	100.00
1848		
9 Jan.	For information about General Valencia's place of concealment	200.00[52]

After the war, Manuel Dominguez, leader of the Mexican Spy Company, fled to New Orleans with his family. With the war over and the United States troops leaving, he was a marked man.[53] Colonel Hitchcock appealed to Senator Jefferson Davis of Mississippi for the United States government to provide assistance for the fugitives. Davis introduced a bill for their relief. It was referred to committee and died there.

Hitchcock's second appeal was written to Jefferson Davis from New Orleans on 9 January 1849. He had found Dominguez and his family of nine living without furniture in a single third-story room on the outskirts of the city. Hitchcock believed this was wrong because Dominguez had been living decently in a comfortable house when he came into the service of the United States Army. Furthermore, he had stayed loyal to the United States, even when offered high rewards from the Mexican government. Hitchcock described to Davis the important and dangerous role of the Spy Company. He ended his letter to Senator Davis with a request that Congress provide some proper allowance, but nothing ever happened in this matter.[54]

General Scott had a full-time secret service manager. He had approximately 200 full-time, well-paid (a total of $16,566.50), professional criminals operating as covert intelligence collectors. Foreign residents, Mexicans from all levels of society, government officials, and military personnel from the highest to the lowest were all part of Scott's vast army of spies. He needed advance information in order to survive. Scott understood his situation and worked at providing that information from the day he received his orders to the day he left Mexico.

Notes to Chapter 9

    1. Arthur D. Howden Smith, *Old Fuss and Feathers* (New York: Greystone, 1937), pp. 254–255.
    2. Eugene Irving McCormac, *James K. Polk — A Political Biography* (Berkeley: University of California Press, 1922), p. 463.
    3. Sellers, *Polk, Continentalist*, pp. 438–439.
    4. U.S. Congress, Senate, *Lieutenant General Scott*, S. Ex. Doc. 34, 34th Cong., 3rd sess., 1854, p. 24.
    5. Pletcher, *Diplomacy*, p. 476.
    6. Smith, *Mexico*, 1:544.
    7. U.S. Congress, Senate, *Lieutenant General Scott*, p. 21.
    8. Brooks, *History of the Mexican War*, p. 306.
    9. Pletcher, *Diplomacy*, p. 493.
   10. Smith, *Mexico*, 2:65.
   11. Ibid., 2:48.
   12. Ibid., 2:19.
   13. U.S. Congress, Senate, *Lieutenant General Scott*, p. 21.

14. Quaife, *Polk Diary*, 2:465–467.
15. Ibid., 2:468.
16. Ibid., 2:472.
17. Philip Shiver Klein, *President James Buchanan* (University Park: Pennsylvania State University Press, 1962), p. 188.
18. Quaife, *Polk Diary*, 2:478.
19. Ibid., 2:480.
20. Ibid., 2:482–483.
21. Smith, *Mexico*, 2:65.
22. U.S. Congress, Senate, *Lieutenant General Scott*, pp. 21–24.
23. Lloyd Lewis, *Captain Sam Grant* (Boston: Little, Brown, 1950), p. 223.
24. Douglas Southall Freeman, *R. E. Lee, A Biography* (New York: Charles Scribner's Sons, 1951), 1:250.
25. U.S. Congress, Senate, *Lieutenant General Scott*, pp. 21–24.
26. Hitchcock, *Fifty Years*, p. 336.
27. Ibid., p. 263.
28. Ibid., p. 264.
29. Ballentine, *English Soldier*, p. 221.
30. Hitchcock, *Fifty Years*, pp. 264–265.
31. Ibid., p. 265.
32. Ibid., p. 337.
33. Wallace, *General Worth*, p. 130.
34. Ibid., p. 141.
35. Grant, *Memoirs*, 1:136.
36. Robert Anderson, *An Artillery Officer in the Mexican War* (New York: G. P. Putnam's Sons, 1911), p. 211.
37. Smith, *Mexico*, 2:72.
38. George W. Hartman, *A Private's Own Journal* (Greencastle, Pennsylvania: E. Robinson, 1849), p. 15.
39. Charles Winslow Elliott, *Winfield Scott — The Soldier and the Man* (New York: Macmillan, 1937), p. 529.
40. Hitchcock, *Fifty Years*, p. 339.
41. Bill, *Rehearsal*, p. 257.
42. Callcott, *Santa Anna*, pp. 264–265.
43. Elliott, *Winfield Scott*, pp. 495–496.
44. Pletcher, *Diplomacy*, p. 509.
45. Reeves, *Tyler and Polk*, p. 319.
46. U.S. Congress, Senate, *Lieutenant General Scott*, pp. 21–24.
47. John Francis Hemtramek Claiborne, *Life and Correspondence of John A. Quitman* (New York: Harper and Brothers, 1860), 1:332–333.
48. Callcott, *Santa Anna*, p. 266.
49. Peck, *Sign of the Eagle*, pp. 105–106.
50. Winfield Scott, *Memoirs of Lieut. General Scott, LL.D.* (New York: Sheldon, 1864, 2:498.
51. Grant, *Memoirs*, 1:148.
52. U.S. Congress, Senate, *Lieutenant General Scott*, pp. 21–24.
53. Hitchcock, *Fifty Years*, p. 334.
54. Ibid., pp. 341–343.

Chapter 10
Conclusion

Tactical covert operations made a significant contribution to the winning of the war on the battlefield. The cumulative effect of these operations on the outcome of the war can only be appreciated when the operations are segregated.

The United States faced many problems in conducting these numerous and varied covert operations. Very few individuals in the United States military spoke Spanish. The military was locked into American civilians of unknown loyalty and character who spoke Spanish, or Mexicans who spoke English.

To put American spies in position or to communicate with them in the field was a slow and frustrating operation. Transportation and communications were by the most primitive means. In many parts of Mexico it was difficult, if not impossible, for an American to travel. As all the fighting was in Mexican territory, cover was a real problem for American agents. Every American was suspect.

The United States government had no trained personnel to conduct covert operations. The army did not have a staff function to collect, analyze, evaluate, and disseminate information. General George Washington, the only officer with experience running covert intelligence collection operations, had long since departed.

Because Mexico was being invaded, it had inherent advantages in conducting covert intelligence collection operations and counter-espionage operations against the invading armies. First, there were the sheer numbers. The small American armies, even in the remote areas, were surrounded by Mexicans. Every movement of the American forces was witnessed by hundreds or thousands of the local population. Even in the American camps, Mexicans were everywhere: selling food, handling mules, and doing all the odd jobs that a camp of soldiers generates.

Language, culture, and knowledge of the terrain were all Mexican assets. Interior lines of communication and transportation provided the Mexican government and military with secure and relatively rapid means of managing covert operations and counter-espionage operations.

American covert operations were very successful, notwithstanding the problems of the Americans and the advantages of the Mexicans, and there are significant reasons for this. Long-range planning enabled the Americans to surmount transportation and communication problems. Frémont departed for California in the summer of 1845, almost one year before the war started. General Taylor arrived at Corpus Christi on 31 July 1845 and received his first report from the covert intelligence collection operation of Kinney on 12 August 1845. In November 1846, prior to sailing from New York, Scott made arrangements for spies to collect information in Mexico, and he never stopped initiating covert intelligence collection operations to provide information for future battles.

The creative and imaginative Americans used every resource available for their covert operations. The formation of the Mexican Spy Company converted a threat to Scott's lines of communication into a valuable asset. Beach, Magoffin, and Frémont were all allowed to operate under the broadest instructions.

Behind all this planning, preparation, management, and execution of covert operations against the Mexican nation was James Polk. When Polk entered office, he had firm policy objectives. He was the driving force that put all these operations into motion and kept them grinding away until the Mexican nation agreed to his demands.

Polk's covert operations at the strategic and presidential level were instrumental in his administration adding the last one-third to the national domain, matching the successes of the negotiators of the treaty with Great Britain (1783) and the treaty with France (Louisiana Purchase, 1803).[1] During the Polk administration, Texas, California, Nevada and Utah, nearly all of Arizona and New Mexico, and portions of Colorado and Wyoming were added to the Union and at the same time, subtracted from Mexico.

Polk's presidential power was increased by the use of secrecy while the electorate lost power. Covert operations conducted by the president change the fiber of a republic. In a republic the supreme power rests in all the citizens entitled to vote. The electorate must be knowledgeable, and their elected representatives must be accountable for the system to work. Secrecy defies accountability, and negates knowledgeability. If the government is allowed to operate in secrecy, power moves from the electorate to the few. As Polk took land from Mexico to add to the United States, he also took power from the people of the United States. Polk changed the rules and the relationship of the president to the people and the other branches of government.

Merrill D. Peterson, in his book *The Great Triumvirate*, described the enigma that was Polk; "A narrow, secretive, lumpish and colorless man, Polk was also a man of clear views and gritty determination. Measured by results, no four-year presidency in American history so fully realized its goals."[2]

Polk died a few months after leaving office. At that time James Buchanan wrote, "He was the most laborious man I have ever known; and in a brief period of four years he assumed the appearance of an old man."[3]

In 1888 George Bancroft gave his evaluation of the Polk administration: "His [Polk's] administration viewed from the standpoint of results, was perhaps the greatest in our national history, certainly one of the greatest. He succeeded because he insisted on being its center and in overruling and guiding all his secretaries to act so as to produce unity and harmony."[4]

Notes to Chapter 10

1. Malone Rauch, *Empire for Liberty*, 1:559.
2. Merrill D. Peterson, *The Great Triumvirate* (New York: Oxford University Press, 1987), p. 418.
3. Klein, *President Buchanan*, p. 193.
4. McCoy, *Polk and the Presidency*, p. 225.

Treaty with Mexico (1848)

Article V

The boundary line between the two Republics shall commence in the Gulf of Mexico, three leagues from land, opposite the mouth of the Rio Grande, otherwise called Rio Bravo del Norte, or opposite the mouth of its deepest branch, if it should have more than one branch emptying directly into the sea; from thence up the middle of that river, following the deepest channel, where it has more than one to the point where it strikes the southern boundary of New Mexico (which runs north of the town called Paso) to its western termination; thence, northward, along the western line of New Mexico, until it intersects the first branch of the river Gila (or if it should not intersect any branch of that river, then to the point on the said line nearest to such branch, and thence in a direct line to the same); thence down the middle of the said branch and of the said river, until it empties into the Rio Colorado; thence across the Rio Colorado, following the division line between Upper and Lower California, to the Pacific Ocean. . . .

Bibliography

Primary

Anderson, Robert. *An Artillery Officer in the Mexican War.* New York: G. P. Putnam's Sons, 1911.

Ballentine, George. *Autobiography of an English Soldier in the United States Army Comprising Observations and Adventures in the United States and Mexico.* New York: Stringer and Townsend, 1853; reprint ed., Chicago: R. R. Donnelley and Sons, 1986.

Benton, Thomas Hart. *Thirty Years View.* 2 vols. New York: D. Appleton, 1857.

Chamberlain, Samuel E. *My Confession.* New York: Harper and Brothers, 1856.

Cooke, Philip St. George. *The Conquest of New Mexico and California.* New York: G. P. Putnam's Sons, 1878; reprint ed., New York: Arno, 1976.

Doubleday, Rhoda, ed. *Journals of P. N. Barbour and His Wife M. I. H. Barbour.* New York: G. P. Putnam's Sons, 1936.

Drumm, Stella M., ed. *Down the Santa Fe Trail, The Diary of Susan Shelby Magoffin.* New Haven, Conn.: Yale University Press, 1926.

Edwards, Frank S. *A Campaign in New Mexico with Colonel Doniphan.* Philadelphia: Carey and Hart, 1847.

Emory, W. H. *Lieutenant Emory Reports.* Albuquerque: University of New Mexico Press, 1951. A reprint of Lieutenant W. H. Emory's *Notes of a Military Reconnaissance.*

Frémont, John Charles. *Memoirs of My Life.* Chicago: Belford Clarke, 1886.

_____. *Narratives of Exploration and Adventure,* ed., Allan Nevins. New York: Longmans, Green, 1956.

Furber, George C. *The Twelve Months Volunteer.* Cincinnati: J. A. and U. P. James, 1850.

Grant, Ulysses S. *Personal Memoirs of U. S. Grant.* 2 vols. New York: Charles L. Webster, 1885.

Hartman, George W. *A Private's Own Journal.* Greencastle, Pennsylvania: E. Robinson, 1849.

Hawgood, John A., ed. *First and Last Consul — A Selection of Letters.* San Marino, Calif.: Huntington Library, 1962.

Henry, William Seaton. *Campaign Sketches of the War with Mexico.* New York: Harper and Brothers, 1847; reprint ed., New York: Arno, 1973.

Hine, Robert V., and Lottinville, Savoie, eds. *Soldier in the West — Letters of Theodore Talbot.* Norman: University of Oklahoma Press, 1972.

Hitchcock, Ethan Allen. *Fifty Years in Camp and Field.* New York: G. P. Putnam's Sons, 1909.

Howe, M. A. De Wolfe. *The Life and Letters of George Bancroft*. 2 vols. New York: Charles Scribner's Sons, 1908.

Hughes, John T. *Doniphan's Expedition*. Cincinnati: U. P. James, 1847.

Jones, Anson. *Memoranda and Official Correspondence Relating to the Republic of Texas*. New York: D. Appleton, 1859; reprint ed., New York: Arno, 1973.

Kenly, John Reese. *Memoirs of a Maryland Volunteer*. Philadelphia: J. B. Lippincott, 1873.

Livingston-Little, D. E. *The Mexican War Diary of Thomas D. Tennery*. Norman: University of Oklahoma Press, 1970.

McCall, George A. *Letters from the Frontiers*. Philadelphia: J. B. Lippincott, 1868; reprint ed., Gainesville: University of Florida Press, 1974.

McIntosh, James T., ed. *The Papers of Jefferson Davis*. 3 vols. Baton Rouge: Louisiana State University Press, 1981.

Manning, William R., ed. *Diplomatic Correspondence of the United States — Inter-American Affairs, 1831–1860*. 12 vols. Washington, D.C.: Carnegie Endowment for International Peace, 1937.

Maury, General Dabney H. *Recollections of a Virginian*. New York: Charles Scribner's Sons, 1894.

Meade, George G. *The Life and Times of George Gordon Meade*. 2 vols. New York: Charles Scribner's Sons, 1913.

Montaignes, François des. *The Plains*, ed. Nancy Alpert Mower and Don Russell. Norman: University of Oklahoma Press, 1972.

Moore, John Bassett, ed. *The Works of James Buchanan*. 12 vols. Philadelphia: J. B. Lippincott, 1909.

Peck, John James. *The Sign of the Eagle*. San Diego: Union-Triune, 1970.

Polk, James K. *Presidents' Papers Index Series*. Washington, D.C.: Library of Congress, 1969. Reel 38.

Quaife, Milo Milton, ed. *The Diary of James K. Polk*. 4 vols. Chicago: A. C. McClurg, 1910.

Revere, Joseph W. *A Tour of Duty in California*. New York: C. S. Francis, 1849.

Royce, Josiah. *California*. Boston: Houghton, Mifflin, 1886.

Scott, Winfield. *Memoirs of Lieut. General Scott, LL.D.* 2 vols. New York: Sheldon, 1864.

Scribner, Benjamin F. *Camp Life of a Volunteer*. Philadelphia: Grigg, Elliot, 1847; reprint ed., Austin: Jenkins, 1975.

Semmes, Raphael. *Service Afloat and Ashore During the Mexican War*. Cincinnati: W. H. Moore, 1851.

Spence, Mary Lee, and Donald Jackson, eds. *The Expeditions of John Charles Frémont*. 2 vols. Urbana: University of Illinois Press, 1973.

Taylor, Fitch W. *The Broad Pennant*. New York: Leavitt, Trow, 1848.

Watterson, Henry. *Marse Henry*. 2 vols. New York: George H. Doran, 1919.

Williams, T. Harry., ed. *With Beauregard in Mexico*. Baton Rouge: Louisiana State University Press, 1956.

Secondary

Alstyne, R. W. Van. *The Rising American Empire*. New York: Oxford University Press, 1960.

Bancroft, Hubert Howe. *History of Arizona and New Mexico, 1530–1888*. San Francisco: History, 1889; reprinted ed., Albuquerque: Horn and Wallace, 1962.

Bauer, K. Jack. *Surfboats and Horsemarines*. Annapolis, Md.: United States Naval Institute, 1969.

_____. *The Mexican War 1846–1848*. New York: Macmillan, 1974.

Bayard, Samuel John. *A Sketch of the Life of Com. Robert F. Stockton*. New York: Derby and Jackson, 1856.

Bill, Alfred Hoyt. *Rehearsal for Conflict*. New York: Alfred A. Knopf, 1947.

Bishop, Farnham. *Our First War in Mexico*. New York: Charles Scribner's Sons, 1916.

Brackett, Albert G. *History of the United States Cavalry*. New York: Harper and Brothers, 1865.

Brooks, Nathan Covington. *A Complete History of the Mexican War*. Philadelphia: Grigg, Elliot, Baltimore, Hutchinson and Seebold, 1849; reprint ed., Chicago: Rio Grande, 1965.

Callcott, Wilfred Hardy. *Santa Anna*. Norman: University of Oklahoma Press, 1936; reprint ed., Hamden, Conn.: Archon Books, 1964.

Chambers, William Nisbet. *Old Bullion Benton*. Boston: Little, Brown, 1956.

Claiborne, John Francis Hemtramek. *Life and Correspondence of John A. Quitman*. 2 vols. New York: Harper and Brothers, 1860.

Clarke, Bennett Champ. *John Quincy Adams*. Boston: Little, Brown, 1932.

Clarke, Dwight L. *Stephen Watts Kearny, Soldier of the West*. Norman: University of Oklahoma Press, 1961.

Copeland, Fayette. *Kendall of the Picayune*. Norman: University of Oklahoma Press, 1943.

Curtis, George Ticknor. *Life of James Buchanan*. New York: Harper and Brothers, 1883; reprint ed., Freeport, New York: Books for Libraries, 1969.

Cuttings, Elizabeth. *Jefferson Davis, Political Soldier*. New York: Dodd, Meadland, 1930.

Cutts, James Madison. *Conquest of California and New Mexico*. Philadelphia: Carey and Hart, 1897.

DeVoto, Bernard. *The Year of Decision, 1846*. Boston: Little, Brown, 1943.

Dulles, Allen. *The Craft of Intelligence*. New York: New American Library, 1965.

Dyer, Brainerd. *Zachary Taylor*. Baton Rouge: Louisiana State Univ. Press, 1946.

Elliot, Charles Winslow. *Winfield Scott—The Soldier and the Man*. New York: Macmillan, 1937.

Fehrenbach, T. R. *Lone Star*. New York: American Legacy, 1983.

Freeman, Douglas Southall. *R. E. Lee, A Biography*. 4 vols. New York: Charles Scribner's Sons, 1951.

Frost, J. *The Mexican War and Its Warriors*. Philadelphia: H. Mansfield, 1850.

Gettys, Warner E. *Corpus Christi—A History and Guide*. Corpus Christi: Caller Times, 1942.

Goetzman, William H. *Army Exploration in the American West, 1803–1863*. New Haven, Conn.: Yale University Press, 1959.

Goodwin, Cardinal. *John Charles Frémont*. Stanford, Calif.: Stanford University Press, 1930.

Hamilton, Holman. *Zachary Taylor*. New York: Bobbs-Merrill, 1941.

Howard, Oliver Otis. *General Taylor*. New York: D. Appleton, 1892.

James, Edward T., ed. *Notable American Women*. 3 vols. Cambridge, Mass.: Belknap Press of Harvard University Press, 1971.

Jenkins, John S. *History of the War Between the United States and Mexico*. Auburn: Derby, Miller, 1849.

Jones, Oakah L., Jr. *Santa Anna*. New York: Twayne, 1968.

Klein, Philip Shiver. *President James Buchanan*. University Park: Pennsylvania State University Press, 1962.

Lewis, Lloyd. *Captain Sam Grant*. Boston: Little, Brown, 1950.

McCampbell, Coleman. *Texas Seaport*. New York: Exposition, 1952.

McCormac, Eugene Irving. *James K. Polk—A Political Biography*. Berkeley: University of California Press, 1922.

McCoy, Charles A. *Polk and the Presidency*. Austin: University of Texas Press, 1960.

McElroy, Robert McNutt. *The Winning of the Far West*. New York: G. P. Putnam's Sons, 1914.

McMasters, John Bach. *A History of the People of the United States*. 8 vols. New York: D. Appleton, 1910.

Malone, Dumas, and Basil Rauch. *Empire for Liberty*. 2 vols. New York: Appleton-Century-Crofts, 1960.

Mansfield, Edward D. *The Mexican War: A History of Its Origin*. New York: A. S. Barnes, 1848.

Merk, Frederick. *Manifest Destiny and Mission in American History*. New York: Alfred A. Knopf, 1963.

Montgomery, H. *The Life of Major-General Zachary Taylor*. Philadelphia: Henry T. Coates, 1847.

Myers, William Starr. *General George Brinton McClellan*. New York: D. Appleton-Century, 1934.

Nevins, Allan. *Frémont*. 2 vols. New York: Harper and Brothers, 1928.

Neu, C. T. *Annexation of Texas in New Spain and the Anglo-American West*. 2 vols. Lancaster, Pennsylvania: Lancaster, 1932.

Nichols, Edward J. *Zach Taylor's Little Army*. Garden City, N.Y.: Doubleday, 1963.

Nye, Russel B. *George Bancroft, Brahmin Rebel*. New York: Alfred A. Knopf, 1945.

Peterson, Merrill D. *The Great Triumvirate*. New York: Oxford University Press, 1987.

Pletcher, David M. *The Diplomacy of Annexation*. Columbia: University of Missouri Press, 1973.

Price, Glenn W. *Origins of the War with Mexico*. Austin: University of Texas Press, 1967.

Reeves, Jesse S. *American Diplomacy Under Tyler and Polk*. Baltimore: Johns Hopkins University Press, 1907.

Remini, Robert V. *Andrew Jackson and the Course of American Democracy, 1833–1845*. 3 vols. New York: Harper and Row, 1984.

Ripley, Roswell S. *The War with Mexico*. New York: Harper and Brothers, 1849.

Rives, George Lockhart. *The United States and Mexico*. 2 vols. New York: Charles Scribner's Sons, 1913.

Robinson, Fay. *Mexico and Her Military Chieftains*. Glorieta, N.M.: Rio Grande, 1970. First published in 1847.

Rogers, Fred Blackburn. *Montgomery and the Portsmouth*. San Francisco: John Howell—Books, 1958.

Sellers, Charles G., Jr. *James K. Polk, Jacksonian 1795–1843*. Princeton: Princeton University Press, 1957.

————. *James K. Polk, Continentalist, 1843–1846*. Princeton, N.J.: Princeton University Press, 1966.

Singletary, Otis A. *The Mexican War.* Chicago: University of Chicago Press, 1960.

Smith, Arthur D. Howden. *Old Fuss and Feathers.* New York: Greystone, 1937.

Smith, Justin H. *The War with Mexico.* 2 vols. New York: Macmillan, 1919.

_____. *The Annexation of Texas.* New York: Barnes and Noble, 1941.

Spencer, Ivor D. *The Victor and the Spoils.* Providence, R.I.: Brown University Press, 1959.

Stephenson, Nathaniel W. *Texas and the Mexican War.* New Haven, Conn.: Yale University Press, 1921.

Wallace, Edward S. *General William Jenkins Worth.* Dallas: Southern Methodist University Press, 1953.

_____. *Destiny and Glory.* New York: Coward-McCann, 1957.

Webb, Walter Prescott. *The Texas Rangers.* Boston: Houghton Mifflin, 1935.

_____, ed. *The Handbook of Texas.* 2 vols. Chicago: R. R. Donnelly and Sons, 1952.

Weems, John Edward. *To Conquer a Peace.* Garden City, N.Y.: Doubleday, 1974.

Young, Otis E. *The West of Philip St. George Cooke, 1809–1895.* Glendale, Calif.: Arthur H. Clark, 1955.

Government Documents

U.S. Congress, Senate. *Claims on Mexico.* S. Doc. 411, 27th Cong., 2nd sess., 1842.

_____, Senate. *Report of the Secretary of the Navy.* 29th Cong., 1st sess., 1845.

_____, House. *Contingent Expenses of State Department.* H. Doc. 11, 29th Cong., 1st sess., 1845.

_____, House. *Hostilities by Mexico.* H. Doc. 196, 29th Cong., 1st sess., 1846.

_____, House. *Presidential Message.* H. Ex. Doc. 187, 29th Cong., 1st sess., 1846.

_____, House. *Contingent Expenses of the State Department.* H. Doc. 8, 29th Cong. 2nd sess., 1846.

_____, House. *Receipts and Expenditures of the Government—Ending 30 June 1846.* H. Doc. 10, 29th Cong., 2nd sess., 1846.

_____, Senate. *Expenditures from the Appropriations for the Contingent Expenses of the Military Establishment for the Year 1846.* S. Doc. 143, 29th Cong., 2nd sess., 1847.

_____, House. *Secretary of War Marcy, Letter to Colonel Kearny.* H. Ex. Doc. 60, 30th Cong., 1st sess., 1847.

_____, House. *Contingent Expenses of State Department.* H. Ex. Doc. 3, 30th Cong., 1st sess., 1848.

_____, House. *Presidential Message.* H. Ex. Doc. 25, 30th Cong., 1st sess., 1848.

_____, House. *Mexican War Correspondence.* H. Ex. Doc. 60, 30th Cong., 1st sess., 1848.

_____, Senate. *Secretary of War Marcy, Letter to Colonel S.W. Kearny.* S. Ex. Doc. 18, 31st Cong., 1st sess., 1849.

_____, House. *Contingent Expenses of State Department.* H. Ex. Doc. 5, 30th Cong., 2nd sess., 1849.

_____, Senate. *Select Committee on Mexican Claims.* S. Rep. Com. 182, 33rd Cong., 1st sess., 1852.

_____, Senate. *Lieutenant General Scott.* S. Ex. Doc. 34, 34th Cong., 3rd sess., 1854.

_____, Senate. *Claims Presented under Convention of 4 July 1868.* S. Ex. Doc. 31, 44th Cong., 2nd sess., 1868.

Journals

Adams, Ephraim Douglass, ed. "British Correspondence Concerning Texas." *The Southwestern Historical Quarterly* 20 (1917): 50–99.

Kelsey, Rayner W. "The United States Consulate in California." *Academy of Pacific Coast History* 1, no. 5 (1910).

Nelson, Anna Kasten. "Mission to Mexico—Moses Y. Beach, Secret Agent." *The New York Historical Society Quarterly* 59 (July 1975): 227–245.

Reilly, Thomas William. "Jane McManus Storms: Letters from the Mexican War, 1846–1848." *Southwestern Historical Quarterly* 90 (July 1981): 21–44.

Smith, Justin H., ed. "Letters of General Antonio López de Santa Anna Relating to the War Between the United States and Mexico, 1846–1848." *Annual Report of the American Historical Association for the Year 1917* (1920), pp. 355–431.

Stenberg, Richard R. "President Polk and the Annexation of Texas." *Southwestern Social Science Quarterly* 14 (March 1934): 333–356.

_____. "The Failure of Polk's War Intrigue of 1845." *Pacific Historical Review* 4 (March 1935): 39–69.

Index